France at the Flicks

France at the Flicks
Trends in Contemporary French Popular Cinema

Edited by

Darren Waldron and Isabelle Vanderschelden

CAMBRIDGE SCHOLARS PUBLISHING

France at the Flicks: Trends in Contemporary French Popular Cinema, edited by Darren Waldron and Isabelle Vanderschelden

This book first published 2007 by

Cambridge Scholars Publishing

15 Angerton Gardens, Newcastle, NE5 2JA, UK

British Library Cataloguing in Publication Data
A catalogue record for this book is available from the British Library

TABLE OF CONTENTS

ACKNOWLEDGEMENTS

This book is the outcome of a conference organised jointly between Manchester Metropolitan University and the University of Manchester on 12th and 13th January 2006. We would like to thank all the contributors who made this conference a success. We are very grateful to the Languages Department at Manchester Metropolitan University and the School of Languages, Linguistics and Cultures for their ongoing and enthusiastic support. Our gratitude also goes to MERI at MMU, the Alliance Française and the Cornerhouse cinema, both in Manchester. Finally, we would like to acknowledge the excellent work undertaken by Jonathan Hensher in translating the three French articles included in this volume.

PREFACE

This book has been conceived for students and researchers of contemporary French popular cinema. It focuses on recent trends in "mainstream" film in France and thereby makes a very useful contribution to the field. It is also intended as a pedagogical support for tutors and lecturers of French and Film Studies alike. The volume's strength lies in the diversity of its subjects and methodologies and, most importantly, in that it combines case studies not only of films which were distributed outside of France, but also productions which enjoyed major success with domestic French audiences. For convenience, film titles are provided in French in each article; their English translations can be found in the filmography at the end of the book. All quotations from the French have been translated by the authors unless otherwise indicated.

INTRODUCTION

DARREN WALDRON
(UNIVERSITY OF MANCHESTER)
AND ISABELLE VANDERSCHELDEN
(MANCHESTER METROPOLITAN UNIVERSITY)

In the last twenty years, academic studies of French cinema have gradually departed from largely auteurist and aesthetic approaches, with an increasing number of scholars turning their attention towards popular aspects of film in France. Such a shift reflects the prominence of Cultural Studies, a burgeoning field in Anglophone academic institutions which has also started to make inroads in Film Studies in France, as the work of several French scholars within this volume illustrates (see Moine, Molia and Nacache). Concerns about the question of legitimacy–whether mainstream cinema is a valid subject for scholarly investigation–which discouraged researchers from approaching this as an area in its own right have dissipated, paving the way for many of us who are interested both in what attracts large audiences in France and, more generally, in the evolution of the "popular".

This new interest in popular European cinema was driven forward by Richard Dyer and Ginette Vincendeau's edited volume *Popular European Cinema*, published in 1991. Here, the authors brought together different perspectives on mainstream film in Europe and provided an important consideration of how to define the popular within a non-Hollywood context. Dyer and Vincendeau distinguish between two ways of appreciating what the popular signifies: "[t]he popular can refer to things that are commercially successful and/or to things that are produced by, or express the thoughts, values and feelings of 'the people'" (1991, 2). The latter–what the authors term "anthropological concerns"–are very much influenced by folklore and local forms of cultural expression which have spanned the centuries. The former–what Dyer and Vincendeau term as "market concerns" –relate to reception and economics. It is this category which is of significance for the study of mainstream cinemas since, as Dyer and Vincendeau affirm, "there can be no understanding of popular film without reference to the market, because popular cinema has only existed in a market economy" (1991, 4).

Within the area of French Film Studies, Phil Powrie's *French Cinema in the 1980s: Nostalgia and the Crisis of Masculinity* (1997) explores three of the most mainstream genres of the 1980s–comedy, the *polar* and heritage film–and provides a landmark study of popular cinema in France. The heritage film can be identified as mainstream principally through its success with audiences. By contrast, the comic film and the *polar* bridge the "anthropological" and "commercial" because they remain the genres which attract the greatest numbers of spectators and utilise informal, everyday language and stereotypes. Powrie examines these genres through the prism of nostalgia and the crisis of masculinity, two themes with which, in his view, mainstream French film of the 1980s was preoccupied. His later edited volume which explores trends in French cinema in the 1990s, *French Cinema in the 1990s: Continuity and Difference*, though not explicitly concentrating on the popular, includes a number of crucial case studies of mainstream films, including *Gazon maudit* and *Nikita*.

More recently, Lucy Mazdon's edited volume, *France on Film: Reflections on Contemporary French Popular Cinema*, published in 2001, is the first book to make mainstream French cinema its principal area of interest, as its title explicitly states. Mazdon's introduction considers how the popular can be defined within a contemporary French cinema context, thereby providing a key text within the field. Mazdon problematises the distinction between art and mainstream cinema (2001, 5) and argues that the films discussed within the volume question the received view among international audiences that French cinema is synonymous with notions of quality and art-house productions (2001, 1). Mazdon is also one of the first scholars in the field to identify the paradox within contemporary French cinema whereby individual films revive mainstream conventions traditionally associated with the Hollywood of the past–she cites *Taxi* (Gérard Pirès, 1997) as an example (2001, 5). This characteristic constitutes a recurrent feature of more recent French popular successes, such as *Les Rivières pourpres* (Mathieu Kassovitz, 2000) and *Le Pacte des loups* (Christophe Gans, 2001), and illustrates the increasingly transnational feel of contemporary French mainstream film (see Hayes and O'Shaughnessy 2005a; Tarr 2007). Many of the contributors to this volume develop this point, as will be seen.

Yet Mazdon's volume, while important, is not without its limitations, as Martin O'Shaughnessy reveals in his review of the book (2002), and these are common to works which map out new perspectives within established fields. One of O'Shaughnessy's comments concerns the fact that there is no overarching definition of the popular to which all contributors to the book subscribe (2002). Another limitation, according to O'Shaughnessy, is that its dual focus on the popular and on national identity cannot easily be reconciled (2002). Finally, Mazdon's volume includes films which, in many circles, may not be considered popular–Catherine Breillat's *Romance* (1999) could be cited as an example.

Elsewhere in the study of European cinemas, mainstream film has attracted critical attention among scholars. This is particularly the case in work on contemporary Spanish cinema. Antonio Lázaro-Reboll and Andrew Willis provide a fruitful discussion of the popular which can be applied to some extent to the French context. Their categories are informed by the work of Raymond Williams, for whom a first dimension of the popular is something that is "organically produced from within social groups or communities, whereby the popular is something of the people" (Williams (1976, 198-9) as summarised in Lázaro-Reboll and Willis (2004, 4-5)). Similarities with Dyer and Vincendeau's "anthropological" concerns are therefore evident. Williams' second aspect of the popular, as summarised by Lázaro-Reboll and Willis, is something that is "enjoyed or consumed by large numbers of people, but not produced by them" (2004, 5). Lázaro-Reboll and Willis, then, echo Dyer and Vincendeau's postulation that the "commercial" is a fundamentally defining characteristic of the popular.

The interpretation of the term "popular" in the present book adopts these dimensions of the people and the market. However, it should be said that we are not interested in long deliberations of what the popular may signify, partly because its fluidity as a term resists clear and exact definition. Rather, it is our intention to focus on trends in the popular and how these reveal fundamental changes in recent French cinema, which is precisely what the contributions here reflect. Below, we outline what we think these developments are in their most general sense, and we use the films mentioned by our contributors, as well as other important mainstream releases, to guide us. Unlike Mazdon, the issue of national identity is not a central concern, although this does arise in some of the chapters. Our approach recognises the transnational and global influences on recent shifts in contemporary French popular cinema; indeed, the influences of Hollywood and other media have been instrumental in the commercial success of many of the films released in recent years in France and which are discussed in this volume. Additionally, while it may be said that some articles here mention productions which can be located at the periphery of the popular, the majority of these case studies concern movies which are resolutely mainstream, either in terms of their narrative, casting of actors, themes and mode of address or in that they were enjoyed by a wide public.

An original aspect of this volume is that many of the articles examine films which were successful domestically, but which did not achieve an international distribution; examples include Joseph McGonagle's study of *La Vérité si je mens 1* and *2* (Thomas Gilou, 1997 and 2001, 4.8 and 7.7 million spectators respectively), Carrie Tarr's discussion of *L'Esquive* (Abdellatif Kechiche, 2004) and Jacqueline Nacache's examination of the critical reception of *Boudu* (Gérard Jugnot, 2005). Existing work in the field–including, but not restricted to Mazdon's volume–tends to perceive the popular through the prism of films which have achieved some success, critical or other, outside of France. The inclusion of productions which resonated with a domestic as opposed to an international audience, therefore, gives an insight into the types of films successful with a French movie-going public, and enriches our knowledge of the characteristics and pleasures which appear to have a broad appeal in France. The book also includes studies of French releases which have reached an international audience and which have been widely incorporated onto film syllabuses outside of France. Thus, the collection of articles sheds light not only on how the popular is defined among and by French audiences, but also on the characteristics of French cinema which chime with spectators abroad.

If popular cinema can be mainly understood in its relation to the market, as Dyer and Vincendeau have argued, then the recent phenomenal box office success of a series of French films must be our first area of interest. Included in this category are, for instance, *Les Rivières pourpres* (3.2 million spectators), *Un long dimanche de fiançailles* (Jean-Pierre Jeunet, 2004; 4.38 million spectators), *Le Pacte des loups* (5.6 million spectators) and *Les Bronzés 3* (Patrice Leconte, 2006; 10.22 million spectators).[1]

Nevertheless, contemporary French cinema also counts among its biggest audience successes films which articulate a localised, people's culture, and thus represent the second main dimension of the popular. Many of these target a teenage audience, such as *Astérix et Obélix: mission Cléopatre* (Alain Chabat, 2002) and *Brice de Nice* (James Huth, 2005; 4.4 million spectators). Astérix, clearly, is the quintessential *gaulois* hero, but he is also France's most famous comic strip figure; yet, *Astérix et Obélix: mission Cléopatre*, which is a sequel to *Astérix et Obélix contre César* (Claude Zidi, 1999) sidelines the central protagonist, placing peripheral characters in the main roles, the most important being Numérobis/Edifis played by Jamel Debbouze. Debbouze is widely regarded as the favourite film star of young French audiences.[2] His presence in the cast brings with it references to the humour he developed in a series of comic programmes on Canal+ in the 1990s, as well as nods to youth culture and the language of the *banlieue* which, in recent times, has captured the imagination of young people more broadly.

French popular cinema also counts among its recent releases films which were designed for large audiences, but which ultimately did not succeed in reaching them, a category that Lázaro-Reboll and Willis also identify in relation to the Spanish context. *Blueberry: L'expérience secrète* (Jan Kounen, 2004; 800,000 spectators) and *Vidocq* (Pitof, 2001; 1.89 million spectators) were expected to succeed at the box office, but failed to match expectations. In addition, ticket sales for *Boudu*, while exceeding the key audience threshold of one million tickets–1.3 million people saw the film in cinemas–were relatively disappointing in comparison to forecasts which anticipated higher receipts.

Surprise successes–films which surpassed the expected audience figures of their makers–also feature in contemporary cinema in France. Productions encompassed by this category include *Le Fabuleux destin d'Amélie Poulain* (Jean-Pierre Jeunet, 2001), *Chouchou* (Merzak Allouache, 2003), *La Vérité si je mens 1* and *2*, *Brice de Nice*, *L'Auberge espagnole* (Cédric Klapisch, 2002) and *Les Choristes* (Christophe Barratier, 2004). These films clearly resonated with audiences who actively sought to see them, rather than being motivated by expensive promotional campaigns or reviews. *Les Choristes*, for example, attracted an audience of around 700,000 spectators every week during its first five weeks at the cinema and achieved a figure of just under nine million after thirty-five weeks of general release. A number of recent successes owe their popularity to the timeliness of their release, thus allowing them to capture the *air du temps*. *Brice de Nice* inspired young audiences with its in-jokes and slapstick humour. *Le Fabuleux destin d'Amélie Poulain*, the object of an intensive promotional campaign, also fits into this sub-category, albeit in a different way in that it reassured French audiences keen to escape into its fantasy world from an atmosphere of pessimism at the beginning of the presidential campaign for the 2002 elections. The film remained in the French top ten for 22 weeks and sold 8.85 million tickets. Moreover, *Le Fabuleux destin d'Amélie Poulain*'s significant success with international audiences can be partly attributed to the trauma which followed the events of 11th September 2001–its distribution and exhibition in the United States coming just after the attacks on the Twin Towers.

Of significant importance in relation to the French context, and an area which is central to this volume, are films which have clear mainstream credentials, but which also assert their legitimacy as part of a

French quality cinema. Given the prominence of the *exception culturelle* in film discourses and constructions of French cinema, such ambiguity may seem rather unsurprising. Many recent French successes sit on the cusp between a cinema of popular appeal and one that conveys both a style associated with its director and which often addresses serious social issues. Films such as *Le Goût des autres* (Agnès Jaoui, 2000), *Chaos* (Coline Serreau, 2001) *Ma femme est une actrice* (Yvan Attal, 2001) and *Il est plus facile pour un chameau...* (Valeria Bruni-Tedeschi, 2003) can be described as *comédies de mœurs*, an established sub-genre that tackles questions of class, gender and sexuality through the medium of light entertainment, but which also bears the personal, authorial signature of the director. Particularly pertinent in this respect is *Le Goût des autres* which, as Sarah Leahy reveals, examines the theme of class as expressed through cultural taste and distinction. Interestingly, as Leahy argues, this film probes the very judgements that are at the heart of comparisons of so-called legitimate and popular culture. Consequently, the questions it articulates are of significant importance to constructions of a popular cinema and its relations to other areas of French film.

If *Le Goût des autres* probes the boundary between popular and legitimate culture from within its diegesis, *Boudu* challenges this from an extra-diegetic perspective. On the one hand, this film is a remake of a classic from French cinematic history–*Boudu sauvé des eaux* (1932)– which was directed by the widely-acclaimed "godfather" of French cinema, Jean Renoir. On the other hand, it was marketed to attract large audiences, particularly through its casting of Gérard Depardieu as the central protagonist, and also as it was directed by Gérard Jugnot who started out as a comedian in the irreverent, but mainstream *café-théâtres*. Yet, the career of this remake testifies to the fact that a film's economic achievements cannot only be measured by its box office takings; *Boudu* managed to attain a television audience figure of 7.5 million when it was broadcast on TF1 in the prime-time Sunday evening slot on 13 May 2007. Television plays a crucial role in the financing and exhibition of French films and we will return to this subject later.

Another category of popular films requires identification: those which, in many respects, may not initially seem likely to attract large audiences. Such films are distinguished from the earlier group of surprise successes in that they portray themes and social issues which are generally not deemed mainstream. One such film is *L'Esquive*, which explores the topical issue of youths growing up in the *banlieue*. Directed by a relatively unknown director, with a small budget, *L'Esquive* casts unknown actors and its dialogue makes use of street slang, all characteristics which are not easily reconcilable with the popular. Like *Le Goût des autres*, its narrative examines the relationship between a classic cultural text–here a Marivaux play–and the working classes, who in this case live on a council estate on the outskirts of Paris. However, the film did achieve relatively high box office takings, as Carrie Tarr notes in her chapter: 80,000 people went to see it in the space of two weeks in 2005 and 188,000 tickets were sold before the 2005 Césars where it won four awards including best film, director and most promising actress. Such a figure may seem modest, but *L'Esquive*'s performance is remarkable given that little, if anything, in the way of a promotional campaign preceded its release; it owes its success, then, to the benefits of a strong reception among those who went to see the film when it was first released and who then recommended it to other people they knew–"word of mouth". *L'Esquive*'s audience rose to 283,000 after its re-release which followed the Césars. Clearly, fewer than 300,000 spectators do not make this film popular in the same way as, for example, *Les Choristes*, which, incidentally, did not receive any major awards, but it reveals that small budget films can achieve success and popularity and that this may not be immediate, but gradual and accumulative.

It is also perhaps worth mentioning *Indigènes* (Rachid Bouchareb, 2006) in this context; clearly, this film counts among its cast Djamel Debbouze as well as a number of other rising French stars. Yet it focuses on the plight of Maghrebi soldiers whose contribution to the liberation of France has been relatively unacknowledged by the French government, a subject, then, which many audiences may find controversial and rather serious. *Indigènes*, like *L'Esquive*, gains its popularity from the positive "word-of-mouth" campaign which preceded its awards at both the Césars and the Cannes film festival in 2006, eventually allowing it to reach an audience of three million (Loustalot 2006, 7).

Two further films–*Balzac et la petite tailleuse chinoise* (Dai Sijie, 2002) and *Depuis qu'Otar est parti* (Julie Bertuccelli, 2003) –destabilise the notions of both popular cinema and of French film, since not only were they not hits with the general French public, but they are also set outside France and include strong references to classic French literature and culture, again viewed from abroad. Yet, as Deirdre Russell and Binita Mehta argue respectively, these films construct a view of France and its culture that is shared by ordinary people, thereby examining the ways in which France penetrates the everyday lives of individuals in other countries.

Increasing audiences, deepening crisis

Many of the box office figures for the above-mentioned films demonstrate that audience demand for domestic productions has risen fairly sharply in recent years. 2001 was a key turning point, with a steep increase in the number of films produced in comparison with previous years, greater audience takings and therefore a larger share of the market for French films. In 2006, the market share represented by French productions exceeded that of American films for the first time since 1984.[3] This comes after decades of Hollywood dominance at the French box office. For some, this, and the fact that the number of tickets sold is rising every year (see Hayes in this volume), may be a sign that French cinema is no longer experiencing a "crisis". Yet, a form of crisis still exists, even if this has been displaced.[4] The new, larger audiences for French films tend to be attracted to a limited range of movies; as Michel Ciment argues, 90% of the tickets sold in 2006 were for only 10% of the total output, despite the significant rise in the number of productions–240 in 2005 (Ciment 2006, 78). As Hayes points out in this volume, funding for projects in France has grown significantly, with a third of finances being invested in films with budgets of over 15 million euros. Hayes attributes this to television channels which are keen to invest in films which will, eventually, secure large television audiences.

The rise in budgets of 240% between 1996 and 2006, and the concentration of finances on a limited number of productions, has created an atmosphere of concern, as illustrated by Jean-Michel Frodon's regular articles in *Cahiers du cinéma* (2006, 11-15 and 2007, 37).[5] For Frodon and other critics of recent French films, the term "popular" is associated with a multifaceted crisis, evident not only in these exaggerated production costs, but also in that films enjoy far shorter runs at cinemas than in the past. Some see this as the result of recent developments in the consumption of cultural products, particularly in that cinemas have become merely one location of reception among many (we will return to this point later). Pascal Mérigeau, an established film critic writing for the French press, deplores the fact that French cinema has, like so many others, become a commercial enterprise. Mérigeau argues that films tend to be "products shown on cinema screens but destined for television",[6] with a few exceptions such as Jacques Audiard and Kechiche:

> When audiences make films like *Amélie Poulain*, *Les Choristes*, *Fauteuils d'orchestre* or *La Doublure* triumph at the box office, they are universally casting a vote for pre-television cinema. And these films conform to the image the spectators have of what cinema is. (2006, 65)[7]

In a noted speech made at the Césars in March 2007, Pascale Ferran–who, incidentally, received five awards for her film *Lady Chatterley*–outlined the negative effects of this commercialisation of cinema.[8] For Ferran, there is room in the French film industry for popular, big-budget films and for very small-scale "auteur" films which inhabit the margins of the cinephile market, but what Ferran refers to as films from the "middle ground" find themselves being squeezed out and denied the possibility of gradually gaining the favour of spectator groups. An example of such a film could be *Indigènes* which, while eventually reaching a budget of €14 million, took three years to secure its funding (Loustalot 2006, 7). Critics agree with Ferran, and speak of a polarisation of the French film industry between the blockbuster and the *film d'auteur*.[9] It should also be noted, however, that not all small auteur films receive the necessary funding for the project to come to fruition; first-time directors are privileged, but struggle to secure monies for their second and subsequent films.

Beyond the question of budgets, critics have been reticent about the success of blockbusters in France. Some have decried what they see as excessive repetition of the same commercial and production strategies. This includes devoting an increasingly large proportion of a film's finances to publicity. According to the Centre National de la Cinématographie, advertising budgets doubled between 2000 and 2005.[10] Marketing for Jeunet's *Un long dimanche de fiançailles* accounted for 3.5 million euros out of a total budget of 45 million (Priot 2005, 104). Increasingly, producers use business plans and approach large conglomerates to sponsor their projects, which, in return, are able to use the films as ways of advertising their own products. An example of this is *Arthur et les minimoys* (Luc Besson, 2006) for which Besson and his production company EuropaCorp negotiated promotional contracts with major business partners.[11] *Arthur* was released in France in December 2006 with a record budget for a French film of 65 million euros after nearly a year of commercial preparation using a variety of supports, including partnerships with a bank (BNP Paribas) and a mobile telecommunications company (Orange). Customers and spectators alike could watch clips from the film on the Orange website and BNP Paribas bought the rights to use the face of Arthur in their own promotional material in order to rejuvenate their image, with every branch featuring posters of the charismatic central character. *Arthur* was an instant box office hit in France with 1.5 million viewers in its first week of release at 956 cinemas, culminating in a total audience figure of 6.3 million. Other common and recurring strategies include the use of familiar stars and recognisable genre conventions. As a consequence, originality and the creative impulse have been said to suffer, there being little space for individual artistic expression within such restrictive financial, production and promotional practices (Frodon 2007, 38). Frodon observes what he terms an "anti-auteur ideology" among certain powerful production teams and television channels. This has contributed to the "bipolarisation" (Frodon 2007, 38; see also Vulser 2007) of the film market already mentioned in reference to Ferran's speech cited above.

Critics keen to laud and retain the specificity of French cinema are also concerned about the cultural hybridity of some of these large blockbusters. Films such as *Les Rivières pourpres* and *Taxi 3*, both produced by Besson, are said to be the products of a globalised culture, not only in terms of financing, but also in terms of the representations within the diegesis, referencing Hollywood perhaps more than French culture. Besson is the most common victim of this disdain for the transnational shift in film funding and production, particularly with regard to his use of financial formatting of the type mentioned above in relation to *Arthur et les minimoys*.[12] Perhaps the most notorious example of a film which was perceived as challenging assumptions about a national cinema is *Un long dimanche de fiançailles*. An adaptation of a French novel, the film recounts an important period of French history and is shot in French with French actors, but its funding came indirectly from the USA and it benefited from a marketing strategy worthy of a Hollywood blockbuster, raising a polemic in critical debates as to how "French" Jeunet's movie actually was. Although its release marked an important moment in contemporary French cinema history, it failed to match the long-term box office success of *Le Fabuleux destin d'Amélie Poulain*; its audience figure of 4.35 million was achieved after approximately six weeks of general release (Priot 2005).

A further criticism which results from the recent emphasis on big blockbuster movies is the perceived limitation in the types of scripts that are being made into films, thus recalling the polemical debates of the 1950s, in particular Truffaut's lampooning of the *tradition de qualité* in his infamous article of 1954. Such a paucity of plots and themes has, in some ways, led to a return to genre films, many of which are the object of mixed success; again, *Boudu* and *Les Rivières pourpres* may be cited as examples.

Often, an audience's perception of genre films differs from that of the critical establishment. For Nacache, the attitudes of film journalists can be narrow-minded, their language denigrating popular cinema, not only as being of little valid interest, but also as potentially damaging French cinema's international image. Frequently, terms such as "ringard" (behind the times, cheesy), "vulgaire" (common), and "franchouillard" (salt-of-the-earth-French) pepper the reviews of mainstream productions. This last word carries more negative connotations than its English-language translation suggests. When critics use this term, they convey their stereotypical perception of the French popular character or attitude and therefore articulate a highly judgemental view of certain sectors of the French population. It seems that these reviewers are reluctant to recognise the key changes which have occurred in French cinema in recent years. These include the transformation of production practices–particularly the use of digital special effects–which have adopted new strategies to counteract the dominance of Hollywood in the 1980s and 1990s (Austin 2004). Other media have played an increasingly powerful role in this shift, which we will now outline briefly.

The role of other media and developments in film exhibition and reception

The relationship between French cinema and its small-screen counterpart has always been complex. In recent years, it can be said that French cinema has become increasingly dependent on television for its funding, as already mentioned. In fact, it is estimated that French television channels now account for 90% of film financing. Not surprisingly, then, television companies exercise great power over the choice of projects which get approval. For instance, films with tried and tested formulas–such as comedies–are privileged over more personal projects (Frodon 2007, 37). Productions which do not risk alienating audiences with subject matter than could offend, or forms which could surprise, spectators are prioritised–the aim being to enable these films to be screened during the prime-time periods of television consumption and to maximise their audiences.

    In addition, as alluded to above, another trend which affects cinema consumption, in France as well as elsewhere, is the proliferation of "new" media through which audiences can watch films. The 1980s saw the introduction of video and witnessed a reduction in the size of audiences as a consequence, as spectators were presented with the option of renting and watching films in the comfort of their own home. During the 1990s, a shift from video to DVD was evident and soon individuals were presented with the possibility of purchasing films for almost the same price as a cinema ticket, but in a form which has a far better quality of image than video, contains much more information than is possible to access either through video or at the cinema and which is durable and flexible–it can be viewed on a number of different devices from DVD players to computers. From the late 1990s, new developments in technology have allowed individuals to install cinema-like entertainment systems in their own homes, thus providing some of the pleasures afforded by a film auditorium–surround sound, large screens, widescreen, digitalised images which enhance picture clarity and so on. In addition, the Internet has increased access to film, allowing individuals not only to watch films, but also to purchase them through downloads (or other, less legal means). More recently, innovations in mobile telephone technology have paved the way for films to be viewed on a micro-screen and at times when they would not normally have been watched. Such changes alter not only the contexts of film reception, but also its modes; individuals can start watching a film, but pause it until later, thus forcing a break in the moment of reception. Film appears to have become more commercial, as Mérigeau asserts; it is also a commodity which can be accessed almost anywhere, in a range of different contexts and which can be picked up and dropped at will. As a result, ticket sales at the cinema account for an ever-decreasing percentage of the total recovery costs for a film project.

These new sources of exhibition and reception can now be said to threaten the traditional picture house, thereby presenting cinema managers with the dilemma of finding ways to continue to attract audiences. Movie buffs tend to remain faithful to the practice of watching films in cinemas, but these often erudite spectators are as much attracted to art-house productions as they are to mainstream blockbusters. As a result, producers and cinema managers alike have had to emphasise the specificity of the experience of watching films on the big screen and bring home the many pleasures it offers which cannot be replicated on DVD, through home cinema devices, the Internet or mobile phones. The spectacular, through the use of special effects, appears to be perceived as the area where cinemas can enhance the viewing experience. This has led to the proliferation of multiplexes, as discussed in Hayes' chapter. Multiplexes, due to their size, are often situated on the periphery of French cities and they provide audiences with an unprecedented choice of films which are screened with the latest technologies in image and sound. Consequently, the spectacle has been redefined since the arrival of the multiplex, with audiences now anticipating an experience that will wow and overwhelm them. The imperative need to impress the audience has led genres with their roots in more modest and intimate media forms to invest in the high-tech. Hence, the comic film has shifted from its theatrical aesthetics to the use of special effects in order to bring in large audiences and, in particular, young spectators. As has been mentioned, *Astérix* and other adaptations of the comic strip or *bande dessinée* provide good examples of this.

This desire for innovation beyond the traditional blockbuster has become a contemporary characteristic which resolutely moves French cinema forward, a point which both Moine and Molia develop in their chapters. Yet contemporary French popular film is also characterised by an attraction for the codes and conventions of the past, a classic cinema of the pre-New Wave period. Vincendeau and Russell examine this in their chapters. Such a nostalgic return to a distant time is articulated through a revisiting of genres, a continuing perception of period dramas as quintessentially espousing a French world view and the release of remakes of past classics (see Nacache). Established themes and stylistic devices are revived without necessarily being modernised and a nostalgic atmosphere and aesthetic is often created. As the contributors argue, this particular trend appears to reveal a France which lacks the confidence to look to the future and to assume its place in a globalised, transnational world; a France which is withdrawing into itself.

If one of the strengths of this volume is the fact that it provides an up-to-date examination of trends in contemporary popular cinema within France itself, another is the varied methods deployed by the different authors in their engagement with many of the films mentioned. Some adopt a mainly textual analysis approach; Tarr, Mehta and McGonagle all provide studies of the representations of ethnicity in contemporary popular cinema in *L'Esquive*, *La Vérité si je mens 1* and *2*, *Chaos* and *Depuis qu'Otar est parti* respectively. Similarly, Leahy examines the theme of class and cultural distinction in *Le Goût des autres*, Vincendeau explores the relationship between *La Cage aux Rossignols* and *Les Choristes* and Michelle Scatton-Tessier probes the place of advertising techniques in *Le Fabuleux destin d'Amélie Poulain* and *Un long dimanche de fiançailles*. Russell analyses the personal filmmaking practices evident in *Les Choristes*, *Ma femme est une actrice* and *Balzac et la petite tailleuse chinoise*, therefore combining an approach which is part-based in auteur discourses with film analysis and a study of critical reception.

Industrial concerns and contexts are the focus of the chapters by Hayes and Higbee: Hayes examines the emergence of a new exhibition market in France over the last ten years and its consequences, while Higbee considers the ways in which the influences on Mathieu Kassovitz's work reflect shifts in understandings of popular French cinema. Some of these influences clearly emanate from the United States, and the often choppy relationship between Hollywood and French cinema forms the focus of the articles of Moine and Molia; Moine investigates the grafting of foreign generic conventions onto recognisably French material in *Taxi* (Gérard Pirès, 1998), *Le Pacte des Loups* and *Le Fabuleux destin d'Amélie Poulain*, while Molia discusses specifically the emergence and development of the French "superproduction" genre and what this owes to Hollywood. In his chapter, Tim Palmer analyses the relationship between art-house film and popular cinema in France through the case study of *Il est plus facile pour un chameau…*; for Palmer, Bruni-Tedeschi's film sits at the frontier of both art-house and popular cinema–it is, as Palmer suggests, a "pop-art" product. Finally, although reception is a concern for many of the articles here, it provides the central focus of the chapters by Nacache and Ingrid Stigsdotter. Nacache explores the paradoxical and, at times, destructive preconceptions of French film critics through her case study of the reviews of *Boudu*. Stigsdotter also engages with critical reception, this time the reviews of *Le Fabuleux destin d'Amélie Poulain* in the British press. Stigsdotter's article makes an important addition to the methodological diversity of this volume in that it also provides a study of audience responses to the film among a group of British spectators. While a fairly established approach to the study of reception exists in work on British and American media products, little detailed and focused research has been carried out on the actual reactions among spectators to French films (Waldron 2004, 121). The range of case study material, the inclusion of factual data and the different methodologies employed clearly combine to provide what we believe is an original overview of the state of popular cinema in France today and how it is viewed, both in France and abroad.

---

[1] The statistics provided are from the CNC unless otherwise indicated.

[2] Debbouze was voted most popular actor by 6-14 year-olds in 2003 and 2004. See Vanderschelden (2005) for a more detailed account of his career. See also Martin (1998) and Herzberg and Johannès (2006).

[3] Source CNC *Bilan 2006*, May 2007.

[4] For a provocative report on the theme of crisis affecting contemporary French cinema, see Cluzel (2003).

[5] For full budget information on key recent films see Priot (2005).

[6] "[D]es produits télé diffusés sur grand écran mais destinés au petit." (Mérigeau 2006, 64). See also Mérigeau's overtly polemical pamphlet, *Cinéma: autopsie d'un meurtre* (2007).

[7] "Quand le public fait un triomphe à "Amélie Poulain", aux "Choristes", à "Fauteuils d'orchestre" et à "La Doublure", c'est le cinéma d'avant la télé qu'il plébiscite. Et ces films-là correspondent à l'idée que les spectateurs se font d'un film de cinéma. "

[8] The transcript of the speech was reproduced in *Le Monde*, 26 February 2007 (Ferran 2007). See also Péron (2007). Ciment talks of a "cinéma intermédiaire" (2006, 80); Ferran about a "cinéma du milieu" (2007).

[9] See Ciment (2006, 79-80); Frodon (2006); Vulser (2007).

[10] *La Promotion des Films*, CNC March 2006.

[11] See telling review titles such as: Bonnard and Lepage (2006) "*Minimoys, maxifric*"; Bouzet (2006) "*Minimoys, maximarché*"; and Lorrain (2006) "*Minimoys* et maxibusiness".

[12] For more information on transnational and postnational cinema, see Ezra (2004), Danan (2000, 2006) and Tarr (2007).

CHAPTER ONE

SCREEN GRAB: POPULAR CINEMA AND THE TRANSFORMATION OF FILM EXHIBITION IN FRANCE

GRAEME HAYES

In the mid-1990s, it was common for film professionals and politicians of the left and right alike to refer to multiplexes as "les porte-avions du cinéma américain", invading "aircraft-carriers" ready to unleash Hollywood fodder on a subdued public. The consistently strong performance of French cinema at the domestic box office over the last ten years, supported by a wide range of state regulatory measures, has since calmed most of these initial fears. Indeed, according to official figures from the Observatoire de la diffusion et de l'exploitation cinématographiques, a monitoring body set up in 1995 by then culture minister Philippe Douste-Blazy in response to the unease about the development of multiplexes, the national market share of French films has increased as multiplexes have spread: whereas over the five years 1996-2000 French films attracted 32% of total admissions, in the five years 2001-05 this figure rose to an average of 37.3% (Observatoire 2006, 8), and in 2006 reached 45%, only 0.8% lower than the market share claimed by American films (CNC 2007). Moreover, France produced over 220 films in each of the three years 2003-2005 (compared to 160 in 1996), and has produced over 200 films every year bar one since 1999 (Observatoire 2006, 3). Meanwhile, as of the end of 2005, there were 140 multiplexes across France, including at least one in every conurbation of 100,000 inhabitants; only seven of these multiplexes are not owned by French concerns, and only one of these–AMC's complex in Dunkirk–is American-owned.[1] An authorisation procedure introduced in 1996 has enabled the central state to intervene in cinema-building applications and protect multiplexes from potentially harmful competition by guaranteeing them local geographical monopolies, in turn enabling the constitution of "national champions" –essentially EuroPalaces (a fusion of Pathé and Gaumont, with the former holding two-thirds and the latter one-third of shares) and UGC–with the capital to invest in exhibition markets elsewhere in Europe, particularly Italy and Spain (see Hayes and O'Shaughnessy 2005 for further discussion).

In France, French "popular" cinema has flourished in the multiplex era, particularly if we define popular as commercially successful. Indeed, high levels of investment in the modernisation of theatres have unquestionably attracted mass audiences back to the cinema. From the 124 million registered in 1994 (the year after the first multiplex was opened in France), admissions rose to 195 million in 2004 and, despite the disappointing results for 2005 of 174 million, recovered to 188 million in 2006. Most spectacularly, the unheralded *Les Choristes* (Christophe Barratier, 2004) attracted 8.6 million spectators in 2004, and further sold over one million soundtrack CDs and over two million DVDs, generating a total return of over 100 million euros for a production budget of only 5.3 million euros. More widely, 88 French films attracted more than a million paying spectators over the 2001-05 period, compared to 47 in the five years from 1996-2000 (Observatoire 2006, 10), while there are an increasing number of medium-large budget films being produced in France. Given also the increasing centrality in production decisions of television channels seeking mass-market films which will attract subsequent audience share, the signs are that there is a developing trend towards the concentration of total production investment in films with higher than average budgets (Bray and Catalayud 2005, 201-4, Bénabent 2006, 52-4). Thus, though 60% of French films had budgets of 5 million euros or less in 2005, 61.1% of investment was devoted to films with budgets of 7 million euros or greater (compared to 50.5% in 2002), and nearly a third of investment went to the dozen films with budgets of 15 million euros or more (CNC 2006a, 8-9).[2]

Nonetheless, there remain key concerns over the effect of multiplexes. They have provided the conditions for a sustained resurgence in French popular cinema, not simply in the quantitative terms of commercial success, but also by extending access to film socially and geographically; but they have also reinforced the dominant position of national programming circuits, especially UGC and EuroPalaces. Since 2000, this position has been further reinforced–especially in the key Paris market–by the introduction of loyalty cards (UGC's *Carte Illimitée* and Gaumont/MK2's *Le Pass*). While these developments have delivered high, stable audience levels, providing the commercial returns necessary for the production of a French popular cinema capable of competing with

Hollywood, at least at the domestic box office, they have also brought one key aspect of what we might term Americanisation: the development of saturation, or platform, release strategies. The last ten years or so have been remarkable for the inflation seen in the number of prints on which films are released, and the concomitant shortening of time that films have to find an audience. As I will argue, by entrenching the dominant position of national programming circuits, multiplexes have therefore afforded audiences outside central Paris rapid access to new mass-market releases, screened in modernised, state of the art theatres. But they have also brought into sharp focus questions over who defines what popular cinema might be. Given the widespread success of French films at the domestic box office, this question is not posed in terms of a Franco-American opposition, but rather in terms of access to and the prospects of independent cinema.

How multiplexes have transformed the geography of mass-market film

Multiplexes brought the financial investment and technological modernisation underpinning the startling renaissance in cinema-going in France over the last decade; they have also brought first-run mass popular cinema to audiences outside the major urban centres. The spread of multiplexes has followed deliberately urban and peri-urban logics, with a number of predominantly rural *départements* (from the Vosges to the Creuse and the Gers) still awaiting their first multiplex; yet 68 of France's 95 *départements* now have at least one multiplex (compared to 47 in 2000), and only one of metropolitan France's 22 administrative regions (Corsica) is now unequipped (CNC 2006b, 24-8). This model of spatial development has had key consequences for the pattern of audience figures. Indeed, figures from the Observatoire (2005, 9-11) show that the increase in cinema admissions over the 1996-2004 period has been disproportionately low in Paris:

Screen Grab: Popular Cinema and the Transformation
of Film Exhibition in France

	1996		2004		change 2004/1996	
	Admissions millions	% of total admissions	Admissions millions	% of total admissions	millions	%
France	**136.7**	**100%**	**194.8**	**100%**	**+58.1**	**+42.5%**
Paris	**26.3**	**19.2%**	**30.3**	**15.6%**	**+4.0**	**+15.3%**
Ile de France (not incl. Paris)	**16.9**	**12.3%**	**27.9**	**14.3%**	**+11.0**	**+65.0%**
Petite couronne (inner suburbs)	7.8	5.7%	14.3	7.3%	+6.5	+82.0%
Grande couronne (outer suburbs)	9.1	6.6%	13.6	7.0%	+4.5	+50.4%
Outside Paris and its region	**93.6**	**68.5%**	**136.6**	**70.1%**	**+43.0**	**+46.0%**
Conurbations of >100,000	57.0	41.7%	83.3	42.7%	+26.3	+46.1%
Conurbations of <100,000	36.6	26.8%	53.3	27.4%	+16.3	+45.8%

Table 1: Evolution of cinema admissions 1996-2004

As the table shows, the increase in cinema admissions has overwhelmingly been a product of absolute increases in provincial cinema audiences, while audiences in the capital's suburbs–particularly in the "petite couronne" adjacent to the périphérique motorway ring–have produced the highest relative increase in admissions. These figures are consonant with the pattern of development of multiplexes. Though central Paris boasts UGC's Les Halles and Bercy complexes, which together accounted for more than 6 million admissions in 2004, it has only six multiplexes in total, accounting for 36% of the capital's total admissions in 2004. By contrast, the modernisation of France's cinema exhibition has been concentrated in the Parisian suburbs, where there are now sixteen multiplexes, and in the provinces. Multiplexes now account for one out of every two tickets sold in France, but three out of four in conurbations of between 100,000 and 200,000 people, while over a quarter of France's multiplexes are sited in agglomerations of fewer than 100,000 inhabitants.

The supporters of multiplexes frame this as the balanced development of social access to culture. Given the centrality of cinema to projections of national identity in France, it is important to underline that by extending access to commercial cinema into the suburbs, multiplexes can be seen as playing a valuable role in the construction of cultural cohesion, social integration, and democratic legitimacy. For Dominique Lefebvre, former chief adviser to Jack Lang at the ministry of culture in 1992-93, this is a process of cultural democratisation. As socialist mayor of Cergy in the northern Paris suburbs (since 1995), Lefebvre has actively supported the construction and subsequent extension of a UGC Ciné-Cité multiplex in the new town of Cergy-le-Haut (also within his constituency); this decision has locked him into an often bitter local dispute with the ASCUt, a thousand-strong spectators' association formed in 2002 to defend the neighbouring Utopia cinemas in Pontoise and St Ouen l'Aumône (see Hayes 2005). For the ASCUt, the new multiplex threatened cultural diversity by programming some of the more accessible art-house and subtitled films that the independent Utopia cinemas would normally screen. According to the spectators' association, though this programming policy might seem superficially progressive, it was simply economic bullying: UGC was really intent on reducing local competition by depriving Utopia of the receipts on which its financial security depends, and which also enable it to screen less immediately commercially viable films. For Lefebvre, in contrast, the two cinemas were not only compatible but provided a vital component in spectator choice, access to culture, and balanced infrastructural development; rather than a threat, the type of "quality" programming offered by UGC constitutes a key element of municipal urban, cultural and education policies. Not only would the new multiplex play a vital role for the local community ("un rôle important de proximité") and for the "quartiers très populaires" in particular–such as the 25,000 inhabitants of the nearby Saint-Christophe/Axe Majeur high-density housing estate–but it would also act as an anchor development helping to attract other cultural and leisure facilities to the under-resourced suburbs.[3] For Lefebvre, the three weeks of rioting which hit France's suburbs in autumn 2005 serve to confirm this view, increasing the strategic importance of municipal cultural policy for social integration.[4]

First-run popular cinema now has a base in the Parisian *banlieue* as well as in small to medium-sized provincial towns (particularly through the CGR circuit). Not only have multiplexes brought mainstream cinema to mass audiences, then, but they have also by the same process transformed the geography of film distribution in France. In this sense, multiplexes can be seen as central to the construction of a popular cinema, where popular is identified in terms of social access to culture. Further, this is not only the case for the socially, culturally and economically disadvantaged suburbs, but for the construction of France's cinema audiences as "un peuple", a single entity with equal access to film, irrespective of internal geographical differentiation. Contrasting the current situation with that prevailing thirty years ago is instructive. In 1976, the review *Cinéma* devoted its August-September double issue to a highly critical analysis of the state of French cinema, focusing in particular on the treatment of cinema audiences outside the Paris region. In its study of five provincial towns of varying size–Dieppe, Montpellier, Saintes, Strasbourg and Toulon–the review noted that there were only two real similarities between the Parisian and provincial cinema-going experience: the price of admission and the opportunity to see successful commercial films. In contrast, though films attracting 100,000 or more spectators in their initial Paris run were released nationwide relatively quickly (and major productions were often released simultaneously throughout France), provincial audiences were obliged to wait several months to see less commercially successful films. Films attracting fewer than 50,000 spectators on their Paris run were often not released at all outside the capital, except in *ciné-clubs*. Moreover, when films did reach the provinces, the environment in which they were presented was all too often sub-standard: outdated theatres, poor-quality prints, artificially-inserted cuts to create an interval for selling ice-creams, dubbing rather than subtitles. According to the review, film exhibition outside Paris was–with only a few exceptions–in the hands of "shopkeepers who know nothing about cinema and take spectators for retards", a situation which highlighted "a fundamental absence of cultural policy and the incoherence of a commercial policy which cares little for the product sold" (Gévaudan 1976, 61).

Today, the dominance of national multi-screen cinema circuits enables films to open on screens throughout France at the same time, with little distinction made between Paris, provincial towns and cities, or their outlying suburban areas. One indication of this increasing non-metropolitan exposure is that mass-market films have consistently higher audience penetration in the provinces than they do in Paris. Of course, absolute audience figures are expected to be higher in successful films outside Paris, in line with the overall proportion of French audiences tabulated above; on average, films attracting over one million spectators at the domestic box office did 84% of their business in the provinces in 2004. But there is also evidence that very successful mass-audience films are proportionally more successful outside Paris and its region; in 2004, all four films which attracted over five million spectators (*Les Choristes*, *Shrek 2* (Andrew Adamson *et al.*, 2004), *Harry Potter and the Prisoner of Azkaban* (Alfonso Cuarón, 2004), *Spider-Man 2* (Sam Raimi, 2004)), and ten of the top twenty films, found at least 90% of their audiences outside the Ile de France.

Saturation release strategies and the squeezing of screen space

In other words, therefore, the spread of multiplexes across French provincial towns and cities has enabled the construction of a simultaneous, collective, *national* audience for cinema, while at the same time increasing the potential market penetration of French (as well as foreign) film. Yet–as apparently attractive as this *nouvelle donne* might sound–it is also highly problematic. One of the reasons why commercial films may do better in the provinces than in Paris is that there is also less available film choice outside Paris. American films, for example, receive proportionally more screenings outside Paris than they do in the capital, a trend which is especially pronounced in the Paris suburbs (CNC 2006b, 36). To put it another way: what makes a film popular may have less to do with the textual properties of an individual film than with the prevailing conditions of marketing, distribution and exhibition. In particular, simultaneous-release circuit programming privileges both the screening of relatively few films and a high weekly film turnover.

A key consequence of the multiplexing of French cinemas–as was the case with America's malls in the 1970s–is that it has provided France's major distributors with the control over nationwide exhibition (through vertical integration and programming agreements) and the financial predictability (in terms of expected audience figures) necessary for the introduction of the type of saturation release strategies associated with the "New Hollywood". Famously first deployed by Universal Pictures' release of Steven Spielberg's *Jaws* in 1975, saturation release is characterised by a simultaneous nationwide opening, accompanied by heavy advertising campaigns and promotional tie-ins to create spectator momentum, or what De Vany and Wells term a "non-informative information cascade". In other words, saturation release aims to produce a follow-the-leader effect, where spectator choice is conditioned by purely quantitative factors such as initial audience figures and box office revenues rather than by qualitative factors such as word of mouth or critical opinion (De Vany and Wells 2003, 5). It is also integral to the Hollywood blockbuster business model: given the vast production and marketing outlays on which the blockbuster depends, these films must have an "immediate and massive effect" in the marketplace, or they run the risk of becoming huge–even catastrophic–financial failures (Allen 2003, 108). Saturation release is therefore a distribution strategy designed both to help a major film open (by creating a "media event"), and to ensure that it recoups its investment in the shortest time frame possible.

It is also a seemingly ever-accelerating phenomenon. Again, the comparison with the mid-1970s is instructive. *Jaws*, easily the most popular film of 1976 in France, was released nationwide on 121 prints, which for *Cinéma 76* underlined the role of programming circuits (Pathé-Gaumont and the recently-privatised UGC) and advertising in structuring spectator demand (Rabourdin 1976, 38-40). In the single month of December 2005, by contrast, *The Chronicles of Narnia: The Lion, the Witch and the Wardrobe* (Andrew Adamson, 2005), *King Kong* (Peter Jackson, 2005), *Harry Potter and the Goblet of Fire* (Mike Newell, 2005), *Chicken Little* (Mark Dindal, 2005), *Olé* (Florence Quentin, 2005) and *Kirikou et les bêtes sauvages* (Bénédicte Galup and Michel Ocelot, 2005) were released on 854, 850, 950, 908, 550 and 333 screens respectively. Neither the construction of national programming circuits (which date back to the initial Pathé-Gaumont agreement of 1967) nor saturation release strategies were produced by multiplexes; as Claude Forest (2002, 148-50) points out, significant increases in the number of prints for mass-market films have been observable since the releases of *Jaws* and *The Empire Strikes Back* (George Lucas, 1980). Yet the trend has most particularly accelerated in France since multiplexes were established: between 2001 and 2005, 207 films were released in France on 500 screens or more, compared to 89 between 1996 and 2000. The figures for French films are even starker: in the single year 2005, 18 French films were released on 500 screens or more–compared to a total of 12 French films for the whole of the 1996-2000 period (Observatoire 2006, 22-4).

Mass-market films in particular now benefit from the greater geographical coverage afforded by simultaneous national release; and whereas in the 1970s provincial audiences were treated as "sous-spectateurs" (as *Cinéma 76* had it), they can now see films in state-of-the-art conditions at the same time as their Parisian counterparts. Yet there is a downside to this evident gain. Because new mass-market releases monopolise screens, the runs of previously-released films are shortened, in turn creating extra pressure on new releases to make a profit as quickly as possible before they too are displaced. This situation is exacerbated by one of the very markers of the recent success of French cinema: with well over two hundred French films produced every year, it is seemingly impossible for each of them to find an audience. Whereas in 1996, 387 films (of all nationalities) were released in France, in 2005 there were 530, and in six of the seven years since 1999 the figure has exceeded 500. Joëlle Farchy reports that in the 1960s, a film's screen career typically lasted two to three years; in the 1970s, a film would take 80% of its receipts in its first four months; but by 2002, it took 80% of receipts in its first four weeks (Farchy 2004, 47). And logically, given the very short time frames available, there is therefore an incentive for distributors to increase the number of prints on which a film is released. This is a particularly vicious circle, exacerbated by the tendency for releases to be bunched at key points of the year, such as the mid-term school holidays in February and October, and in early December. In three separate weeks in 2005, films in their first and second week of release took up over 75% of the country's available cinema screens (Observatoire 2006, 28-31).

The combined effects of increased film production and print numbers on the one hand, and ever-shortening film runs on the other, affect different sections of the market differently. Mass-market films, irrespective of their nationality, have clearly benefited from the new strategies, and are able to extend their lives through the "multi-streaming" opportunities provided by the DVD and subscription television markets. Other films–the vast majority of France's domestic film production–have rather less to gain, however, especially given the highly oligopolistic nature of the French distribution sector. While 95 different distribution companies each released at least one film in France in 2005, the top five distributors accounted for 50% of total audiences, and the top nine, 75% (Observatoire 2006, 43). These companies are all either American conglomerates (UIP/United International Pictures, Warner, Fox, BVI/Buena Vista International), Franco-American partnerships (Gaumont Columbia, TFM), or French groups which are either vertically-integrated, like Pathé, or horizontally-integrated, like Mars, which is tied to pay-television broadcaster Canal+.

Over the past five years, French television channels have sought to exploit this new context by establishing their own distribution companies: Canal+ bought Mars from Bac Films, SND was established by M6, and TFM–the distributor, notably, of popular hits *Brice de Nice* (James Huth, 2005) and the Edith Piaf biopic *La Môme* (Olivier Dahan, 2006), both of which attracted more than 4 million spectators at the domestic box office–is an alliance between TF1 and Miramax. In contrast, independent distributors–already identified by the 2000 Goudineau report as the most precarious of all the industry's sectors–appear increasingly vulnerable. Noting that 75% of French films do not recover even their production costs, even after public funding has been taken into account, Goudineau recognised that maintaining a plurality of distribution forms is necessary to maintain the diversity of French cinema, which in itself therefore implies making distribution an economically viable industry (Goudineau 2000, 65-6). Yet despite the adjustments to the state aid system introduced by Goudineau, the rapid developments in the distribution and exhibition markets have only increased the problems of independent distributors. For example, according to the Distributeurs Indépendants Réunis Européens, DIRE–a lobbying structure established in June 2005 to bring together the eight largest independent French distributors–independents are particularly squeezed by the "output deals" concluded between France's major distribution companies and American studios, the terms of which stipulate that films must be released on between 200 and 400 prints, even where these figures cannot seemingly be justified by the predicted returns (DIRE 2005, 5). Rather than being able to release a film on a relatively restricted number of prints which could be re-used in a staggered national release, distributors must decide whether to incur the increased print costs of a simultaneous national release. Even at marginal cost–and the DIRE estimates the average cost of a print at 1000 euros–multiplying the number of prints on which a film is released substantially heightens the financial risk, especially to small distributors.

Finally, not only are an increasing number of films left to fight over a decreasing number of screens and shortened screen time, but they are also obliged to fight over a limited number of column inches in the general and specialist press. This situation is made worse by a developing tendency amongst the major distributors towards "technical releases". These are films–almost exclusively Hollywood films–released with high promotional budgets but on very few prints (often fewer then five), with the objective not of financial viability in cinemas, but of securing the public visibility to maximise both the film's subsequent career on television (whether subscription or free-to-air) and its DVD sales. Such "technical releases" are a significant phenomenon–the DIRE calculates, for example, that they constituted seven out of seventeen cinema releases in the last week of September 2005, with Gaumont Columbia Tristar alone releasing three films (*Deuce Bigalow: European Gigolo* (Mike Bigelow, 2005), *Beauty Shop* (Billie Woodruff, 2005) and *Madison* (William Bindley, 2001)) on three or fewer prints (DIRE 2005, 5-6). While these release strategies clearly do not pressurise screen space, they do pressurise media space. The consequence, according to the DIRE, is that films are becoming ever more dependent on the extent of their advertising in order to find an audience. Here, again, the trend is towards economic concentration, the strengthening of the market dominance of the major distributors and exhibitors, and concomitant squeezing of independent film.

In line with Laurent Creton and Anne Jäckel's (2004, 217-9) detection of an increased emphasis on marketing and promotional tie-ins from the mid-1990s onwards, the last five years or so have seen an explosion in the range and cost of film advertising in France, both within and outside cinemas.[5] Above all, this is a consequence of the diversification of advertising across media platforms (internet, 3G mobile telephones...), and the introduction of branding and secondary revenue streaming, particularly for mass-market family films. To take two recent examples: Pathé's Franco-British co-production of *Le Manège enchanté/The Magic Roundabout* (Dave Borthwick *et al.*, 2005) benefited on its release in France in February 2005 from saturation advertising across different platforms (public transport, children's magazines, FM radio, the Disney TV channel) and merchandising licences issued to Intermarché, Quick, Toys'R Us, Berchet, Jémini, Ferrero Kinder, Nathan and Ravensburger. A partnership with Banette saw 2000 *boulangeries* re-decorated to sport the film's bright colours, while 40,000 primary schools received a four-page brochure suggesting in-class activities based on the film; amongst a series of prizes awarded to primary schools for the best pictures of the film's characters, class CE1 of Charbonnières les Vieilles won a trip for all thirty pupils to Futuroscope. Meanwhile, Luc Jacquet's *La Marche de l'Empereur*, released in January 2005 by Disney subsidiary BVI France, similarly targeted audiences, but this time playing on its educational content, with Canal+ screening a documentary on penguins in the

Antarctic which was shot concurrently with the film, France Info concentrating on the film's themes, the WWF holding a competition for schools to win 1,000 free cinema places, and Barclay releasing the film's soundtrack. The use of a database (Cinebase) with 300,000 email addresses further enabled the distributor to target a family audience for the winter holiday period.

Though the use of such sophisticated and expensive strategies tends to remain the preserve of the bigger budget productions, the development of multiplexed national exhibition circuits has also produced a generalised trend towards increased film-release costs. According to figures produced by the DIRE, monies spent on film advertising in France increased from 129 million euros in 1999 to 290 million euros in 2004. This is particularly a consequence of increases in charges for in-cinema advertising imposed by the national circuits, exploiting their dominant market position. Perhaps most significantly, whereas in 2000 film trailers were screened free by exhibitors up to six weeks before release date, over the last few years exhibitors such as UGC, CGR, MK2 and EuroPalaces have gradually introduced a number of different trailer packages, at an average cost of 100,000 euros per trailer for a two-week run prior to film release. The total "in-cinema" advertising spend by distributors consequently increased from 5.5 million euros in 1998 to 34 million euros in 2004 (DIRE 2005, 6-8). Given the differences in financial power, the increases in these costs further skew the market in favour of American films over French ones, and in favour of the major horizontally- and/or vertically-integrated distributors over independent ones.

These issues were sharply brought into focus by the 2005 *Césars*, the French film industry's annual awards ceremony, held–like the Oscars on which it is closely based–on the last weekend in February. Ahead of the ceremony, competition for the principal awards was widely billed in the press as a straight run-off between French cinema's two popular box office successes of 2004, *Les Choristes* and Jean-Pierre Jeunet's *Un long dimanche de fiançailles*, which garnered twenty nominations between them, after combined figures of some 13 million admissions. On the night, these two films collected seven awards; yet these were mostly second order, technical awards (such as best sound, photography, and costumes). Unexpectedly, four Césars, including best film and best direction, went to Abdellatif Kechiche's *L'Esquive*, while Gilles Porte and Yolande Moreau's *Quand la mer monte* picked up the awards for best actress and best first film, and Mathieu Amalric won best actor for his role in Arnaud Desplechin's *Rois et reine*. This was, for *L'Humanité*, "the victory of quality over quantity" or, to paraphrase *Libération*, that of auteur individualism over characterless success.[6]

Collecting the award for best first film, Gilles Porte used his speech to criticise the multiplex circuits which had declined to screen his film, depriving it of the chance to reach a wider audience: "Who are these people who decide for spectators what is and what isn't a popular film?" Indeed, a common feature of *L'Esquive*, *Quand la mer monte* (positioned 132nd and 150th respectively at the 2004 domestic box office) and *Rois et reine* is that they were all released on relatively few screens, and owed their comparative success to the independent art-house cinemas which invested screen time and space in them. Moreover, these three films were alone amongst French films released on between 50 and 300 prints in 2004 which did not benefit from a significant increase in their exposure, despite encouraging first-week returns and final audience figures which in each case–470,000 for *L'Esquive*, 320,000 for *Quand la mer monte* and 490,000 for *Rois et reine*–substantially outperformed the mean average figure (of 111,000) for films released on between 50 and 100 prints (Observatoire 2005, 27-8).

The screen career of *L'Esquive* is instructive. Shot in Saint-Denis' Francs-Moisins housing estate with a cast of adolescent, non-professional actors largely drawn from similar estates ringing Paris, Kechiche's remarkable film is constructed around the interplay between the language and mores of the youths on the estate and the classical French of Marivaux's eighteenth-century social drama, *Le Jeu de l'amour et du hasard*, which they are putting on in school. Distributed by Rezo films, one of France's major independent film distributors and a founder member of DIRE, *L'Esquive* was released nationally in January 2004 on 61 prints, rising to a maximum of 80 in its fifth week, after which it fell out of *Le Film Français*'s weekly top twenty box office films.[7] Only five prints went to multiplexes: three to UGC Ciné-Cités outside the Paris region, and two to the Paris periphery, at the Mégarama Villeneuve-la-Garenne in the Hauts de Seine (92) and the UGC Ciné Cité at Rosny-sous-Bois in Seine Saint-Denis (93). By February 2005, *L'Esquive* had sold 280,000 tickets; as is customary, it was then re-released in the first week of March for a second run to benefit from the attendant Césars publicity, ultimately selling another 190,000 tickets. This time, the film was released on 65 prints, rising to 75 in its second week; and this time, the film was taken by UGC's two flagship central Paris multiplexes, Bercy and Les Halles, and by eleven more multiplexes in the provinces, for the most part in France's major urban centres. No prints were taken by multiplex (or, indeed, any other) cinemas in the Paris suburbs in which the film was set.

Yet in this case the poor take-up of the film by the national circuits was as much the will of the distributor as it was of the circuits. Rezo had from the start considered *L'Esquive* to be a demanding film which would easily get lost in commercial circuits, and had thus, for example, placed the film on its first run in MK2 Beaubourg rather than in UGC Les Halles. For the same reason, the film's initial release in the Villeneuve and Rosny multiplexes were conceived as trial runs to gauge whether it could viably attract a popular, suburban audience.[8] The audience figures were not encouraging, however: at Rosny, France's fourth best-performing cinema in annual box office take, and known for the size of its auditoriums, *L'Esquive* sold a disappointing 950, 850 and then 650 tickets in its three-week run. The choice of cinemas for the film's second release was a conscious and positive decision by Rezo to reward the independent, urban, art-house cinemas which had sustained and supported the film during its first run. Indeed, despite the polemic launched by Porte and Moreau at the Césars ("We talk about the 'exception culturelle'. But we have to give it resources if we want it to exist"), the relationship between independent distributor and commercial exhibition circuit is rarely a case of the straightforward domination of the small and fragile by the big and strong, for individual films at least. Rather, it is one of negotiation, with each side attempting to match a film with a potentially receptive audience. It is therefore perhaps more helpful to couch the relationship in terms of the structural transformations that the development of national multi-screen commercial cinema circuits have brought about in film distribution and the framework within which popular access to film now takes place in France.

Collective and individual responses to the new exhibition context

The trends set out here are by no means limited to France, where we need to retain a sense of perspective about the situation, for three reasons. First, because–as the numerous references to *Cinéma 76*'s audit in this chapter testify–fears about French cinema's abandonment to market principles are deep-rooted and recurrent. Second, because French cinema continues to produce films of outstanding quality. By recognising films such as *L'Esquive*, *Rois et reine* and *Quand la mer monte*, the 2005 Césars chose to reward a national cinema that remains capable of producing intelligent, complex, compelling film-making, of a calibre that is rarely matched with consistency elsewhere in the world. Writing in the *Cahiers du Cinéma*, Jean-Michel Frodon (2004, 10-13) refers to French cinema as a sort of eco-system–or "biotope" –within which works of individuality and

originality can take root and flourish, and whose breadth and vitality is
without equal anywhere in the world. And in *Positif*, Michel Ciment
(2004) likewise underscores the current vitality of French auteur cinema,
pointing out that the ingrained pessimism about the state of French cinema
which is often found amongst the nation's film critics too easily overlooks
the ability of distinctive, intelligent works to find and build large
audiences. Third, perspective is necessary because French cinema remains
a highly regulated, state protected sector. Policy-makers are armed with a
wide array of interventionist mechanisms, and are generally sensitive to
the demands of the film-making community. Canal+, for instance, is still
obliged to invest 75% of its film budget in independent productions, and
17% of this same budget in films with budgets of 4 million euros or less,
this threshold being reduced from 5.34 million euros in a new diversity
clause inserted into the cable channel's renegotiated 2004 charter.
Moreover, though admittedly relatively weak in character, a series of
CNC-enforced programming obligations at least ensures that cinemas in
France which enjoy programming agreements with major groups (such as
UGC and EuroPalaces) are unable to show any one film on more than two
screens, and that a minimum of 40% of screenings in any nationally
networked cinema must be devoted to European-produced films. Above
all, there is still a considerable distance between the material conditions
within which French cinema operates and, for instance, the type of
production, distribution and exhibition markets which prevail in the UK,
where film funding rules are primarily designed to attract North American
investment capital, 73% of cinema screens are in multiplexes, the five
largest exhibitors operate over 70% of all screens, and where on one
weekend in the middle of December 2005, the top six films at the national
box office occupied 2096 of the total 3342 screens available.[9]

For many film professionals, however, the danger is that this distance
appears to be narrowing. Here, three types of response have been
predominant: individual efforts by filmmakers to promote their films; the
organisation of festivals to promote films which have had little exposure;
and calls from representative organisations–in particular the SRF (Société
de Réalisateurs de Films), ACID (Agence du Cinéma Indépendant pour sa
Diffusion, a filmmakers' collective established in 1993), and the DIRE–
for greater state intervention.

Thus in September 2005, members of the ACID organised *Jamais trop
tard pour bien voir*, a two-week festival in eight cinemas in Normandy
and Ile de France, showcasing ten films released in 2003 and 2004. The
films, including Claire Simon's *Mimi* (2003) and Alain Guiraudie's *Pas de
Repos pour les braves* (also 2003), were selected on the basis of their

audience figures (under 30,000 admissions) and release conditions (few prints, short screen runs), and their qualities, privileging "avowedly original works characterised by a highly personal approach to cinematic composition".[10] The ACID's initiative sought not just to promote films which would otherwise have vanished without a trace, but also to highlight the apparent lack of interest at the CNC in solving the problem.

Typically–and unsurprisingly given the highly regulated structure of the French film industry–filmmakers and distributors have sought to modify the effects of the new film market by calling for further and more stringent regulatory responses from the state. Most publicly, on 4 March 2004 *Le Monde* published "Libérons les écrans" (Free Our Screens), a somewhat provocative text drawn up by the ACID and signed by nearly two hundred French filmmakers; the appeal called for the state to protect cultural diversity by limiting the number of prints of any one film to a maximum of 528, or 10% of France's total screens. An initial exploratory response from the CNC to this appeal produced few results however, especially as exhibitors criticised the proposal on the basis that major distributors would simply react to it by withdrawing releases from provincial cinemas, effectively returning France to a two-tier geographic release process.[11] Frustrated by the lack of response, the SRF and ACID set up a working group which in September 2005 produced a joint position paper designed to stimulate debate within the profession.

Forecasting that "a whole range of independent films (both feature and documentary) with 'small release budgets' are threatened with extinction because they aren't sufficiently exhibited in theatres: the public has neither the time nor the freedom to see them", the joint SRF/ACID document calls for a fundamental review of the conditions in which films are released.[12] In the context of the CNC's review of state film funding mechanisms launched in late 2004, the proposals particularly focus on reforming the distribution of state subsidies for film exhibition.[13] Chiefly, the SRF/ACID propose to limit *by population area* the number of screens on which a film may be released, thus refining the proposals of "Libérons les écrans" to avoid geographical concentration. Further, they propose to increase the levels of state subsidies distributed to art-house cinemas, recognising the social utility and public service mission of the "travail de proximité", or community work, that they undertake. In return, the state subsidy for art-house cinemas should be better targeted. In practice, this means linking the level of subsidy to the conditions in which eligible films are released– in other words, the smaller the number of prints and the lower the budget on which a film is released, the higher the subsidy should be. But it also means–with 71% of French films classified as art-house in 2004–

reforming the method by which films are classified in order to reduce the number benefiting. It is likely that this last proposal in particular would meet stiff resistance from the AFCAE, whose members rely on the more commercially viable art-house films in order to survive.

Finally, there is some evidence that filmmakers are increasingly accompanying their films "on tour". Of course, organising discussion and debate around films forms a key cornerstone of the *mission de proximité* of *art et essai* cinemas, and they must demonstrate to the CNC that they have fulfilled this part of their remit in order to qualify for state funding. However, it seems that given the twin dynamics highlighted in this chapter–the increased costs to distributors of film release (number of prints, advertising) and the reduction in opportunity for a film to build an audience (fewer available screens, shorter screen runs, more difficult access to press coverage)–personal appearances are becoming increasingly important strategies for filmmakers. Broadly, there are two types of personal appearance: promotional appearances which are generally designed to guarantee press coverage, particularly in the local media; and the *film plus débat*, which is more generally associated with "social issue" films and with politically committed cinema, and which is more focused on creating a relationship between film and audience, or "entrer en communion avec les gens" as the Dardenne brothers put it.[14]

It thus appears that from the economic concentration of exhibition and distribution there has emerged a sort of oppositional counter-circuit, based in municipal and independent art-house cinema, and in which cinema can fulfil its culturally and socially integrative function. Yet for a popular national cinema that wishes to entertain a wide audience while asking intelligent questions about the state of contemporary France, the choice of exhibiting films outside the mainstream evidently restricts the audience potential of a film. For a committed Republican filmmaker such as Malik Chibane, for example–whose most recent film *Voisins, voisines* was released in July 2005, and who accompanied his film in over twenty debates in cinemas–to leave the national circuits would be an abandonment of cinema's transformative potential:

> Films made by and for the minority ("la marge") simply preach to the converted. My strategy is radically different... In the neighbourhood where I grew up in Goussainville, I experienced the perverse effects of the structures designed to help you, but which end up fragilising and infantilising you. Throwing in the towel and abandoning the commercial circuits would be like leaving the battlefield in the middle of the battle. I still have a few illusions about my country, about the importance and necessity of culture, about its capacity to make us to live together better.

Films belong to the nation, they are snapshots placed in the family album.
Deserting the cinema of the commercial circuits means giving up existing
in the here and now.[15]

Prospects

Given the recent (20 October 2005) approval of the Convention on the
Protection and Promotion of the Diversity of Cultural Expressions by the
UNESCO General Conference, it is clear that France and French cultural
exceptionalism have become key international counter-models to
competing free-trade visions. Yet even within France, the state's
regulatory interventionism has not been able to keep track with either fast-
moving technological change or the innovative, market-concentrating
strategies of the major French and Franco-American concerns.
Multiplexes have clearly brought a number of benefits to French cinema,
which can now boast a renaissance in audience figures supporting wide
and varied film production, while also taking a domestic market share
which is seemingly beyond the reach of other European nations: for
example, in 2005 home-grown films took only 24.8% of the domestic
market in Italy, 16.7% in Spain, and 17.1%. in Germany.

But if there are now bigger audiences for popular film in France, then
this is not the straightforward positive-sum game that it appears at first
sight to be. The evidence also suggests that the new exhibition and release
strategies have not simply increased total audiences, but are essentially
defensive measures designed to shift audiences *between* films by crowding
out smaller releases, and protect the major production investments. Thus if
French audiences have returned to cinemas, and French films continue to
get made, then it is still the major economic concerns, through their
increasing control of distribution and exhibition, which decide what
qualifies as popular cinema. On these lines, the gap between the cultural
exception and real cultural diversity appears a wide one. It is probable
that, unless state intervention can produce more radical solutions than
those it has so far achieved, future technological developments
championed by the majors–such as the digitisation of film exhibition–will
widen this gap further still. The current debate over film print numbers is
soon set to be surpassed by digitisation, which though increasing the
quality of the film audience experience, also raises fears about the
increased ability of major groups to dictate programming. It is likely that
the current debate on screen capture is setting out battle lines for future
struggles.

We may wonder, also, about the security of the multiplex boom. Given the geographical saturation of the French multiplex market, the main exhibitors–UGC and EuroPalaces–have recently been expanding abroad; UGC's flagship is now, for instance, in Rome. The structure of the French regulatory system gives such dominant groups a competitive advantage, by protecting them from competition (effectively creating local monopolies). Ominously, however, there are signs that multiplexes–if one leaves aside the mastodons of Bercy, Les Halles etc.–are failing to meet their break-even audience targets. This situation is all the more worrying in that the main operators have recently followed other areas of French industry by selling the physical structures of the cinemas to pension funds in order to raise funds for overseas expansion.[16] At the end of the contract–typically of about twelve years–the pension fund will be able to convert the premises. This may be a particularly attractive option where multiplexes are sited as retail anchors in shopping centres, should the popular cinema boom end.

Despite state action and a national cultural and regulatory commitment to maintaining French cinema as a counter-model to Hollywood, many of the features associated with free markets in film exhibition and distribution–economic concentration, cultural polarisation, the fragilisation of independent actors–have been produced in France through the physical, technical and economic transformation of the conditions of supply. Multiplexes have clearly extended access to first-run film, but they have also narrowed the nature of what can be accessed; on this level, French cinema can legitimately said to have become *fast food*. With the benefit of thirty years of hindsight, *Cinéma 76*'s acerbic broadsides at the economic concentration of French cinema seem both prescient... and a little quaint.

---

[1] AMC stands for American Multi-Cinema, Inc.

[2] These figures refer to French productions or majority French co-productions only.

[3] Lefebvre's position is most coherently set out in the municipal document, "CDEC du 18 mars 2003: Demande d'extension du cinéma UGC Ciné Cité de Cergy-le-Haut. Position de la Ville de Cergy".

[4] See Letter to Constituents from Dominique Lefebvre, dated 15 November 2005. The letter is a general response to those who had sent the mayor a pre-formatted letter of complaint drawn up by the ASCUt, accusing Lefebvre of acting in the private commercial interests of UGC rather than in the general public interest.

[5] "Les distributeurs révolutionnent la promotion des films", *Ecran Total*, 23 November 2005.

[6] See "Des Césars à petit budget", (Anon. 2005) and "Un court samedi de retrouvailles", (Anon. 2005).

[7] Distribution details for *L'Esquive* supplied by Rezo films, and used with thanks.

[8] Interview with Florent Bugeau, Rezo films, December 2005.

[9] Box office screen figures for 16-18 December as listed by *The Guardian*, Film & Music, 23 December 2005, p.10.

[10] See http://www.jamaistroptardpourbienvoir.com/.

[11] Interview with Catherine Legave, Déléguée générale de la SRF, Paris, September 2005.

[12] "Diffusion des films indépendants en salles", Document du groupe de travail SRF/ACID, Paris, September 2005, 1.

[13] Launched in the wake of the Paris administrative tribunal's October 2004 decision to prohibit access to the *compte de soutien* of Jean-Pierre Jeunet's *Un Long dimanche de fiançailles*, on account of its part-funding by Warner France, a subsidiary of the American Time Warner conglomerate.

[14] Quoted in Francis Fourcou's film *J'aime la vie, je fais du vélo, je vais au cinéma* (2005).

[15] Private email correspondance, November 2005.

[16] See "Outsourcing: Le grand chambardement", *Nouvel Economiste*, 13 May 2005, pp.23-5, and "L'externalisation des murs d'exploitation prend un nouvel essor", *Les Echos*, 17 February 2005, p.28.

CHAPTER TWO

GENRE HYBRIDITY, NATIONAL CULTURE, GLOBALISED CULTURE

RAPHAËLLE MOINE

The practice of combining generic features drawn from a national cultural tradition with a form, references and generic paradigms that are at least perceived as belonging to a globalised neo-Hollywood model, constitutes one of the defining tendencies of contemporary French popular cinema. This cinematic cross-fertilisation results in the production of hybrid films which simultaneously reflect a national and global culture, borrowing as they do from both French and neo-Hollywood generic traditions. The variety of critical interpretations applied to these films is a testament to their hybridity, as critics seem unable to decide whether to concentrate on their relation to national identity or on their international character, regardless of whether they are panning the films in question or hailing them as a success. Borrowings from American cinema and the influence of Hollywood did not, of course, wait until the 1990s to make their presence felt in French cinema, as may be seen for example in a number of French crime thrillers, in particular gangster films, from the 1950s and 1960s. However, this hybridity raises a specific set of issues: firstly, these "American-style French films" belong to a variety of different genres; secondly, they are often produced with the express aim of using "Hollywood methods" to draw in certain audience categories who are turning their backs on French cinema; finally, the dual French and American style of these films results in an ambivalent critical reception which focuses on debates around questions of identity relating specifically to contemporary France. Admittedly, by exposing what is "national" and what is "global", the heterogeneity of these films invites a re-examination of globalisation and the validity or otherwise of copying the formulas of a dominant neo-Hollywood model. Sometimes, as in the case of *Le Fabuleux destin d'Amélie Poulain* (Jean-Pierre Jeunet, 2001), a film's "Frenchness", thrown into relief by its contrast with technological production methods that are perceived as being "typically Hollywood", may itself become the object of lively debate.

In this chapter, I will focus on three examples that are emblematic of this phenomenon: *Taxi* (Gérard Pirès, 1998), *Le Pacte des loups* (Christophe Gans, 2001) and *Le Fabuleux destin d'Amélie Poulain*. All these films graft foreign elements onto recognisably French material, yet each of them achieves this acculturation using different formulas and generic configurations. It is therefore important to determine not only what syncretic forms this hybridising gives rise to, but also which elements of the films in question belong to a specifically French tradition of popular cinema, as these films' generic and cultural hybridity does not always result in a perfectly unified and homogeneous end product. Lastly, an analysis of the critical reception of *Le Fabuleux destin d'Amélie Poulain* will provide useful indications as to the difficulties involved in defining "French popular cinema" in present-day France.[1]

Mapping contemporary French popular cinema

The notion of "popular cinema", despite the widespread use of this term, is by no means straightforward. For this reason I have chosen, in this preliminary analysis, to use it in a specific and quite uncontroversial sense, taking a popular film to be a film that is seen by a large number of people, and that thus reaches a broad public (it is worth noting that the words "popular" and "public" both derive from the same Latin root, *populus*). The marker of popularity, understood in this way, is therefore success at the box office. Today this obviously depends on the industrial and promotional resources behind the film, although this backing, while often necessary, is never an absolute guarantee of success. The last ten years have seen a number of big-budget, widely distributed French films which have nevertheless played to near-empty cinemas: one only has to think of Jacques Dorfman's *Vercingétorix* (2001), for example, crowned both "turkey of the year"(navet de l'année) and "flop of the century" (bide du siècle) by *Télérama* (27 January 2001, 41) Although differing production costs necessarily mean that a film's commercial success should be seen in relative terms (a low-budget film will turn a profit with lower ticket sales than a big-budget production such as *Les Bronzés 3* (Patrice Leconte, 2006), which needed to sell 3 million tickets in order to break even) it is reasonable today to measure a film's popular success in terms of how many million tickets it sells.

Taxi, with 6.98 million tickets sold (and 10.3 million for its sequel), *Le Pacte des loups*, with 5.1 million, *Le Fabuleux destin d'Amélie Poulain* with 8.52 million, all belong to the select circle of films whose ticket sales pass the 4 million mark. Only between five and seven films per year have achieved this over the last decade, with in general only one or two of them being French films, except in 2001 when, exceptionally, 4 French films– *Le Fabuleux destin d'Amélie Poulain*, *Le Pacte des loups*, *Le Placard* (Francis Veber, 1999), *La Vérité si je mens ! 2* (Thomas Gilou, 2001)– reached this mark.[2] The three films under discussion here, then, attracted a very wide public, but were not the only French films to have achieved record figures against the backdrop of an increasing tendency for ticket sales, in France as elsewhere, to be shared out among a small handful of films. When one examines the list of these highly successful (popular, in the primary sense of the word) French films, it becomes clear that they fall into two groups which, through their separate generic identities, articulate nationality and genre in different ways.

The first group is comprised of films marked by their strong generic emphasis on national identity, proving that Hollywood-style production values or borrowings from Hollywood are not the *sine qua non* of success for a French film. Comedy, a genre that remains well represented, with admittedly mixed results, in French cinema, occupies the top positions in both the first rank of box office successes with *Jet set* (Fabien Onteniente, 2000), *Pédale douce* (Gabriel Aghion, 1996), *Le Placard*, *La vérité si je mens ! 1* and *2*, *Le Dîner de cons* (Francis Veber, 1998) and the second rank of films that "make do" with passing the million mark in ticket sales namely *Meilleur espoir feminin* (Gérard Jugnot, 2000), *On connaît la chanson* (Alian Resnais, 1997) and *Le Goût des autres* (Agnès Jaoui, 2000). Also found in this category are a number of "heritage films" (films patrimoniaux), and the commemorative function of these films, whether nostalgic or critical in character, and their emphasis on questions of identity is manifest. In this sense, the phenomenal success of *Les Choristes* (Christophe Barratier, 2004) should be placed in the context of contemporary French debates on schooling, in particular the "failure of modern teaching methods" and the return to favour in the public consciousness of traditional education.[3] This nostalgia for schooling "as it used to be" (pre-1968?) is touched on in other successful audiovisual productions. These films focus on traditional-style schools and are always situated in a rural setting which does not represent the real sociological and demographic character of contemporary France, but instead clearly refers to a pastoral France symbolically associated with the past. This is the case for the reality TV shows *Le Pensionnat de Chavannes* and *Le Pensionnat de Sarlat*, broadcast on M6, in which present-day young people are supposed to live and study under the "harsh rules" of a

1950s/1960s boarding school. It is also the case for Nicolas Philibert's documentary *Être et avoir* (2002), which was seen by more than 1.8 million cinemagoers, an exceptional tally for a documentary. The film follows an academic year in a small rural primary school with only one class, a type of school that was once widespread, but is now rapidly disappearing, where the teacher, Gérard Lopez, for all his evident kindness, is presented as a schoolmaster in the traditional mould on account of his age (approaching retirement), his background (he is a perfect example of a teacher with working-class roots) and his choice of pedagogical methods.

A second group of highly successful films is comprised of hybrid films which combine a plurality of generic identities and are linked to different cinematic and cultural identities, French/neo-Hollywood, French/global. This group obviously includes *Taxi*, *Le Pacte des loups* and *Le Fabuleux destin d'Amélie Poulain*, but also *Vidocq* (Pitof, 2001), certain films produced by Luc Besson, such as *Yamakasi* (Ariel Zeitoun & Julien Seri, 2001) and *Wasabi* (Gérard Krawczyk, 2001), and *Astérix et Obélix: mission Cléopâtre* (Alian Chabat, 2002). The latter film revisits the universe of the famous Gaulish village of its comic-book inspiration but, unlike the earlier work produced by Claude Zidi (*Astérix et Obélix contre César*, 1997), it adapts a story that is not set in France, and that sees Astérix (Christian Clavier) and Obélix (Gérard Depardieu) relegated to the periphery of the narrative. In the spirit of Goscinny and Uderzo's books, allusions, parody and knowing references abound, but they relate as much to a globalised culture as a French one. For example, a geranium growing in the desert is an allusion to *La Grande Illusion* (Jean Renoir, 1937), while a female union activist by the name of Itineris is a reference to the then-current French context.[4] However, the cruel Roman leader Caiüs Céplus walks on to the music from *Star Wars*, proclaims that "the Empire is striking back", and in silhouette resembles Darth Vader. The sequence which features him is, moreover, a very interesting mixture of national and globalised references. It shows the Darth-Vader-style strangulation by Caiüs Céplus of the unfortunate centurion Antivirus, but the dialogue privileges French references as, in his anger, Céplus gets Antivirus' name wrong and calls him "Centurion AffaireDreyfus". The dual anchoring of these films in a national space and a globalised space helps explain their ability to draw in a wide and varied public, since viewers can "get into" these films and interpret them using a variety of different systems of reference. This strategy functions well within the framework of the home market. Yet, the localised cultural references may well inhibit the films' chances of reaching an international audience because they confront spectators with codes and conventions that they would not normally associate with French cinema. By extension, such films are often more difficult to understand for an international audience which may not grasp their implicit references.

Taxi: the double heritage of the "action comedy"

Written and produced by Luc Besson, *Taxi* was directed by Gérard Pirès, who made his name with such 1970s comedies as *Fantasia chez les Ploucs* (1970) and *Elle court, elle court la banlieue* (1973). It is therefore the work of a pair who can be identified with two different eras in cinema, and with two different genres, French "sociological" comedy and the American action film. On the film's release, the press emphasised, as it does for every new film produced by Besson's EuropaCorp, that this was a "producer's" film, conceived, put together and promoted in the American fashion:

> Luc Besson has set himself up overnight as a producer in the Hollywood sense of the term. Following Steven Spielberg's example, he has brought together in one company all the different areas of expertise involved in the production line of a film: after selecting a script, the different teams set out a budget and, using Luc Besson's name, raise the funds needed to make the film, recruit film crews, and organise the film's distribution and promotion in France and abroad. This model of vertical integration leaves nothing to chance: even spin-offs such as trailers and "the-making-of" books are under the control of EuropaCorp. (Anon. 2002) [5]

Taxi is based around the contrasting and complementary pairing of its two principal protagonists. Émilien is a rather introverted policeman who cannot manage to pass his driving test, is shy with girls and remains under the thumb of his mother, who each week prepares all his meals for him in advance. Daniel is a former pizza-delivery man turned taxi driver who does not like the police, is an extrovert, constantly contravenes the highway code but is a "great driver", has a girlfriend and, to the best of our knowledge, no mother. Émilien lives in the old town, Daniel in a warehouse in a gritty suburb, and so on. Everything seems to separate these two characters who will nonetheless team up with each other, one because he does not want to lose his licence, the other because he needs a good driver, in order to take on the German Mercedes gang. However, it is also an action film, enlivened throughout by car chases, crashes and armed confrontations between the gangsters and the police. The film thus combines dialogue and a plot typical of the comedy genre with the "visual punch" of spectacular scenes filmed with the countless point-of-view tracking shots that are typical of contemporary neo-Hollywood action films.

Taxi, then, exploits a staple comic French comedy formula, namely the pairing of two psychologically and sociologically contrasting male heroes, as is the case in *La Chèvre* (Francis Veber, 1991), *La Grande Vadrouille* (Gérard Oury, 1965) or *Les Visiteurs* (Jean-Marie Poiré, 1993). It was rather accurately described in *Les Échos* of 14 April 1998 as "a *Chèvre*" (an allusion to Veber's film) "which has apparently had a particularly successful facelift".[6] This notion is further confirmed by the presence of supporting parts (the police commissioner in *Taxi*, the military father-in-law in *Taxi 2*), that are very reminiscent of the iconic faces of classic French popular cinema ("les *gueules* du cinéma français") This firm grounding in an identifiably "national" genre is also visible in the stereotypical image of Marseilles that the film conveys: mixed, working-class North Marseilles is contrasted with middle-class, petit bourgeois South Marseilles, old boys with strong Marseillais accents sit around reading the paper, and on several occasions Notre Dame de la Garde appears in the background as an authenticating landmark. This could allow the film to be read as a modernised "*pagnolade*" (in the tradition of Marcel Pagnol's films). However, the automotive adventures of the two heroes also evoke neo-Hollywood action comedies, a subgenre that has met with continuing success since the 1980s. This subgenre constructs a different representation of Marseilles in the film, a portrayal that is culturally non-specific and emptied of its local connotations. Only the characters in secondary roles have Marseilles accents, while the main and supporting characters do not, and during the very numerous action scenes the landscape shifts to a universe of motorway intersections, emblematic of a universal modernity, on which the racers battle it out.

Yet, two factors help to smooth over this simultaneously generic and national hybridity and organise it into a "coherent" form. These are the use of music and the manner in which the comedy dialogue is linked to the action sequences. The composition of the film's soundtrack, produced by celebrated Marseilles rap group IAM, serves to illustrate the film's permanent state of oscillation on both the generic and national level. IAM are representatives of a musical form that is a widely globalised US import, yet in their song lyrics and in interviews they ceaselessly emphasise their origins and life in Marseilles. French rap is very different from its American counterpart, and often claims a strong local identity through the rappers' choice of names and their lyrics (and this identity is most often linked to the *banlieues* of Paris). IAM's originality stems from the fact that they promote their regional Mediterranean and Marseilles credentials and their success extends beyond fans of the rap genre. As for the way in which action and comedy sequences are linked, this owes less to the Hollywood genre of the neo-Hollywood action comedy, with which one can assume younger audiences would be familiar, than to the French tradition of the "*comédie d'action*", an older form that is quite independent of contemporary action comedies.

To reprise the distinction between the syntax and the semantics of genres proposed by Rick Altman (1992), *Taxi* inserts *semantic* elements from the action film into the rather traditional *syntax* of French comedy. For example, the meeting between Émilien and Daniel begins with a quick comic scene in which Émilien is embarrassed at being given advice by his mother in front of the taxi driver. This evolves into a sequence which, in typical comic style, is based on the mismatch between the two characters, with Daniel, at the wheel, telling Émilien, his increasingly irate passenger, all about his contempt for the police and his utterly illegal automotive exploits. It is only after several long minutes that the action sequence gets started, when Daniel, who is in turn annoyed by the frosty reception given to him by his passenger, decides to show him how he is able to turn his ordinary taxi into a customised racing car. The end of the sequence re-establishes the comic order: the car stops, Émilien vomits, Daniel laughs, then stops laughing when Émilien shows him his police I.D. *Taxi* thus operates the shift between comedy and action in the opposite manner to that employed by the neo-Hollywood action comedy, which inserts semantic elements from the comedy genre into an action film syntax. The spectacular visuals are therefore the only element that conforms to the Hollywood action comedy model, as the narrative structure is radically different, referring back to a popular French cinematic tradition which appeared in the 1960s with *L'Homme de Rio* (Philippe de Broca, 1963) or even, in a more overtly comic mode, Hunebelle's *Fantomas* series. These films had already imported elements of the American action film into the comedy genre, grafting foreign semantic elements of action onto the traditional syntax of French comedy, and were occasionally described using the term "*comédie d'action*" by French critics long before the revival of the expression by the contemporary Hollywood action comedy.

The hybridity that characterises *Taxi*, then, admittedly employs novel methods, but its form and guiding principle are not new, which no doubt explains why the vast majority of critics have no difficulty in assigning the generic label of "police comedy" (*comédie policière*) to it, a sign that the alterity of this genre has already been "digested" in a French context.

Le Pacte des loups: giving costume drama a facelift

Like *Taxi*, *Le Pacte des loups* is a "producers' film", with a script based on an idea by Alain Sarde, of Canal+ écriture, an organisation set up to develop genre films and counter Hollywood cinema on its own ground (Chioua 2002, 94). The film is an extreme example of the desire to make a French blockbuster capable of reaching different audience communities, using the cinematic framework of costume drama and a narrative based on a well-known but mysterious historical event (the story of the Beast of the Gévaudan, which terrorised the region in question at the end of the eighteenth century). In a somewhat heritage vein, the film reconstitutes the world of the nobles and peasants of the Lozère region of 1764, and certain salon scenes, where verbal confrontation and wit come to the fore, would not have seemed out of place in *Ridicule* (Patrice Leconte, 1996) or *Beaumarchais l'Insolent* (Edouard Molinaro, 1996).

Le Pacte des loups reprises the characteristics of the swashbuckling films that, in French cinema, reached their peak in the 1950s and 1960s. The stout-hearted hero, naturalist and *chevalier* Grégoire de Fronsac (Samuel Le Bihan), sent by the King to Gévaudan on his return from the Americas to capture the beast, is an enlightened and unconventional minor noble, although not a revolutionary, who is accompanied and assisted in his adventures by a commoner (Bretèque 2005, 177-178). Here the usual class difference between the two characters–as was the case with Planchet the manservant and D'Artagnan the minor noble–is supplanted by ethnic, cultural and geographical difference. Mani (Marc Dacascos), who accompanies Fronsac, is an American Indian. Like any swashbuckling hero worth his salt, Fronsac outwits plots and schemes through his sagaciousness and fighting skill, while falling in love with a young noblewoman whom he obviously saves from the clutches of his enemies before the couple are able to live happily ever after. Finally, the film never takes its sights off a founding myth of France, namely the French Revolution, which is so often used as a narrative horizon in French costume dramas. The film is analeptically narrated against the background of the first revolutionary disturbances by a character (the marquis d'Apcher, played by Jacques Perrin) who was a witness to the events, and both opens and closes with images from the Revolution. It also attributes a political explanation to the ravages of the Beast of the Gévaudan, as the Beast turns out to be a creature manipulated by a group of particularly reactionary nobles in order to foment a climate of terror that will prevent the Monarchy from implementing liberal reforms. The story of the Beast thus becomes the narrative of the origins of the French Revolution!

Into this highly French framework, however, the film imports the methods and the technological arsenal of American blockbusters such as the "bullet time" made popular by the Wachowski brothers' *The Matrix* (1999) and John Woo-style slow-motion sequences, as well as including numerous "genre scenes" which borrow from a vast network of images from Hollywood and wider globalised culture. The Beast itself is straight out of Hollywood horror films of the 1930s, in particular Universal monster features. Slasher movies and other horror sources are borrowed from heavily in the sequences of the Beast's attacks, which are shown right from the beginning of the film. Swashbuckling sword-fights are replaced by kung-fu scenes, a martial art of which Mani, the Indian friend of the hero, proves, rather implausibly, to be a master. Having an Indian character can of course be seen as a reference to Westerns, but the fight sequences themselves belong not only to Asian cinema's tradition of martial arts films but also to the integration of this style of fighting into contemporary Hollywood cinema and computer games.[7]

Without ever adopting the apparent irony which normally accompanies the overt recycling of Hollywood genre films (see Sorin 2002, 108-109), the film shifts scenes from a neo-Hollywood genre into a referential frame that is at once "national" in a geographical sense (the Massif Central) and in a historical and cultural sense (the French Revolution). In this way it modernises a popular French genre (the swashbuckling romance) that is rather outdated but highly charged in terms of national identity, by introducing modern, foreign elements into its syntax, as *Taxi* did within another genre. These fragments of global popular culture allow the film, which takes as its basis a successful European genre (the Heritage film), to reach categories of the public who are not the usual target audience of the Heritage film: young audiences, and male audiences, which explains the predilection of the *Pacte des loups* for borrowing from traditionally masculine genres. Unlike *Taxi*, the film neither aims for, claims, nor achieves any sort of homogeneity, and the fact that this mixture is never presented in an ironic or humorous manner would seem to exclude any reading of it as a parody. *Le Pacte des loups* is certainly not *Mars Attacks!* (Tim Burton, 1996). The genre labels used to characterise the film have differed from one critic to the next, but all have brought out the "bric-à-brac" nature of the cinematic experience it offers. The question of the film's generic and cultural hybridity, while commented upon by critics, has thus always remained a purely aesthetic one.

Le Fabuleux destin d'Amélie Poulain:
revisiting the debate around the "popular"

The case of *Le Fabuleux destin d'Amélie Poulain* differs in a number of respects from that of *Taxi* or *Le Pacte des loups*. Firstly, from a generic point of view, the film in its totality is hard to categorise. One could call it a comedy drama, the term usually assigned to films with a happy ending which do not really belong to a specific genre, or perhaps a tale. However, as he traces Amélie's destiny from one comic scene to the next, from one vignette to the next, Jeunet uses a large generic palette. The film endlessly shifts from comedy to melodrama (with the concierge), to crime thriller (when Amélie investigates), to fantasy (when she dreams). Strictly speaking, it borrows nothing from genres which are identifiably foreign or have neo-Hollywood origins. As far as the film's references go, its décor, geographical boundaries and cultural markers are exclusively French, and images from other contexts only make their way into the film, in a quite literal sense, *as images*, as the photos of the garden gnome and the television images illustrate. Primarily temporal in nature, then, the film's hybridity remains enclosed within a Parisian space and the French national imaginary, and inscribes images of the past in a present-day context.

For example, the film juxtaposes its images with fragments of discourse relating to, and representations of, Paris which are all drawn from a well-known, supposedly universally-shared repertoire with powerful "heritage" connotations. A certain number of the characters' surnames refer to the traditional urban geography of Paris: the concierge who has wept constantly since her husband left her is, as fate would have it, called Madeleine Wallace, like the Parisian water fountains of the same name, while Nino, Amélie's boyfriend, is called Quincampoix, like the Paris street. Many views of the city are borrowed from 1930s French cinema, in particular poetic realism: Amélie skips stones across the still waters of the lock on the Canal Saint-Martin where Jouvet left Arletty in *Hôtel du Nord* (Marcel Carné, 1938); various apartment buildings are irresistibly reminiscent of the studio sets used in Carné's films, in particular *Le Jour se lève* (Marcel Carné, 1939). The montages which utilise lists of likes and dislikes and clips from television documentaries which are by definition temporally non-specific, allows images (or sounds) from the past to be blended with those of the present. The blind old man's crackly record player makes the highly contemporary tunnels of the Abbesses metro station echo to Fréhel's song "Si tu n'étais pas là". The voice of Fréhel, a famous *chanteuse réaliste*, not only evokes its legendary owner, but also conjures up a whole atmosphere from French popular cinema of the 1930s, which regularly used the tired, ageing singer in a manner that was already highly nostalgic, such as in *Pépé le Moko* (Julien Duvivier, 1936) and *Le Roman d'un tricheur* (Sacha Guitry, 1936). Jeunet's recreation of the ambience of French cinema of the 1930s is enhanced by Fréhel's voice echoing through a modern urban décor and a partial remodelling of the French capital according to the cinematic Paris of the past.

The film's cultural hybridity, then, resides chiefly in the relation between its references and its content–which, as we have seen, are French, and its "high-tech" form, which is perceived as exotic. To reprise the formula used by Jérôme Larcher in *Cahiers du cinéma* in May 2001, while "it is hard to imagine a more French film than this one", Jeunet is "the only [filmmaker of his generation] to have managed to make American-style French cinema, a cinema of picturesque imagery revised and corrected through digital editing" (2001, 112).[8]

The first reviews to appear, with a few exceptions quite positive, although not excessively so, commented in particular on the film's duality. On the one hand, these articles emphasise its use of special effects, identifying the film as a successful, but rather formulaic product, and remark upon the fact that Jeunet had just returned from the United States, where he had been filming *Alien: Resurrection* (1997). This sojourn in Hollywood is sometimes taken as an indicator of the director's qualities. However, it also serves as a pretext to recall that Jeunet, now used to American methods of filming, needed to return to France in order to regain the freedom that Hollywood does not offer.[9] On the other hand, the reviews (often the same ones) compare the film to the universe of Raymond Queneau or Marcel Carné, and the photography of Robert Doisneau. In the most positive articles, its poetically "retro" style, often associated with memories of French cinema or with the actress Audrey Tautou, is praised for breathing life into a film where everything is "calculated to the millimetre" (Sotinel 2001), a negative mark of Hollywood-style technical perfection. It is also criticised when, in these same references, critics can only see knowing winks, easy French stereotypes intended for export, "no doubt destined to seduce the American public, always hungry for the picturesque" (Ostria 2001).[10] This hybridity was widely commented upon in the film's first reviews, but disappeared completely from critical discourse once the film became a phenomenon. From this point, the film's Frenchness would become the central issue and the object of lively debates which focused both on the film's "French" dimension, namely its ability to express a national identity, and its "popular" dimension. Two events would bring added emphasis to the film's relation to national identity: the Cannes film festival and the simultaneous success of *Loft Story*, the French version of *Big Brother*. At the opening of the festival, much surprise was expressed at the fact that the French selectors had not chosen *Le Fabuleux destin d'Amélie Poulain*, and the organisers were obliged to explain the film's rejection. This media mini-affair consisted in setting a popular film, which was bringing in audiences but was not supported or promoted by French cinematic institutions, against a *cinéma d'auteur* which was officially recognised by the professional establishment and by a Cannes film festival which seemed the embodiment of a difficult, elitist cinema. By becoming the focus of discussion around the Cannes event for a few days, the film was drawn into this debate and set within the context of a split that has structured French cinema for almost forty years. Its status as a representative of "French popular cinema" was cemented in the context of a specifically French issue of national identity. In the spring of 2001, *Le Fabuleux destin d'Amélie Poulain* shared the headlines in the media debate with another phenomenon, this time from the world of television: *Loft Story*. These simultaneous successes gave rise to a series of comparisons between a so-called "good" popular cinema and a "bad" popular television culture. Another split of great cultural significance, around which a hierarchy in French audiovisual practices is established, was thus made visible: the audiences who had seen *Le Fabuleux destin d'Amélie Poulain* but also watched *Loft Story* were presented as being "Jekyll and Hyde" figures who dreamily contemplate the world of feelings inhabited by the delightful Amélie while satisfying their baser instincts by diving into the *Loft*'s swimming pool with Loana (the show's eventual winner) (Dupont-Monod *et al.* 2001).

The multiplication of these comparisons then reached a climax, as if the film, now crowned with success, was able to crystallise entire swathes of French culture from the last hundred years: Renoir, Doisneau, Carné, poetic realism as a whole, Prévert, Marcel Aymé, Queneau, Georges Perec, Philippe Delerm,[11] Arletty, Bernard Blier and Louis Jouvet (with whom Audrey Tautou, Jamel and Rufus were compared), to name a few. Even Robert Guédiguian's *Marius et Jeannette* (1997) sometimes cropped up on this list. *Le Fabuleux destin d'Amélie Poulain* was thus placed in the perspective of a rather nostalgic, consensual reading of national history and culture. References to its "international" form disappeared, and the film henceforth functioned as a site of regained Frenchness. The identification of *Le Fabuleux destin d'Amélie Poulain* with a certain image of France reached its height at the end of May 2001, following a series of somewhat gushing articles about the film and the private screening organised at the Élysée palace. In the atmosphere of the run-up to the electoral campaign (the presidential and legislative elections of 2002 were a little less than a year away), a series of articles turned Amélie into the emblem of a unified France, at last reconciled with itself. Indeed, "Amélie présidente!" featured among the headings in a special report devoted to the film in *Marianne*. Establishing a clear metaphor of national unity transcending social class, the article emphasised how the French public had been able, thanks to this film, "for once to discover that they shared their tastes with professional film critics" and that it had managed to bring back audiences who had stopped going to the cinema.[12]

We have already seen two commonly understood meanings of the expression "popular cinema", a universal sense (a type of cinema seen by large audiences) and a sense which is more closely related to a specifically French context (a type of cinema opposed to the *cinéma d'auteur*), and it also has a third meaning: "popular film" as film made for and seen by a "popular" public, in the sense of a public composed of lower-income social groups. Whether this latter definition applies to *Amélie* remains to be proved,[13] but what is more important is that broad perceptions of the film saw it as reviving the golden age of the 1930s-1950s, a time when cinema-going among the working classes had not yet declined and the taste for Hollywood cinema had not yet, particularly among this working-class public, usurped the place of popular French cinema.

A raging polemic sprang up in the "Rebonds" section of *Libération* and in the music magazine *Les Inrockuptibles*: was Amélie Poulain's Paris an ideologically acceptable representation of France? David Martin-Castelnau and Guillaume Bigot, both members of the think-tank *Génération République*, published a text emphasising the film's ability to represent ordinary people of modest means "without sarcasm or condemnation", seeing it as a riposte "to the ramblings of Sollers and his *France moisie* (mouldy France)".[14] In the discourse of these defenders of Amélie Poulain, one encounters a fourth meaning of the expression "popular cinema": a cinema which talks about common people. Serge Kaganski replied to this both in *Les Inrockuptibles* and again the "Rebonds" section of *Libération*, levelling his central accusation against the ideological content of the film. Kaganski rails against the reactionary, right-wing vision of Paris as a village "cleansed of its ethnic, social and sexual polysemy" (Kaganski 2001).[15] As far as he is concerned, Jeunet's film was evidence of a dangerous obsession with the past, of a demagogic, "*franchouillard*" (salt-of-the-earth French) nostalgia which delivers a stream of populist clichés about a Paris of shopkeepers and displays, in its elimination of "dirt" from this image by calling the character played by

Jamel Debbouze Lucien, a pervasive phobia of the Other.[16] *Le Fabuleux destin d'Amélie Poulain* is thus clearly linked to French identity here, although this identity is an unwelcoming and hateful one, as spelt out in the concluding phrase: "if Le Pen was looking for a film to promote his vision of France and the French people, *Amélie Poulain* would be the ideal candidate" (Kaganski, 2001).[17]

If I have examined the question of the reception of *Le Fabuleux destin d'Amélie Poulain* at some length, it is because out of these three films, it was the only one in relation to which the question of French popular cinema was raised explicitly and in a sense debated, no doubt because it was also the only one to feature an obvious discrepancy between its technical aspects (modern, American) and its content (nostalgic, French). This is quite exceptional given the character of French film criticism, which in general terms takes a classical cinephile approach to the defence and glorification of the Seventh Art. Whatever one thinks about *Amélie* and its ideological content, its lasting success shows that a contemporary popular French film is not necessarily one that the critics ignore, but can instead be "a film which is talked about, which, for example, has its thematic concerns taken up and amplified by the media, and becomes a defined object in the public consciousness" to quote a definition suggested by Pierre Sorlin (2000, 23).[18] *Le Fabuleux destin d'Amélie Poulain* succeeds in being popular in several different meanings of this term, meanings that were touched upon in the debates surrounding the film, in all likelihood precisely because it was at first regarded as a culturally hybrid film, before this reading was, as we have seen, corrected. This error in framing, or reframing the film on the part of the critics, the shift from a globalised perspective to one focused on questions of French national identity, was what in fact allowed this questioning of the link between the popular and the national. However, these debates bring up another question: is it possible today to make a popular French film which is not, or is not taken to be, populist (yet another, final, possible definition of the term), given that at present any affirmation of a popular French mode necessarily suggests, in cinema and society as a whole, a nostalgic image of the past which obviously poses fewer problems when safely flourishing within the confines of the heritage genre?

Translated from the French by Jonathan Hensher

---

[1] For more information on audience responses, see Stigsdotter in this volume.

[2] Centre National de la Cinématographie (CNC) *Bilan 2001*, May 2002.

[3] For further discussions of *Les Choristes*, see also Vincendeau, Russell and Nacache in this volume.

⁴ This allusion has already become virtually incomprehensible, Itineris being the old name for France Telecom's mobile phone network.

⁵ "Luc Besson s'est improvisé du jour au lendemain producteur, au sens hollywoodien du terme. À l'image d'un Steven Spielberg, il a réuni au sein d'une même société les différents savoir-faire composant la chaîne de production d'un film: après avoir sélectionné un script, les équipes définissent un budget, rassemblent–autour du nom de Luc Besson–les fonds nécessaires à la réalisation du film, recrutent les équipes pour le tournage, en assurent la distribution en France et à l'étranger tout comme la promotion. Une intégration verticale qui ne laisse rien au hasard: même les produits dérivés tels que les bandes-annonces et les livres de tournage sont sous le contrôle d'EuropaCorp."

⁶ "…une *Chèvre* qui aurait subi un lifting particulièrement réussi."

⁷ For example, the design of certain weapons and the choreography of certain fights are inspired by the game *Soul Calibur*.

⁸ "Il est difficile d'imaginer un film plus français que celui-là… le seul à avoir su faire un cinéma français à l'américaine, un cinéma d'imagerie pittoresque revu et corrigé par le numérique."

⁹ See interview with Jeunet (de Bruyn 2001).

¹⁰ "…destinées sans doute à séduire le public américain friand de pittoresque."

¹¹ Author of a highly successful best-seller which listed life's little pleasures, *La première gorgée de bière et autres plaisirs minuscules* (Paris: Gallimard, 1997).

¹² "…se découvrir pour une fois des goûts communs avec les critiques professionnels."

¹³ In the absence of dedicated research, one can only speculate upon the social status of the audience of a given film. One can assume, though, without going too far out on a limb, that there are films which are "less popular" than others in this respect, such as *films d'auteur* that have not achieved wide recognition and are distributed on a small scale, by basing one's conclusions on the sociological character of the few theatres in which these films are distributed (Montebello 2005; Esquenazi 2003).

¹⁴ In his 1999 article "La France moisie", writer and critic Philippe Sollers had attacked what he saw as France's reactionary penchant for sentimental nostalgia.

¹⁵ "…nettoyé de sa polysémie ethnique, sociale et sexuelle."

¹⁶ It is to be noted that when, in *Taxi*, a *beur* character played by a *beur* actor, Samy Naceri, was given the name Daniel, no such polemic ensued.

¹⁷ "Si Le Pen cherchait un titre pour promouvoir sa vision du peuple et de la France, *Amélie Poulain* serait le candidat idéal."

¹⁸ "Un film que la critique ignore… un film qui fait parler de lui, dont les thématiques par exemple, relayées et amplifiées médiatiquement, devient un objet de définition publique."

CHAPTER THREE

PEUT-ON ETRE A LA FOIS HOLLYWOODIEN ET FRANÇAIS ? FRENCH *SUPERPRODUCTIONS* AND THE AMERICAN MODEL

FRANÇOIS-XAVIER MOLIA

A number of young French directors, such as Mathieu Kassovitz, Jean-François Richet and Florent Siri, have, through their work for Hollywood studios in recent years, served to remind us that the opposition between a French *cinéma d'auteur* and an industrial American cinema is not quite so clear-cut as those who talk and write about the subject would often have us believe. More telling yet is the recent emergence of French "*superproductions*" which appear to be modelled on the Hollywood blockbuster. Today's popular cinema, then, has become a mixed zone in which a national tradition of French-style entertainment and the ever-stronger attraction of Hollywood production methods exist side by side, and on occasions become intertwined. The debate surrounding *Un long dimanche de fiançailles* (Jean-Pierre Jeunet, 2004), a French-language film shot in France, but produced by a subsidiary of Warner studios, which consequently had its access to public subsidies blocked by a court ruling (see Vulser 2005), is illustrative of the identity crisis currently gripping French cinema, a crisis which does not appear set to subside, and which stems from one question: can one be at the same time French and "Hollywood"?

Through case studies of two big-budget French films, *Le Pacte des loups* (Christophe Gans, 2001) and *Vidocq* (Pitof, 2001), whose debt to Hollywood cinema has rightly been commented upon, I intend to examine the development of a particular form of cinematic spectacle. This style of film has encountered various difficulties, and at times a good deal of misunderstanding, in establishing its identity as at once a mirror-image of

Hollywood, from which it borrows both its commercial and aesthetic approaches, and a rival to it, insofar as it always affirms a specifically French identity, whether through references to a national cinematic heritage or, in a wider sense, by recycling elements of popular culture.

My work is based on an analysis both of the films themselves and of press articles, interviews and reviews relating to these films. Professional cinema critics are, of course, not entirely representative of the general public, but their output can nevertheless provide important indications as to how the two *superproductions* in question were received and consumed. The comparison I draw between Hollywood cinema and French *superproductions* is taken directly from the discourse examined here. By this I mean that this parallel, before being used in the context of the present analysis, had clearly already played a role in framing these films' reception, as can be seen from many of the articles under examination.[1] In the press, the label "*superproduction hollywoodienne*" so frequently serves to denote and define *French* films that one can, paradoxically, consider it to be a marker of a distinct French cinema genre.

Superproductions: a mirror-image

La Croix described *Le Pacte des loups* as a "comic-book spectacular filmed in the Anglo-Saxon style",[2] while a number of articles considered the western to be the genre to which the film was most indebted.[3] *Vidocq*, meanwhile, was deemed by *France-Soir* to be "a spectacle worthy of American mass-market entertainment",[4] and "a dark and violent serial-killer movie in the American mould" by *L'Humanité*.[5] If a perusal of all the press reviews of *Vidocq* and *Le Pacte des loups* shows us that they were in many cases perceived as productions bearing the mark of the Hollywood film industry, one question nonetheless remains: what is a French "Hollywood" film, if Hollywood is not directly involved in either its production or its financing? Obviously, the expression must be understood in terms of its connotations, insofar as these films "look Hollywood" in the eyes of their commentators. What, though, are the criteria on which this identification is based?

These films' financial and commercial aspects were what first grabbed the attention of commentators. Compared to the usual scale of French productions, *Vidocq*, with a budget at the time of nearly 160 million francs (about 24 million euros), and *Le Pacte des loups*, with a budget of around 200 million francs (30 million euros), appeared extremely expensive films, as even today the average budget of a French film is between 2 and 3 million euros. These figures justify the use of the term *"superproduction"*, and are not far off the going rate for making a Hollywood blockbuster.

The distribution of *Le Pacte des loups* and *Vidocq* was entrusted to two companies regularly sub-contracted by Hollywood studios to distribute their films in France. *Le Pacte des loups* was distributed by Metropolitan, a French company which is the exclusive partner of New Line and, in the same year, dealt with the distribution in France of the *Lord of the Rings* (Peter Jackson, 2001). *Vidocq* was distributed by UFD, a French subsidiary of Fox Studios. Both of these French projects were thus promoted and put into the marketplace using the techniques and commercial savvy usually reserved for the promotion of Hollywood films. The intense marketing campaign (for example, the multiple posters for *Le Pacte des loups* in the Paris metro, each showing one of the main characters, or the distribution of trailers several months before the film's release) and the films' distribution on hundreds of screens (with 725 copies for *Le Pacte des loups*, 655 for *Vidocq*) are typical of the commercial techniques employed by Hollywood blockbuster productions.[6] The practice of "saturation booking" was introduced in Hollywood in the 1970s, and became systematic following the monumental success of *Jaws* (Steven Spielberg, 1975), which at the time came out simultaneously on 409 screens. This distribution process was adopted by exploitation cinema, where producers looked to bank their profits as quickly as possible, before word of mouth and reviews could reveal their film's shortcomings.[7] Moreover, this method, when supported by an advertising drive, surrounds the release of a film with the aura of an "event" and confers a form of omnipresence upon it. At this stage, the media end up presenting the release of a film as an event in its own right, independent of the production's merits, and thereby ensure that it receives a form of free publicity by maintaining its visibility in their output. It should lastly be noted that in France advertising costs do not take up as preponderant a share of the budget as they do in Hollywood productions. What is routine for a Hollywood production, for a French film would be considered exceptional. It is reasonable to conclude that these factors helped to mark out and extol *Vidocq* and *Le Pacte des loups* all the more, given that these films were placed in a market where competition from other French productions, as far as promotion was concerned, was not very strong.[8]

The second main aspect of the parallel drawn between these two films and Hollywood blockbusters concerns their aesthetic features. Critics saw the processes used in their production, in particular the massive use of special effects, and a more general emphasis on the spectacular, as characteristic of the mode of entertainment offered by Hollywood. In a number of interviews, Christophe Gans and Pitof both conceded, each in his own manner, that their work had been influenced by American popular cinema, Gans referring for example to James Cameron and John McTiernan,[9] Pitof to David Fincher.[10] *Vidocq* may thus with justification be considered an heir to *Seven*, a film which, with its expressive use of lighting and a predominantly dull, yellowish colour palette in conjunction with a crime-thriller plot, has been so widely copied, both in Hollywood and France, that it has come to function in many respects as a genre marker in film criticism.[11] In the case of *Le Pacte des loups*, the influence of this Hollywood style takes on a more concrete character, as key production posts were filled by technicians who had previously worked in Hollywood, such as the chief camera operator Dan Lausten, who had shot *Mimic* (Guillermo del Toro, 1997) and *Nightwatch* (Ole Bornedal, 1997), or David Wu, the editor of *Bride of Chucky* (Ronny Yu, 1998). The film's visual identity was in this way placed in the hands of specialists in Hollywood-style cinema. Given this transfer of skills, it would seem reasonable to consider the chase and fight sequences, as well as the film's fantastic, disturbing atmosphere, as fitting into the continuum of Hollywood cinema, where they are par for the course.

The element that the two films are most often accused of borrowing from Hollywood action cinema is their fight choreography. *Le Pacte des loups* seems to lift this element directly from the style of combat which rose to prominence with *The Matrix* (Andy and Larry Wachovski, 1999), a film which had itself adapted the fighting style of Hong Kong martial-arts cinema by engaging the services of choreographer Yuen Woo-Ping. In *Le Pacte des loups*, as well as typical martial-arts moves, one encounters temporal distortions that are put in at the editing stage, slow-motion effects which give the impression that the action has been suspended and serve to lend greater visual impact to scenes of combat which are otherwise based on extremely rapid movement. Hong Kong-based technician Philip Kwok designed the choreography for *Le Pacte des loups* and, like its Hollywood predecessor *The Matrix*, the French film also borrowed techniques and know-how straight from Asian cinema. This borrowing was not so direct in *Vidocq*, as its fight choreography was the work of a French technician, Michel Carliez, although the prominent placing of his name in the film's credits is in itself revealing with regard to the importance given to this aspect of the film. Furthermore, the initial fight in *Vidocq* appears, although as far as I know the director has never explicitly admitted this, to echo the final duel in George Lucas' *Star Wars, Episode I: The Phantom Menace* (1998). The similarities are striking, as, in addition to the kung fu-derived choreography, the French film uses the same scenography, with the fight taking place in a circular space around a well, and also features identical costume-work, with the "bad-guy" wearing a loose, fluttering outfit, his ample cape creating swirls of fabric with every movement. *Vidocq* and *Le Pacte des loups* thus make use of visual and choreographic techniques popularised by contemporary Hollywood cinema, which for this reason can be considered the most obvious aesthetic frame within which to situate these films.

Lastly, a feature of these films often cited to discredit them, and which critics spoke of at the time of their release, is the multigenericity of *Le Pacte des loups* and *Vidocq*, which seems once again to emphasise their links with Hollywood entertainment. It is common to characterise the latter form through its propensity to mix different genres, and one might consider, as Raphaëlle Moine does, that, without inventing this phenomenon, "new" Hollywood has tended to deploy it systematically, thanks in no small part to the refinement of the tools used to analyse potential audiences, allowing the differences in their expectations to be more accurately taken into account, and consequently pushing the Hollywood blockbuster towards an ever more pronounced degree of genre mixing (Moine 2002, 107). *Le Pacte des loups* was duly qualified as an "obese, proliferating object" (objet obèse et proliférant), a "sickly, melancholy blockbuster" (blockbuster malade et mélancolique) by *Les Inrockuptibles* (Père 2001), while Didier Péron, in *Libération*, placed *Vidocq* in the "neo-pompous-gothic-kung-fu" (néo-pompier-gothico-kung-fu) genre, of which *Le Pacte des loups* was, according to him, the first example (Péron and Lalanne 2001). The grotesqueness of this neologism in itself acts as a condemnation of the film's excessive eclecticism.

One could look into the reasons as to why the French reception of this kind of genre-mixing is so frequently hostile, but this would form the subject of a study of cultural history going well beyond the remit of the present article. I would, however, like to suggest two explanatory hypotheses regarding the presence of such a high degree of multigenericity in these two films. It has become habitual, and rightly so, to place particular emphasis on the economic motivations of Hollywood films, which are conceived of as products intended to entertain a wide public, in order to bring in profits. Richard Maltby thus correctly reminds us that "Hollywood's commercial aesthetic is too opportunistic to prize coherence, organic unity, or the absence of contradiction among its primary virtues" (Maltby 2003, 51). The diversity of the genres that are brought together multiplies the possibilities both for recognition and also for comforting pleasure derived from the repetition of a previously assimilated model. The effect of this is to widen the potential audience of the film in question. It seems probable that by combining the fantasy film, crime thriller, kung fu film and costume drama, *Vidocq* and *Le Pacte des loups* followed just such a strategy. However, this plurality of references also fulfils what Rick Altman terms the "pseudo-commemorative" function of genres, a function which he has located in contemporary Hollywood cinema. Here, generic repetition seeks not so much to achieve resonance with the values and institutions of the period in question (as was the case with romantic comedies from the classic era, which confirmed the then-current processes of seduction in Western culture) as to cement a community of viewers together around a shared set of cinematic references. Displaying recognisable elements drawn from a given genre within a film thus, according to Rick Altman, serves to inscribe this film in the history of its medium (Altman 1999, 189-192). Viewers are invited to celebrate their own culture. At the same time, through this technique, the director shows off his knowledge and presents himself as a cinematic memorialist. A marked feature of French *superproductions*, and this is as true of Mathieu Kassovitz's *Les Rivières pourpres* (1999) as it is of Alain Chabat's *Astérix et Obélix: Mission Cléopâtre* (2001), is that they are highly "referenced", liberally quoting other works. However, this reprising of different genres, for the most part, but not entirely, drawn from Hollywood sources, should not hide the fact that these films are driven by a quite different objective, namely that of affirming and promoting a specifically French form of cinematic entertainment.

The *superproduction* as a rival to Hollywood: French specificities

The objective of *Vidocq* and *Le Pacte des loups* would seem to be the gallicisation of the blockbuster form. This can take the form of direct rivalry, with the French films eager to show that they enjoy a form of superiority over their Hollywood model. *Vidocq* clearly seeks to achieve this on the technological level by being the first film in world cinema history to be shot entirely using a high-definition digital camera, made by Sony. Although one has a rather uncomfortable feeling when reading the triumphant cries which greeted this "victory", they are in themselves revealing with regard to the way in which this technological innovation was perceived by the French public, and how it was immediately placed in the context of the competition between French cinema and its American rival. Originally, George Lucas had been set to be the first to use this new equipment for the filming of the second episode of the *Star Wars* saga, *Attack of the Clones* (2002). Pitof's film, by grabbing this "first" in the innovation stakes, thus challenged Hollywood cinema's leadership in terms of technology, a leadership which rests partly on its domination of the world market. Digital filming, as well as providing a differently textured image, also facilitates graphic manipulation, and so allows French know-how in the field of special effects (in this case that of Duran-Dubois studios, who were hired for *Vidocq*) to be shown to its best advantage. The use of this innovation, then, formed part of a strategy to attract audiences which involved showing that "we", the French, can do as well as, if not better than, Hollywood.

Various statements by Christophe Gans, as well as the commercial paratext for *Le Pacte des loups*, express this desire for competition even more clearly. The text on the back of the DVD states that Gans "at last demonstrates that a French production can rival Hollywood cinema".[12] This rivalry would seem to be present within the film itself, through the presence of a traditional figure from Hollywood cinema, the Indian, whom *Le Pacte des loups* not only reprises but, more importantly, "nationalises". The film's Iroquois character, Mani, is the site of an interesting process of cultural hybridisation. He displays various recognisable features of the Indian of the Hollywood western, such as traditional costume, animist beliefs, silence and wisdom, but also other features that are rather Asian (he practises kung fu, although, as has already been mentioned, the film's choreography is more reminiscent of *The Matrix* than of Bruce Lee films) and, in particular, French (unlike the Indians in westerns, he speaks French rather than English, and is explicitly associated with "*la Nouvelle France*", French America). In this respect, *Le Pacte des loups* is not content just to oppose the dominant model of the western, but effects something of a revision of the history of cinema by appropriating the figure of the Indian, and transferring it into a French setting.

In an article signed "O.D.B." published in *Le Point*, the author notes that "[a]fter *Le Pacte des loups* and *Belphégor*, and before *Le Petit Poucet*, the first film directed by Pitof... is part of a new French cinema genre which sets out to knock the dust off the great figures of our cultural heritage using an eye-popping profusion of pyrotechnics" (O.D.B. 2001).[13] What was not lost on journalistic criticism, then, was that these films, so strongly marked by the American model, at the same time affirmed their national specificities: this was Hollywood, but *à la française*. The filmmakers themselves, in the various interviews they gave at the time of these films' releases, continually invoked a French frame of reference, while never denying their debt to Hollywood. Along with David Fincher, Pitof also cited the painter Gustave Moreau as a principal source of inspiration for *Vidocq*'s atmosphere and set designs. However, it was in

Christophe Gans' discourse that this desire to distinguish himself from Hollywood was most clearly expressed. His reasoning was simple: Hollywood's ownership of certain elements (such as, it is perhaps implied, the figure of the Indian) must be challenged, in order to show that these elements have also long been present in European culture. In *Le Figaro*, Gans explained that he had been particularly marked by films which express the idea of "a caste conscious of living its last moments" (d'une caste consciente de vivre ses derniers moments). By way of examples he cited such westerns as *The Wild Bunch* (Sam Peckinpah, 1969) or *The Man Who Shot Liberty Valance* (John Ford, 1962), as well as Asian sword-fighting films. "But", he was quick to add, "these are all profoundly European themes, I don't see why we should have any complexes about re-appropriating them".[14] Further on, he offered a definition of *Le Pacte des loups* which seemed to exclude all reference to Hollywood: "It is a historical fantasy film, in the same vein as the *Angélique* series" (C'est un film de fantaisie historique, dans le goût des *Angélique*).[15] What Christophe Gans rejects in these statements, then, is any claim that Hollywood might have to exclusive rights over certain themes and, more importantly, over popular film entertainment.

Le Pacte des loups and *Vidocq* distance themselves from Hollywood by emphasising their own cultural resources, drawn from France's national heritage. *Le Pacte des loups* thus reactivates a historical reference, the period of the French revolution, and a reference from legend, the famous Beast of the Gévaudan. *Vidocq*, for its part, presses the revolution of 1830 into service, as well as the figure of its eponymous hero. Indeed, one might comment upon the presence in both films of this revolutionary motif, which could subliminally emphasise what is taken to be representative of a rebellious "French spirit", independent and fractious, which more often than not feeds into an anti-Americanism directed particularly against the conformism which is supposedly all-pervasive on the other side of the Atlantic. In this respect, *Vidocq* also, very obviously, plays on its reconstruction through digital images of the Paris of 1830. The use of digital cameras in the shooting, coupled with painstaking research, allowed the recreation of highly detailed views of certain Parisian monuments and districts. At various points, panning shots of, for example, Les Invalides or Montmartre, are inserted into the montage indicating that *Vidocq* is also conceived as a documentary spectacle, intended to show French audiences the image of their capital city, snatched from the jaws of the past thanks to digital wizardry. Historical films aimed principally at the domestic market, *Le Pacte des loups* and *Vidocq* fit into a large network of representations of the nation's past, popularised through the educational system, through other films, and also through television series.

These films are also heirs to a French cinematic tradition, that of the costume drama, which was particularly popular from the 1940s to the 1960s, and in a more general sense draw upon France's national audiovisual heritage. *Vidocq* thus takes its cue from the highly successful television series of the same name, which ran from 1967 to 1974. Most importantly, unlike Luc Besson's *Le Cinquième élément* (1997), a French film (approved by the CNC) which nonetheless starred Bruce Willis and was filmed in English, *Le Pacte des loups* and *Vidocq* take a gamble by relying on actors who are best-known within France: Vincent Cassel, Monica Bellucci, Jacques Perrin in the former film, Gérard Depardieu, André Dussollier, Inès Sastre and Guillaume Canet in the latter.[16] What is particularly remarkable is that these films bring together actors from different generations, and even, in the case of *Le Pacte des loups*, from different branches of cinema, as Vincent Cassel, a regular of big-budget films (such as *Les Rivières pourpres*), is cast alongside Emilie Dequenne and Jérémie Rénier, emblematic actors of the Dardenne brothers' *oeuvre* – a type of film that could not be further removed from the Hollywood blockbuster. A number of popular actors whose faces are well known to the French public also make discreet appearances in inconspicuous minor roles, such as Jean-Marc Thibaut's cripple in *Vidocq*, or Jean Yanne's provincial nobleman in *Le Pacte des loups*. One of the attractions of these French *superproductions*, one of the ways in which they show off their opulence, then, seems to be to bring together a cast which is rich and prestigious in the eyes of French audiences, who end up looking out for every new character in order to see which celebrity is playing the role. A comment in a review of *Vidocq* is testimony to the pleasure to be gained in this way: "the director gambles on providing everything in enormous quantities. Sometimes the result is seductive–when the sets take you by surprise, when even the tiniest of roles is given to a great actor".[17]

However, recognising them is not always easy, and it is a particular feature of these films that while they both press this audiovisual heritage into service, they at the same time seek to shake it up, or "dust it off" as the journalist quoted above put it. For instance, in *Vidocq*, thanks to some impressive make-up work, André Dussollier is unrecognisable as a bald-headed chief of police. The director's commentary on the DVD edition of the film reveals that the actor in question was for some time reluctant to appear in such an unexpected guise. Such surprise effects thus derive from the expectations that French audiences have established from their knowledge of their national cinema. The most spectacular of these surprises is the death of Vidocq himself in the film's opening minutes, which sends not only the character from whom the film takes its title, but also its principal star, plunging into the fiery pit. Even though he reappears in later flash-back sequences, Gérard Depardieu remains the film's absent party, the original victim from whom the diegesis proceeds.

Le Pacte des loups also makes efforts to break down its audience's familiarity with well-known elements of cultural and cinematic heritage. In the commentary that he provides for the DVD edition of the film, Christophe Gans, evidently conscious of the fact that his film primarily targeted adolescent audiences, states how, concerned about avoiding the "museumy" (musée Grevin) character of historical reconstructions, he had looked for "a totally sexy eighteenth century" (un dix-huitième siècle complètement sexy). Like in Hélène Angel's *Rencontre avec le Dragon*, another film from 2001, but a far more modest success, the reconstruction of the past is filtered through a fantastical imagination, culminating in the final fight-scene where the bad-guy uses an exotic sword-whip which, as Christophe Gans himself has admitted, is taken straight from the imagery of Asian sword-fighting films. In his DVD commentary, Gans, speaking about swashbuckling films, explains how he "really wanted to get inside this genre and give it a good kicking".[18] It is this mixing of genres, with the trans-national cross-fertilisation to which it can lead, which becomes, in this film, the principal means of renewing French historical cinema.

Conclusion

"Give it a good kicking": this image gives a sense of the risks involved in this enterprise, in particular as far as the film's public reception is concerned. *Le Pacte des loups* and *Vidocq* are in effect motivated by a double rejection, both of the Hollywood copy and of the French genre film, a double rejection which forms the source of a desire for new hybridisation. In *Vidocq*, it is the star Gérard Depardieu who is the site of the most striking attempt at achieving this hybridisation. Depardieu, a stalwart of heritage roles (Jean de Florette, Cyrano, Rodin, Balzac), this time plays a Vidocq reworked according to the codes of the Hollywood action film, fighting unarmed in the Hong Kong style. The magazine *Aden* was not slow to begin asking questions: "Seeing, as we do here, a final drawn out fight scene, straight out of Star Wars, with Depardieu executing spectacular back-flips worthy of the Matrix... isn't this all a bit silly?"[19] This treacherous remark reveals, in its own way, the commercial risks run by this type of project, which, by attempting improbable transplants between different cinematic traditions, exposes itself to the risk of not finding an audience.

In this respect, the revolutionary paradigm present in both films can be seen in a new light: just as Grégoire de Fronsac explains to Vincent Cassel's character that "times are changing" (les temps changent), *Vidocq* and *Le Pacte des loups* are shot through with a theme of renewal taken up, in aesthetic terms, by the way they plunge traditional representations into crisis. By confronting the old order with the modern order, by mixing up the historical and the fantastic, by refusing either to be American or completely French, both films illustrate, right down to the images they use, the problematic identity of a contemporary French cinema caught between a desire for continuity and rupture, imitation and specificity.

Translated from the French by Jonathan Hensher

---

[1] This study was made possible by the archive of press reviews kept in the Bibliothèque du Film in Paris. This database contains 21 articles on *Vidocq*, and 26 on *Le Pacte des Loups*.

[2] "…bande dessinée grand spectacle mise en image à la mode anglo-saxonne." See P. Royer, 2001.

[3] On the influence of the Western in *Le Pacte des Loups*, see Boujut (2001), Coppermann (2001), J. Roy (2001), E. Libiot (2001) and Père (2001). See also F-X. Molia (2005).

[4] "…un spectacle digne d'un divertissement américain". See A. Dollfus (2001).

[5] "…un film de serial-killer violent et glauque à la mode américaine". See Ostria (2001b).

[6] The figures for the two films' budgets, as declared pre-production to the CNC, and for the number of copies distributed in the first week of release are taken from *Film Français*, n° 2924, 22 February 2002.

[7] For a history of this practice, see Cook (2000).

[8] In point of fact, while *Le Pacte des loups* was indeed a clear commercial success, the success of *Vidocq* was, to say the least, qualified. Ticket sales for *Le Pacte des Loups* reached 5,166,703 in France and *Vidocq* made 1,863,522 as of 1 January 2002 (source: *Le Film Français*, n°2921, 1 February 2002). In Europe and Quebec, the former film had, by 30 November 2001, sold 1,450,556 tickets, compared to only 53,512 for the latter (source: *Le Film Français*, n° 2918, 11 January 2002).

[9] In an interview with *L'Express* "Christophe Gans et l'impact des loups", (anon. 25 January 2001), the director rather humbly declared, with respect to the distance he intended to keep between himself and Hollywood: "Why would I go comparing myself to great filmmakers like James Cameron and John McTiernan? I'd rather be myself here than a nobody over there" (Pourquoi irais-je me mesurer à ces cinéastes formidables que sont James Cameron et John McTiernan? Plutôt être moi-même ici que le dernier là-bas).

[10] He describes his film as "a sort of *Seven* transposed onto the 19th century" (une sorte de *Seven* transposé au XIXè siècle) (in E. Fois 2001), while his chief set designer, Jean Rabasse, explained that he "had *Seven* in his sights" (*Seven* en point de mire) in his work for this production (in G. Douguet, 2001).

[11] For example, a critic writing about *Rivières pourpres 2: Les Anges de l'Apocalypse* (Olivier Dahan 2003), notes that in this film one encounters "a gothic aesthetic seen 1000 times over since *Seven*" ("une esthétique gothique vue et revue 1000 fois depuis *Seven*") (R. Gianorio, 2004).

[12] "...démontre enfin qu'une production française peut rivaliser avec le cinéma hollywoodien."

[13] "Après *Le Pacte des loups*, *Belphégor* et avant *Le Petit Poucet*, le premier film réalisé par Pitof... s'inscrit dans un nouveau genre du cinéma national qui tente de dépoussiérer les figures du patrimoine culturel avec une profusion de pétarades pyrotechniques."

[14] "Mais ce sont des thèmes profondément européens, je ne vois pas pourquoi il faudrait avoir le moindre complexe à se les réapproprier."

[15] Quotation taken from Tranchant and Gans (2001).

[16] One could argue that the presence of, respectively, Vincent Cassel and Gérard Depardieu in the two films is evidence of a internationalising distribution strategy, as both actors are well known abroad thanks to films such as *Les Rivières pourpres* for the former, and *Cyrano de Bergerac* (Jean-Paul Rappeneau, 1989) or *1492* (Ridley Scott, 1992) in the case of the latter.

[17] "...le metteur en scène mise sur une surabondance de tout. Parfois, cela séduit–quand un décor surprend, quand le moindre petit rôle est tenu par un grand acteur" (Anon. 2001).

[18] "Je voulais vraiment donner des coups à l'intérieur de ce genre."

[19] "Voir comme ici un long combat final, tout droit sorti de *Star Wars*, avec Depardieu exécutant des sauts périlleux arrière dignes de *Matrix*... est-ce bien raisonnable? " (Anon. 2001).

CHAPTER FOUR

FROM *LA CAGE AUX ROSSIGNOLS* (1945) TO *LES CHORISTES* (2004): CHANGES AND CONTINUITIES IN FRENCH POPULAR CINEMA

GINETTE VINCENDEAU

There is little consensus about the meaning of the term "popular", especially in the cinema. We only have to look at the recent *Dictionnaire du cinéma populaire français* (Dehée and Bosséno 2004) which includes entries on films and filmmakers that its editor Yannick Dehée considers "limit cases", to see a confused picture, in which "popular" is frequently equated with "favourite", "cult" or "well-loved". We are on safer ground with box office figures, even though some "popular"–genre, mainstream–films fail commercially. Nevertheless, as Jostein Gripsrud put it in the introduction to *The Aesthetics of Popular Art*, "The greatest importance of popular art lies precisely in its popularity" (Gripsrud 1999). Films that do well at the box office have important economic implications; they create jobs, raise the salaries of their stars, boost national cinema audiences and DVD sales, and may even involve the legal system (for example, *Les Choristes*, one of the films discussed in this article, made Gérard Jugnot the best paid actor of 2004, while in the wake of the unexpected success of the film the parents of one of the young singers took the production to court). But popular films also matter because we tend to assume that there is a link between their popularity and the taste or mentality of their audience, even if the nature of this link is unclear. This is because the cinema navigates uneasily between the two main paradigms that are used to define the popular, namely the commercial paradigm and the anthropological paradigm. As V.F. Perkins says, "Popular cinema brings with it the sense of 'popular culture', but only the 'mass culture' sense... There is no folk cinema to parallel folk music or folk-tale since access to

the apparatus of production is so restricted by its cost and complexity."
Yet, he continues, "it also strains belief to suppose that the interests of
cinema-goers have been without influence on the form and content of
movies" (Perkins 1992, 194).

Studying popular cinema is also fraught with difficulties on account of
its low cultural capital, a problem magnified when talking about French
(or European) cinema as opposed to Hollywood. Popular French films
contradict established notions of French cinema as a quality, auteur
cinema, which means that they tend to be considered inferior to both
popular Hollywood cinema and French art cinema. Concurrently, in
ideological terms they are invariably thought to be beyond the pale–
conservative as well as nostalgic, as is indeed the case for the two films I
have chosen to discuss as a case study.

La Cage aux rossignols was seen by five million spectators, which
made it the top French film of 1945, ahead of the now much more famous
Les Enfants du paradis (both were beaten only by Chaplin's *The Great
Dictator*, made in 1940 but only released in France in 1945). *Les Choristes*
was the surprise hit of 2004, with 8.5 million spectators. Apart from the
two films' commercial success, there is a strong link between them insofar
as *Les Choristes* is a remake, or rather an adaptation of the 1945 film. A
comparison between the two should thus be particularly useful in charting
changes but also continuities in popular French cinema of the post-war
period in terms of themes and critical reception.

In my choice of sample I have also deliberately chosen two films that
span the whole of the post-war period, for two reasons. One is practical:
1945 marks the beginning of precise and reliable statistics in French
cinema. The other is that the post-war period includes the New Wave,
which introduced a separation, in audience and critical practice, between
popular and auteur cinema. I am interested in the effect of this break on "a
certain tendency of the French cinema", to use François Truffaut's
infamous phrase to qualify French mainstream cinema (Truffaut 1954,
224-237), given that my two sample films appeared on either side of it.

La Cage aux rossignols and *Les Choristes* essentially tell the same
story, in both cases in flashback. The plot concerns a middle-aged school
supervisor (*pion*), Clément Mathieu–played by Noël-Noël in *La Cage aux
rossignols*, and by Gérard Jugnot in *Les Choristes*. Mathieu gets a job in a
disciplinarian boarding school for difficult adolescent boys. At first he
experiences discipline problems, but rapidly he tames and charms the boys
by teaching them to sing as a choir, despite hostility from the headmaster.
In both films one boy emerges as a star soloist, Laugier (Roger Krebs) in
La Cage aux rossignols, Pierre Morhange (Jean-Baptiste Maunier) in *Les*

Choristes. Also, in both films Mathieu develops a romantic interest in a woman, the boy's cousin Micheline (Micheline Francey) in *La Cage aux rossignols*, his mother Violette Morhange (Marie Bunel) in *Les Choristes*. The choir steadily improves and triumphs when performing in front of Madame la Comtesse, the school benefactor. Mathieu seems vindicated in his unconventional pedagogical methods, until a fire breaks out in the school. No boys are hurt, thanks to Mathieu disobeying the rules that forbid him to take the children out without the director's permission, and yet he is dismissed. Back in the present of the film, Mathieu in *La Cage aux rossignols* marries Micheline. In *Les Choristes* he is rejected by Violette but at the last minute he adopts Pépinot (Maxence Perrin), a boy from the school.

As well as having similar plots, *La Cage aux rossignols* and *Les Choristes* display many similarities, especially in terms of their "classicism", their use of children and music, and the prominence of their central star. Both films have classic-realist, old-fashioned, easy-to-follow stories with an uplifting narrative about progress, social cohesion and redemption: the boys go from bad to good as Mathieu brings out their inner, Rousseauesque goodness, while Mathieu himself is redeemed by his good influence on the boys. Both films are technically accomplished but *simple*. They do not use special effects (the digital effects that are used in *Les Choristes* are designed to make the film look more "realistic" –for example in blending some sets and natural locations for the school décor; they are thus invisible to the spectator). These films are therefore not extraordinary monuments of remarkable technical or stylistic accomplishment, unlike some of their contemporaries (such as *Les Enfants du paradis* in 1945 or *Un long dimanche de fiançailles* in 2004). Mise-en-scène, combining location shooting and studio work, is understated. Jean Dréville, the director of *La Cage aux rossignols*, claimed his film was his return to "content over form" (Guiguet and Papillon 1987, 131) and Jean-Pierre Jeancolas has qualified *Les Choristes* as "an old man's film made by a young man",[1] both pronouncements emphasising the stylistic classicism, or conservatism of each film at the time of its production. While technically flashy or monumental films command a lot of critical attention, *La Cage aux rossignols* and *Les Choristes* show that across a whole time span, unassuming and less stylistically flamboyant films can elicit more widespread popularity.

At the same time as they belong stylistically to classic-realist modes of filmmaking, both films undeniably also possess a fairy-tale, utopian dimension which smoothes over cracks in verisimilitude, such as, for instance, the miraculous speed with which the behaviour of the delinquent boys improves. In this respect *La Cage aux rossignols* and *Les Choristes* correspond to what Michèle Lagny has isolated as a characteristic of popular European cinema in a very different genre, the *peplum*, that is to say films that have "simple themes... in a narrative that is effective and didactic at the same time." (Lagny 1992, 169).

Generically, *La Cage aux rossignols* and *Les Choristes* are *comédies dramatiques*, meaning gentle comedies with elements of melodrama, an eminently French genre. Both films are the antithesis of vulgar, carnivalesque comedies and in this sense they fit within the French tradition of respectable family comedies that have frequently triumphed at the French box office–two notable examples being *Le Corniaud* (11.7 million spectators in 1965) and *La Grande vadrouille* (17.2 million in 1966). This partly explains the lack of serious critical attention these films have received, since French critics interested in comedy consistently prefer more extreme and therefore supposedly "subversive" examples of the genre–for instance Italian comedies of the 1960s and 1970s by the likes of Dino Risi (*I mostri*, 1963) and Marco Ferreri (*La Grande bouffe*, 1973), the films of Luis Buñuel, or more recent French films with macabre and/or sexual elements such as *Delicatessen* (Marc Caro and Jean-Pierre Jeunet, 1991) and *Le Derrière* (Valérie Lemercier, 1999).

The presence of children is central to both our films. The success of *Les Choristes* is widely acknowledged as having been boosted by repeated viewings instigated by children. Thematically, narratively and visually, children in general have strong appeal for filmmakers: they are innately attractive and they have huge emotional power, able to go from comedy to drama in an instant. Symbolically, they evoke universal questions of identity and of evolution. As a group they signify the future, as individuals they signify the past, a use both films put them to. In addition to my two case studies, it is noteworthy that a significant number of the top-scoring French films of the post-war period focus on children and adolescents, among the most famous being *Jeux interdits* (René Clément, 1952), *Les 400 coups* (François Truffaut,1959), *La Guerre des boutons* (Yves Robert, 1962), *La Gifle* (Claude Pinoteau, 1974), *La Boum* (Claude Pinoteau, 1980), *Diabolo Menthe* (Diane Kurys, 1977), *Trois hommes et un couffin* (Coline Serreau, 1985), *Au revoir les enfants* (Louis Malle, 1987), *La Gloire de mon père* (Yves Robert, 1990), *Le Château de ma mère* (Yves Robert, 1990), *Le Maître d'école* (Claude Berri, 1981), *Le Plus beau métier du monde* (Gérard Lauzier, 1996), *Un indien dans la ville* (Hervé Palud, 1994), *Être et avoir* (Nicolas Philibert, 2002). Although further comparative research in international top box office films would be needed to be categorical about this point, this list suggests that the presence of children is an important characteristic of popular French cinema.

Music was equally crucial to the success of *La Cage aux rossignols* and *Les Choristes*. Both films evidently mobilise music and singers in thematic, aesthetic and marketing terms. The symbiotic relationship with other leisure and art forms, in particular radio, the stage or television, has been a constant feature of popular cinema. In 1945 *La Cage aux rossignols* helped popularise the choir of "Les Petits chanteurs à la croix de bois" who became a performing and recording success story. In 2004, the CD of *Les Choristes* enjoyed record sales and the press reported new choirs springing up all over France as a result of the film (Dupont 2005). Individual viewers may object to the style and quality of the music in either case, but music undeniably enhances the emotional appeal of both films, since it structures the films' internal coherence, narrative progression and climax. In *La Cage aux rossignols* music makes Mathieu a successful teacher and writer; in *Les Choristes* it makes him a successful teacher and surrogate father, while Morhange becomes a famous conductor.

It is also acknowledged that popular films can function to democratise a highbrow form–in the case of our two films classical music, as Disney did with *Fantasia* (1940). This is akin to what Michèle Lagny and Malgorzata Hendrykowska have discussed in different contexts as the instructional, or pedagogical function of popular cinema (Lagny 1992, 163-180; Hendrykowska 1992, 112-125). Both films mix classical music (*La Nuit* by Rameau) with contemporary scores composed for the film which, especially in *Les Choristes*, pastiche classical choral song. Music also provides opportunities for moments of *mise-en-spectacle*. Without being "musicals" as such, both *La Cage aux rossignols* and *Les Choristes* include moments of musical spectacle that interrupt the narrative and yet are perfectly integrated within it. In this respect they fit into a long and important tradition in classical French cinema (Vincendeau 2004, 137-152). In addition, like other popular genres, from the *peplum* to the disaster film, they illustrate the survival of the "cinema of attractions" within popular cinema up to the present day, even in apparently unspectacular genres.

La Cage aux rossignols was directed by Jean Dréville, a respected filmmaker at the time but one who is now largely forgotten and who is certainly not a canonical auteur. *Les Choristes* was the first feature film directed by Christophe Barratier, a musician by training (he is also the nephew of producer Jacques Perrin, who plays the older Morhange in the film). In both films the high-profile creative role is filled, instead, by a male star at the height of his career who, moreover, in each case was strongly involved in the film's production.[2] Both stars started out in other media (Noël-Noël on the pre-war cabaret stage as a *chansonnier*; Jugnot in the 1970s *café-théâtre*). Both already had, when they made the two films under consideration here, a string of popular movies under their belts, configured as series: Noël-Noël starred in the *Ademaï* comic series in the 1930s (*Ademaï aviateur*, 1933; *Ademaï au moyen âge*, 1934; *Ademaï bandit d'honneur,* 1943), Jugnot in the *Les Bronzés* series (*Les Bronzés*, 1978; *Les Bronzés font du ski*, 1979).[3] Such antecedents create an essential *complicity*, a strong bond between audience, star and film which is fundamental to the popular appeal and status of the films.

At the time they made *La Cage aux rossignols* and *Les Choristes* respectively, Noël-Noël and Jugnot were middle-aged, physically unassuming stars, with similar star personas as "ordinary" men, their lack of virility emphasised by their narrative role as, respectively, failed writer and failed musician. The recurrent success of such "unglamorous", apparently unimpressive, stars in popular cinema is not new, nor is it a uniquely French phenomenon (in 1930s Hollywood for instance, Greta Garbo and Marlene Dietrich appeared as top stars but it was the distinctly less glamorous Marie Dressler or Mickey Rooney who were the box office winners), but the magnitude of their success tends to be hidden by their low critical status. Figures of identification rather than objects of desire, these stars are, in their "ordinariness", arguably more–or at least equally– representative of grassroots French cinema tastes than more glamorous and critically feted stars such as Catherine Deneuve, Isabelle Adjani, Alain Delon or Jeanne Moreau.[4] While these stars regularly generate new studies, Noël-Noël remains unsung, as I suspect Jugnot will be. In certain areas, then, popular French cinema is critically portrayed in inverse proportion to its importance to the audience.

Having examined the common elements in the two films which point to important continuities in popular French cinema across the post-war decades, we can now turn to equally important differences between them, which are illuminating in themselves as well as in relation to the wider evolution of popular French cinema. As already mentioned, both films are narrated through a long flashback. However *La Cage aux rossignols* has a much longer framing story in the "present", in which Mathieu tries in vain to publish his novel, called "La Cage aux rossignols". His friend Raymond (Georges Biscot) manages to trick the newspaper where he works into serialising the novel. Meanwhile, Mathieu's fiancée Micheline convinces her mother, thanks to the serialisation of the novel, that Mathieu is worthy of marrying her (previously the mother considered him a total failure, as shown in the scene where she witnesses him carrying a publicity board on his back). After the long flashback to the events in the school, set in 1935 (10 years before the narrative present of the film), *La Cage aux rossignols* ends with the marriage of Mathieu and Micheline, while the young choir boys escape from the school in order to sing at the wedding.

In *Les Choristes* by contrast, the framing story is minimal. In New York, an orchestra conductor (the older Morhange) learns of his mother's death and returns home to France for the funeral. There he is given Mathieu's (unpublished) memoirs by his former school friend, Pépinot. We quickly move into the flashback (set in 1949, more than 50 years before)–about ten minutes into the film instead of 25. The longer prologue in *La Cage aux rossignols* is partly due to the fact that Dréville collapsed two novels into his script. Still, this long opening sequence also shows that the earlier film essentially sets its action in the present, or in a very recent past, whereas in *Les Choristes* the accent is distinctly on a distant past clearly connected to the childhood of men now in late middle age. Moreover, the 2004 film is unable to call forth its own classicism without a self-conscious nod towards the earlier film. Indeed, the temporal differences just mentioned are also reflected in the films' divergent styles.

Despite the 10-year gap between past and present in *La Cage aux rossignols*, the film looks and feels contemporary with its shooting period at the end of the war (location scenes were shot in Fontevrault in June 1944). The understated, classic-realist mise-en-scène in part derives from the material restrictions of the time, but also, as indicated earlier, because of Dréville's desire to keep things simple. By contrast, *Les Choristes* dwells on the past through the stylistic features of heritage cinema, with its careful recreation and celebration of past décors and objects. So, for example, the move into the school at the beginning of the flashback is signalled by a drawing which "morphs" into a live shot, while *La Cage aux rossignols* begins the scene with a simple shot of the school gates. *Les Choristes* indulges in close-ups of lovingly displayed objects such as a music sheet case, an old-fashioned pen and ink well, the boys' vintage sweaters and copperplate writing on the blackboard. Self-consciousness about representation marks one of the key changes in popular cinema on either side of the New Wave break. This is true across various genres– thrillers, film noir, comedies and melodramas alike, all marked by pastiche, parody or, as in this case, simply a heightened showcasing of décors and objects (a comparison between Marcel Pagnol's *Manon des sources*, shot in 1952, and Claude Berri's remake of 1985, generates similar conclusions).

Self-consciousness in *Les Choristes* extends to the representation of the children. In *La Cage aux rossignols* they tend to be shown as a relatively indistinguishable mass. The constraints of shooting an existing choir do not entirely account for this, nor do they explain why the soloist emerges only later in the film and is comparatively played down. The representation of children in the 1945 film addresses a collective identity at the time of the reconstruction of France following the devastation of the war. By contrast, *Les Choristes* favours an individual focus more in tune with the early twenty-first century–alluding both to the fragmentation of real-life families and the concurrent elevation of the child as *l'enfant roi* (the "child king"). *Les Choristes* builds up Morhange from the very start. The action in the "present" begins with his older self, and in the flashback he is immediately treated as a budding star narratively and visually. Another key change is that, unlike in *La Cage aux rossignols* where the topic is absent, *Les Choristes* raises the threat of paedophilia but only in order to defuse it. A scene in the toilets shows a teacher being suspicious of Mathieu's presence in the lavatory with the boys–the spectator, on the other hand, knows that his intentions are entirely pure. Yet, paradoxically, in *Les Choristes* there is a blatant visual fetishisation of the boys in general and of Morhange in particular, through lingering close-ups of lovely faces, hair, legs, etc. Their visual fetishisation is more intense and at times takes an almost sexual slant. In the 2004 film the young actors were chosen for their looks and acting ability since their singing was dubbed using a real choir; the only exception was the soloist Morhange (Jean-Baptiste Maunier), although he too was cast for "his physique" as well as "his voice" (Boulaire 2004). In *La Cage aux rossignols*, by contrast, as already mentioned, the boys were pre-selected by their membership of the "Petits Chanteurs à la croix de bois" choir.

The different treatment of the framing story also affects the endings, where *La Cage aux rossignols* and *Les Choristes* ascribe a very different narrative trajectory to the adult male hero. At the end of *La Cage aux rossignols* Noël-Noël marries his beautiful fiancée, while in *Les Choristes* Jugnot is rejected by Morhange's mother and adopts Pépinot. For Noël Burch and Geneviève Sellier, who are among the very few historians to have written about *La Cage aux rossignols*, the star Noël-Noël is an actor of "low virility", and the character Mathieu is evidence of "the glorification of masculine weakness… a veritable cliché of Occupation cinema" (Burch and Sellier 1996, 156). This is true insofar as Mathieu begins the story as a failed writer, and a lowly *pion* in a third-rate boarding school. Indeed, in both films the dialogue underlines the stigma of the character's social and sexual failure in relation to his age. Nevertheless, throughout *La Cage aux rossignols* Mathieu/Noël-Noël is elegant, attired in well-cut suits and desired by a beautiful woman. As in his other hit movie *Le Père tranquille* (René Clément and Noël-Noël, 1946), Noël-Noël's apparently weak masculinity is a front, a disguise that serves to hide his male power.[5] Mathieu's lack of virility at the beginning is in fact a ploy to set the stage for his redemption through the successful musical education he gives the children, further validated by his transformation into star novelist and fulfilled bridegroom. Mathieu/Noël-Noël thus emerges as a pivotal figure between the "weak male" of the Occupation period and the more hopeful and forward-looking hero of Liberation cinema. He is, noticeably, a figure on the move, a man with a future. This aspect is particularly striking when we compare him to Jugnot's Mathieu in *Les Choristes*. On the one hand Jugnot is distinctly less handsome and elegant than Noël-Noël; on the other hand the film repeatedly emasculates him as a character, in ways that are absent from the 1945 film. Jugnot's Mathieu is pitted against a grotesquely disciplinarian director and he is later challenged by a sinister delinquent youth; although he is a successful teacher he continues to be a failed musician and, finally, he is sexually rejected–although this point adds pathos to his character, making him a more vulnerable figure.

Burch and Sellier do not fail to note that *La Cage aux rossignols* largely eliminates women, and that Mathieu is glorified as a "mothering father" (Burch and Sellier 1996, 165). While this is true, the comparison with *Les Choristes* again throws new light on the different manners in which both films eliminate women, as well as on the films' different takes on education. Contrary to the charge of conservatism levelled at *Les Choristes* in particular, Mathieu's methods in both cases embody a view of education that is liberal and anti-authoritarian. The boys are nurtured and redeemed not by brutal authority but by collegiality, by the "feminine" vehicle of music and the loving care of the music teacher. Indeed in 1945 *La Cage aux rossignols* was acknowledged as taking a discreetly anti-Vichy stance, its methods seen as closer to the progressive Uriage school experiment.[6] In 2004, however, *Les Choristes* was predictably considered nostalgic and de facto conservative in its portrayal of education. Yet, in the most interesting article generated by the film, the semiologist Mariette Darrigrand argued in *Libération* for the film not to be seen as nostalgic, but rather as an example of "a modest utopia" (Darrigrand 2005)–a utopia rooted in the failure of current pedagogical methods in French schools. A writer in *Marianne* also spoke of the film as "the utopia of the renewed efficiency of pedagogy" (Cohen and Konopnicki 2004).

As Richard Dyer has argued, utopia is a key component of popular entertainment films (Dyer 1992, 17-34), but along with Dyer we must interrogate what kind of utopia we are dealing with. The startlingly obvious fact that *Les Choristes* is an all-male story does not seem to have been considered by the film's reviewers, including Darrigand (2004). And, interestingly, the 2004 film marginalises women even more than the 1945 film, in which Mathieu's marriage implies a role for women, albeit the traditional one of bringing forth a new generation. It is also noticeable that in the opening story, *La Cage aux rossignols* gives space to Micheline and her mother; the two women's reading of Mathieu's memoirs takes us into the past, whereas in *Les Choristes* this function is performed by two men, the older Morhange and Pépinot. We may link the increased marginalisation of women in *Les Choristes* (as well as the adoption of Pépinot at the end) to other successful films of the last 20 years or so that focus on children and/or school, such as *Trois hommes et un couffin*, *Le Maître d'école*, *Un indien dans la ville*, *Le Plus beau métier du monde*, and *Être et avoir*, in which the same strange gender substitution takes place. In these films the adult male characters take over the traditionally feminine role of mothering, at a time of a huge increase in female single parenthood. Furthermore, the repeated focus on male teachers evidently flies in the face of the social reality of an overwhelmingly female profession. Ironically, the erasure of the female in *Les Choristes* is echoed in its production: the "making of" documentary available on the DVD of the film reveals that quite a few girls sang in the choir we hear on the soundtrack, dubbing the all-male group of children we see on screen.[7]

Finally, we need to get back to Mathieu and the two stars who embody him. Although Noël-Noël was popular in the 1930s, he rose to new heights of stardom during the war, a phenomenon in part connected to the fact that one of his rivals at the box office, Jean Gabin, had emigrated to Hollywood. But the Gabin-Noël-Noël shift represents something more profound than the lucky break afforded by the German occupation. Noël-Noël heralds the arrival of the *classe moyenne* centre stage, replacing the working-class hero of the pre-war period epitomised by Gabin. This shift is symbolically replayed in the opening scenes of *La Cage aux rossignols*. In this prologue, it is thanks to his canny working-class friend Raymond, played by comic silent-film star Georges Biscot, that Mathieu gets his novel published, but the friend is quickly eliminated. Sixty years later, Jugnot shows the perenniality of this figure, illustrating how popular culture, as expressed in the cinema, is no longer "working-class" but triumphantly "middle-class".

La Cage aux rossignols and *Les Choristes* show significant continuities in French cinema and society in terms of the role and importance of the representation of children, anxieties about parenting and education and the nature of popular spectacle. In particular, the perenniality of middlebrow, gentle, comedies with "ordinary" male figures and children at their centre is well illustrated by these two films. But their differences are also enlightening, in terms of the more recent film's greater stylistic self-consciousness, its more individual focus and its paradoxical relationship to gender.

At this point it may be useful to return to the films' contemporary critical reception. In 1945 *La Cage aux rossignols* was highly praised for its simplicity, its lack of stylistic experimentation, its transparency. In other words its "classical" aesthetic project was well understood and accepted by dominant critical practice. The only significant hostility to the film was political (the communist critic Georges Sadoul, somewhat predictably, criticised it for its lack of social realism, in particular its failure to evoke "the problem of deprived children") (Sadoul 1945). In 2004, on the other hand, there is strong evidence of a cultural distinction operating in relation to popular French cinema, one that we can trace back to the time of the New Wave. Although there was some modest praise in the quality press (*Le Monde* praised "a fine popular film, made with care and respect" (Anon. 2004)[8]), generally the film's reception was absolutely symptomatic of the familiar critical divide that greets popular French cinema in France–praised in the mainstream press and the popular, fan-directed magazines such as *Studio Magazine* and *Première*, but trashed by the specialist, cinephile press (*Les Cahiers du cinéma, Positif, Les Inrockuptibles, Libération*). And here, contrary to the reception of *La Cage aux rossignols*, critical hostility was both political and aesthetic. Politically, *Les Choristes* was accused of Pétainisme–an interesting irony in view of the fact that the 1945 film had been perceived as anti-Pétain in its view of education–and generally of being right-wing. *Les Inrockuptibles* accused the film of populism and quipped "*Les Choristes* sing for Raffarin [the right-wing Prime Minister at the time]" (quoted in Suzer 2004). The difference in reception also demonstrates a greater cultural snobbery towards popular French cinema in the French critical establishment. In *Marianne*, for example, the writer Alain Rémond wrote a whole piece "about" *Les Choristes* devoted to boasting of *not* having seen the film (Rémond 2004), while several reviewers, including Jean-Michel Frodon, tainted it with the brush of being "pre-televisual" (Frodon 2004a, 35). *Télérama*, a weekly television listing magazine read primarily by the educated middle-classes, enshrined this division by publishing the results of its 2004 survey: while its readers preferred *Les Choristes* and *Un long dimanche de fiançailles*, its critics favoured the auteur films *Rois et Reine* (Arnaud Desplechin, 2004) and *L'Esquive* (Abdellatif Kechiche, 2003).

On the brink of the technological revolution of digital cinema, the onslaught of television reality shows (including *Le Pensionnat de Chavagnes*, set in a school, which echoes *Les Choristes*) and youth-oriented cult films such as *Brice de Nice* (James Huth, 2005) and television shows like *Star Academy*, the continued box office success of films like *Les Choristes* shows that a central trend in popular French cinema still upholds a middle-class, middlebrow and middle-aged utopia, as long as it remains firmly male and heterosexual.

---

[1] Jean-Pierre Jeancolas, paper on "Le jeune cinéma français", delivered at the Studies in French Cinema conference, London, 16 April 2004. The same idea recurs in the press reception of the film.

[2] Noël-Noël co-wrote the script of *La Cage aux rossignols*, while Gérard Jugnot was associate producer of *Les Choristes*. The press surrounding the release of both films gives pride of place to the stars, who give many more interviews than the directors.

[3] A third instalment, *Les Bronzés 3: amis pour la vie*, was shot in 2006.

[4] *La Cage aux rossignols* was more popular in the provinces, while its "rival" at the 1945 box office, *Les Enfants du paradis* was more popular in Paris.

[5] *Le Père tranquille* is the story of Edouard Martin, a sedate and "ordinary" family man (Noël-Noël), who apparently stays away from politics during the German occupation of France–much to the contempt of his son who dabbles in Resistance activities. However, it is revealed at the end that Martin was the head of the local Resistance network.

[6] The Uriage school (1940-1942), situated in the Alps, was created under Marshall Pétain's regime after the defeat of the French army by the Germans, in order to educate future military cadres in the ideology of Pétain's reactionary "National Revolution". However, the school soon included a wider range of independent and left-wing intellectuals, including members of the Resistance. (See Hellman 1993).

[7] DVD *Les Choristes*, Pathé, DFRS 480893, © 2004.

[8] "…un beau film populaire, fait avec soin et respect".

CHAPTER FIVE

CONTEMPORARY TRENDS IN PERSONAL AND POPULAR FRENCH CINEMA

DEIRDRE RUSSELL

This chapter examines how trends in personal filmmaking may be accommodated within approaches to contemporary French popular cinema. "Personal" stories–whether overtly autobiographical or loosely inspired by the filmmaker's personal experiences–have long been an ingredient of French filmmaking. However, with their roots in avant-garde practices and association with auteurs, personal expression and self-representation may appear at odds with the qualities of "popular" cinema. Personal storytelling is nonetheless relevant to enduring features of mainstream French film, such as the prevalence of portraits of the past and concerns with the representation of identity (particularly national identity). It is also significant for its representativeness of wider cultural trends characterised by, for example, preoccupations with authenticity and the blending of reality and fiction. Autobiographical voices in mainstream cinema can thus be considered in the context of what is sometimes called a "confessional culture" where the communication of personal experience now holds unprecedented value.

The nature and boundaries of popular cinema resist easy delineation. Whether based on box office performance or supposed opposition to the values of auteur filmmaking, discussions of this category of film are plagued by notable exceptions. My approach to "popular" cinema is based largely on notions of *accessibility* and *predictability*. While a "difficult" or innovative film can achieve commercial success (a notable recent example being Michael Haneke's *Caché* (2005)), this unexpected popularity being itself worthy of critical attention, such films are excluded from this category in the absence of popularity as a primary goal. Films comfortably accommodated into this grouping aim for wide accessibility in the interests of attaining as wide an audience as possible; one method is to

employ a set of predicable elements so that the potential audience knows
what to expect, most obviously through genre.

I begin this investigation with a discussion of some of the traditional
facets of autobiographical cinema practice and criticism, addressing why
these may appear to oppose the demands of popular cinema. I then discuss
three recent French films which relate these two categories: Yvan Attal's
romantic comedy *Ma Femme est une actrice* (2001), Dai Sijie's Franco-
Chinese co-production *Balzac et la petite tailleuse chinoise* (2002) and
Christophe Barratier's *Les Choristes* (2004). In these analyses, I argue that
these films do not foreground the concerns traditionally associated with
personal cinema, but instead adopt autobiographical elements to lend a
tenor of authenticity and credibility to storytelling within the conventions
of popular French genres, namely comedy and the heritage/nostalgia film.
Consequently, I hope to suggest why the presence of autobiographical
discourse in mainstream French cinema merits critical attention: in
particular, how these uses of personal material potentially disrupt the
traditional classifications of both autobiographical and popular film.

Autobiographical cinema and criticism

Like the classification of popular cinema, definitions of personal
filmmaking are elusive.[1] Autobiographical films generally fail to fulfil the
definitional requirements of literary autobiography, such as the
unambiguously unified identity of author-narrator and protagonist. In the
absence of a clearly delineated genre, the somewhat vague term
"personal" is often used to describe a range of practices in which the
filmmaker's personal experiences and visions are governing principles.

Regarding scholarly attention, Jean-Pierre Chartier, in his influential
1947 article "Les 'films à la première personne'", first identified the
emergence of "a personal cinema" (un cinéma subjectif) (1947, 35) in the
growth of films told from one character's perspective. Although life-
writing scholars such as Elizabeth Bruss (1980) and Philippe Lejeune
(1987) have disputed the concept of filmed autobiography,
autobiographical projects as a category of film have earned a limited
amount of critical consideration, notably from the European film scholar
Wendy Everett (1996a and 2000). Such scholarly responses to
autobiographical or identifiably "personal" films focus largely on how
they depict subjectivity and articulate the visual dimensions of memory
and selfhood.

Autobiographical discourse is a longstanding feature of France's
cinematic landscape. Indeed, Emma Wilson cites "personal history" as the

"dominant concept in French cinema of the last fifty years" (1999, 19). However, these practices have traditionally been affiliated with avant-garde and art-house film. Autobiographical material has figured widely in experimental cinema since at least Jean Cocteau in the 1930s; Marjorie Keller, in her study of childhood in avant-garde cinema, notes the use of film as a self-exploratory tool by many experimental filmmakers, stating that the "confusion of the terms *personal* and *avant-garde* in reference to these films is not unfounded" (1986, 14). Throughout the 1970s and early 1980s, experimental and underground films continued to dominate the "genre", prompting critics like Dominque Noguez (1987, 15-17), to see autobiographical filmmaking as fundamentally subversive or underground. Even the more well-known autobiographical films, such as Tarkovsky's *Mirror* (1974), Bergman's *Fanny and Alexandre* (1982) and several features by Fellini, are authored by directors who inhabit the art-house, if not the avant-garde, realms of cinema. The same applies to the French filmmakers most associated with autobiographical discourse, such as Diane Kurys, Marguerite Duras and Agnès Varda. Today, the low-budget video-diary or self-portrait remains the leading autobiographical form, examples within French cinema including *Omelette* (Rémi Lange, 1994) and *Demain et encore demain* (Dominique Cabrera, 1997), or, in the US, the unexpectedly successful *Tarnation* (Jonathan Caouette, 2003).

Autobiographical practices are also identified with the *Nouvelle Vague*, and particularly the *politique des auteurs*. For Wilson, the dominance of "personal history" in French film is "directly linked to 'la politique des auteurs' through the notion of cinema in the first person" (1999, 19). Indeed, underlying the emergence of auteurism was the shift in theoretical attention from the "objectivity" of cinema to its subjective potential. The principle of unique vision (and in some cases–most obviously Truffaut's *Les 400 coups* (1959)–specific autobiographical content) associated with the *Nouvelle Vague* and its auteurist underpinnings points to one of the ways in which personal cinema may be seen as fundamentally at odds with popular cinema: auteurs' rejection of the limits of genre. Genres are defined by their familiarity, or as a means of what Sarah Berry calls "popular market segmentation" (1999, 25), providing spectators with horizons of expectations through norms and rules, whereas auteur status implies freedom from such constraints. This suggests that the personal nature of autobiographical filmmaking, aligned with an auteurism in which commercial success and widespread appeal (often afforded through generic expectations) are subordinate to subjective expression and uniqueness, is inherently incompatible with popular "genre cinema".

The overall implication is that the intellectual, intimate tendencies which characterise the autobiographical impulse are irreconcilable with popular cinema's principles of accessibility and recognisable formulas. However, the 1980s and 1990s saw the growth of autobiographical content in French films beyond the boundaries of art-house practices. Everett (1996a and 2001), Wilson (1999) and Phil Powrie (1999) all identify autobiography as a trend of European, or specifically French, contemporary cinema. This is especially demonstrated by the influential 1994 *Arte* television series *Tous les garçons et les filles de leur âge*, a selection of largely autobiographical memory pieces which, Powrie suggests, signalled an "attempted return of the auteur" (1999, 1). The unprecedented popularity of this collection of films (some of which, such as André Techiné's *Les Roseaux sauvages* (1994), became extended cinema versions), explicitly associating the film with the creator, the text with the life, challenges assumptions about the autobiographical mode's incompatibility with widespread appeal. The presence of personal stories within mainstream genre cinema, however, requires different parameters for investigation than those used for auteurist personal films, which suggests the instability of exclusive definitions of autobiographical filmmaking as well as the boundaries between auteur and popular modes. I will now examine the intersection of personal and popular characteristics in three films which challenge such suppositions.

Ma Femme est une actrice: autobiography and the comic play of fiction and reality

Yvan Attal's 2001 feature *Ma Femme est une actrice* employs autobiographical material within the framework of a resolutely popular genre: the romantic comedy. The film stars the director and his wife, Charlotte Gainsbourg, as a married couple, also called Yvan and Charlotte. It details Yvan's neurotic jealousy over the sex scenes his actress wife is filming with a renowned sex symbol, John, in her latest movie.

Attal is reticent about defining his film as autobiographical. He states in interviews that elements of its story and themes are inspired by his own experiences, but that these sources are used in the interests of credibility and humour, rather than veracious self-exploration, and that he is above all concerned with the *relationship* between fiction and reality. He explains:

> I thought it would be a good idea to expand the film by exploring what is real and what is not. So the film is actually meant to be a deeper exploration of that divide and that's why I wanted you to believe that this story is our story–why it's called *My Wife is an Actress* and that she and I

> play characters named "Yvan" and "Charlotte". Every time in the film you
> think you're about to hear Charlotte's last name we have some sound
> covering it so it's like a joke, you see, to play with reality. (Chaw 2002)

Thus, the realism suggested by the title and protagonists' names is undermined by explicitly fictionalised elements (such as Yvan's profession as a sportswriter), with the intention of deriving humour from the confusion. The film opens with a short sequence emulating documentary–cinema's truth-telling format–and several scenes directly point to the play of truth and fiction, such as one located in an exclusive restaurant, situating the fictional scene in a setting full of recognisable celebrities playing themselves. Furthermore, what is and what is not real is the essence of Yvan's anxieties (whether Charlotte is having an affair, whether her acting is merely acting). The relationship between fiction and reality also extends to the artifice, deception and mythmaking which constitute the acting profession and cinema themselves, as exemplified in the scenes on the film set. Similarly, when Yvan argues with an acquaintance about his wife's sex scenes he claims, "it's false, it's cinema" (c'est du faux, c'est du cinéma) and, in an acting studio he joins, students perform a scene from Marivaux's *Les Acteurs de bonne foi*, ending with the lines "and in spite of the comedy, all this is true, they pretend to pretend".[2] This confusion extends to the audience who are invited to guess at which anecdotes are inspired by Attal's experiences, and which are pure fiction. Equally, the film plays with their expectations and interpretations through the editing of scenes in which spectators must reassess what they thought they had seen; a notable example occurs when Yvan attacks John in the park, which subsequently transpires to be a fantasy or dream.

This confusion of fiction and reality is significant to autobiography. One of the perceived "difficulties" of autobiographical film is its apparent dependence on fiction. But this blend of truth and artifice foregrounded in *Ma Femme* sidesteps the fallacy of accurate self-portrayal which characterises the literary genre. It plays with the expectations of truth-telling autobiographical discourse and, above all, exploits its humorous potential by, for example, demystifying and satirising the acting process and the glamorous life of film stars. Crucially, this comic play of fiction and reality, both in theme and form, pertains to many of the mainstays of the romantic comedy genre: miscommunications and misunderstandings, jealousy and infidelity. Humour is similarly derived from the irony of Yvan the filmmaker filming his wife in the sex scenes which torment Yvan the character. In this sense, the use of personal experiences within comedy conventions allows above all for *self-parody* (Attal states that "this character is a caricature of myself" (ce personnage est une caricature de moi-même) (Aiach 2002)). Equally, the subversion of spectators' expectations and interpretations (often through editing) is a basic element of comedy, which the autobiographical posture of the film complements. In addition to enhancing comedy, the autobiographical dimension embellishes the film's "romantic" elements: the depiction of the couple relies in part on the audience's knowledge of Attal and Gainsbourg's relationship; as Attal states, "people know that we are together, so it was fun to play with that" (Cimbalo 2002). The film exploits spectatorial voyeurism in the pleasure of perhaps seeing a glimpse of their private lives (voyeurism also has a thematic role within the narrative), and much of the film's appeal resides in the suggested revelations of the private lives of public figures: the celebrity's advantages in booking restaurant tables, and the inconveniences of autographs and press interviews.

It is tempting to situate *Ma Femme* in a tradition of celebrated autobiographical films about filmmaking, examples of which include *8½* (Frederico Fellini, 1963), *La Nuit Americaine* (François Truffaut, 1973), *Cinema Paradiso* (Giuseppe Tornatore, 1989) and, more recently, Catherine Breillat's *Sex Is Comedy* (2002). Like these films, it addresses filmmaking processes (though here from the actor's, rather than director's, perspective) and the voyeurism of cinematic production and products. However, very little of the "film within a film" is depicted, and rather than expressing an intimate contemplation on cinema's mystical attraction or personal theories about filmic functions and forms, *Ma Femme*'s self-reflexivity, once resolutely associated with the avant-garde, can be seen as an incarnation of the popularisation of this broadly postmodern attitude.

There is, nonetheless, a certain meditation on the acting process. Equally, the subplot involving Yvan's sister and her husband's arguments over circumcising their baby, of little consequence to the primary narrative, is suggestive of Attal's concerns with his Jewishness. Attal concedes that his film may be more autobiographical than he initially thought: "I can see many things that come from me when I watch this film. I see my preoccupations, I even saw things which escaped me in the framing of a shot" (Aiach 2002).[3] The intermittent first-person voiceover also affirms the subjective stance of personal cinema, though this singular subjectivity is undermined by the inclusion of scenes where Yvan is not witness to the events (such as those between Yvan's sister and her husband). The self-exploration associated with the autobiographical impulse is thus perceptible, but firmly subordinate to the demands of the romantic comedy genre. Crucially, the autobiographical inferences invited by the film are employed primarily in the interests of humour, enhancing the characteristics of the genre. In a challenge to the traditional characterisations of our two categories, the personal material and stance complements, rather than compromises, popular appeal.

Balzac et la petite tailleuse chinoise: autobiography, history and heritage

If comedy is an unlikely genre for autobiographical discourse, the relationship between autobiography, in its attention to memory and history, and heritage cinema is more logical. The success of the *Arte* series is representative of this, as is Dai Sijie's *Balzac et la petite tailleuse chinoise*–an adaptation of his own semi-autobiographical best-selling French novel. Despite its Chinese setting and dialogue, the film, in the words of the critic Geoff Andrews, "displays the influence of its French funding at every turn" (2005, 86). Inspired by the author's "re-education" during Mao's Cultural Revolution, it recounts the experiences of Sijie's fictional counterpart Ma and friend Luo in a rural village where they both fall in love with and educate, with a stash of prohibited foreign novels, the local seamstress. As well as celebrating French literature, the film revives the hallmarks of the French heritage genre, such as the lingering attention to the beauty of landscape, the prominence of classical music and the themes of love, friendship and lost innocence. Indeed, Sijie acknowledges the fictionalising process, explaining that "[t]here was a real love story, but not as romantic" (Yu Sen-lun 2002, 11); in other words, truth-telling is again subordinate to dramatic and generic concerns, namely, the sentimental aesthetic of coming-of-age films.

Typically, autobiographical films, unlike *Ma Femme*, are narratives of the past, inspired by and constituting an exploration of the filmmaker's memories, often childhood ones. They are commonly characterised by inquiries into the visual facets of memory and identity, and marked by thematic and formal concerns with time.[4] It is also common for autobiographical films to explore personal experiences and memories against a backdrop of significant historical events or periods. Hence, much scholarly attention to such films is devoted to probing the intersections of personal and collective experience and memory.

Balzac employs several common features of personal filmmaking. The message of adolescent salvation through cinema and literature is reminiscent of other French autobiographical films such as *Les 400 coups, Au Revoir les enfants* (Louis Malle, 1987) and *Les Roseaux sauvages*. The narrative is framed by journeys, a familiar figure in autobiographical films denoting journeys into the past (Everett 1996b, 108), and contains a recurrent water motif, whose symbolic value of the flow of time is noted by Susannah Radstone as a conventional trope of memory (1995, 45).[5] The first-person voiceover is also characteristic of depictions of personal memories, and the narrative is largely driven by Ma's subjectivity.

However, *Balzac*'s engagement with the vicissitudes of history and identity commonly encountered in autobiographical projects is limited. The film is to a degree concerned with historical interrogation and documentation in denouncing the excesses of the Cultural Revolution, but this context is subordinate to more familiar concerns of secret love and emerging maturity; as Sijie acknowledges, "the Cultural Revolution is pushed into the background, it is not the subject of the film" (Haski 2001).[6] Rather than addressing the legacies of histories and their effects on selfhood, the separation of past and present is ultimately made explicit in the film's closing images as Ma's memories are literally submerged by the rivers flooding the village. The concluding contemporary section (absent from the novel[7]), where we see Ma settle in France and revisit the village, also places the events safely in the past, as well as securing the protagonist's French identity and fulfilling mainstream cinema's requirement for resolution and a desire to know "what happened in the future". The straightforward, linear narrative structure (bar a couple of clearly signposted flashbacks) also dispenses with the innovative temporal configurations associated with autobiographical films. In short, *Balzac* shows little interest in the intersections of shared and personal histories, memory phenomena, or the visual constitution of selfhood which dominates much scholarly discussion of autobiographical cinema. Rather, it adopts subjective devices and autobiographical motifs to lend an authentic and personal touch to a film grounded in the conventions of heritage cinema.

In its illustration of the ills of Mao's China, *Balzac* may appear to lack the conservative nostalgia associated with heritage cinema. However, there is a present sense of nostalgia for youth, and the film includes a veritable ode to nostalgia when Ma and Luo as adults watch a video (made by Ma) of the villagers reminiscing sentimentally. This self-reflexive scene is suggestive of how the film's autobiographical status perhaps enhances the genre's nostalgic qualities. *Balzac*'s Chinese setting might also seem to undermine the patriotism aroused in heritage cinema, but while it may not address France's past, it valorises the culture and ideals on which the nation's historical identity is based.[8] The message of the transformative power of France's great writers and culture, furthermore, appeals to the distinctively French ethic of universalism: the characters are at ease with the European culture of the novels, as are the film's Western audience with the story and its narration. The plausibility of the message, furthermore, is arguably guaranteed by the film's autobiographical credentials.

We might expect the film to reveal a compelling aspect of the autobiographical voice: its association with expressing marginal identities and non-canonical tales. As Emma Wilson states, personal cinema may be a privileged means of representing minority identities in which personal experience becomes a marker of authenticity (1999, 21). However, unlike recent French autobiographical films like Yamina Benguigui's *Inch'Allah Dimanche* (2001) or Chad Chenouga's *17 rue bleue* (2001), *Balzac*, along with its praise of Western culture and individualism, reveals no politics of marginalised or diasporic experience. Rather, the film relies on widely recognisable formulas such as the opposition between sophisticated urbanites and naive country-folk. *Balzac* is nonetheless representative of a culture of testimony which asserts the importance of bearing witness, here to the misguidedness of the Cultural Revolution. It also relates, of course, to what scholars such as Naomi Greene (1999) and Emma Wilson (1999) identify as the preoccupation amongst French filmmakers with memory, history and national identity. It is notable, then, that this Franco-Chinese co-production articulates personal memories of a distant land within the codes of French storytelling.

In its uncomplicated depiction of time, history and identity, *Balzac*, as with Attal's film, employs its autobiographical material and subjective stance as a means rather than a focus. *Balzac* not only challenges the irreconcilability of popular film with the autobiographical mode, but also the boundaries of *French* mainstream cinema, wielding its traditions in an atypical setting. It is arguably precisely the personal angle of the film which achieves this: its autobiographical foundations again serve to enhance and nuance existing generic criteria–the demands of historical authenticity and nostalgia in "quality" heritage cinema.

Balzac is representative of what Radstone identifies as contemporary mainstream cinema's interest in narratives "in which male protagonists remember, or 'revisit' the scenes of their youth" (1995, 34). This nostalgic trend finds another expression in the enormously popular *Les Choristes*.

Les Choristes: autobiographical nostalgia

Though ostensibly a remake of *La Cage aux Rossignols* (Jean Dréville, 1945), Christophe Barratier has claimed in several interviews that his debut film *is* autobiographical, relating to his memories of an inspiring music teacher. [9] The narrative, recounting the benevolent Clément

Mathieu's creation of a choir for troubled boys at a rural boarding school in 1949, is even more disengaged from any notable historical contexts than *Balzac*, and similarly eschews explorations of the role of subjectivity and memory in identity formation. As with *Balzac* and many of the films from *Tous les garçons,* in its evocation of a lost past, its rural setting, the return to youth and the centrality of music, *Les Choristes* relies on the conventions and expectations of French nostalgia filmmaking, and it is this couching of personal experience in established narrative modes and themes which assures its highly popular credentials.

Like *Balzac*, *Les Choristes* promotes the edifying potential of the arts, here specifically music, and also employs typical autobiographical motifs and themes, such as the trope of journeys, again at the beginning and end of the film, and the subjective voiceover. However, this latter structuring device is a combination of Mathieu's diaries and the memories of his former pupil Pierre Morhange (Barratier's alter-ego). The main flashback sequence begins and ends with Mathieu's voiceover superimposed over Morhange's, while the brief closing flashback is narrated by Morhange. This use of multiple perspectives contradicts the first-person subjectivity and recollection conventionally found in autobiographical film. Instead, the film employs some of the *features* of the autobiographical mode to lend a personal tone to an otherwise conventional film.

The film appears to belong to a French tradition of autobiographical narratives of wayward schoolboys, examples of which include *Zéro de conduite* (Jean Vigo, 1933)*, Les 400 Coups*, and *Au Revoir les enfants*. However, Barratier claims (Hoggard 2005) that he was more influenced by British and American coming-of-age films such as *Dead Poets Society* (Peter Weir, 1989) and *Billy Elliot* (Stephen Daldry, 2000). The familiar tale of unfortunate schoolchildren, guided by a mentor, achieving redemption through artistic endeavour, has been encountered in so many films that it may constitute a genre in its own right.[10] *Les Choristes* adheres to formulas in its simple characterisation, comic interludes, ode to the unsung hero and message about overcoming humble beginnings to earn success and fame. The narrative structure equally follows well-trodden lines: for example, the choir's progress is shown in customary montage sequences and culminates in a triumphant concert, and the ending offers satisfying resolutions (triggered by Pierre asking, "and the rest"? (et la suite?).

However, Barratier transposes these elements from this largely Anglo-Saxon trend into the codes of French cinema's nostalgia tradition, especially by virtue of the film's 1949 setting. Though the film again demonstrates less nostalgia for the specific time and place depicted than for childhood generally, it retains the "feel-good" factor of escaping contemporary difficulties in the refuge of a supposedly simpler past.[11] The centrality of reminiscence–personal nostalgia–is set up from the beginning with the nostalgic emblem of an old school photograph. The nostalgic qualities of pastoral scenery are also in evidence, as is the prominence of family (Morhange is ultimately reunited in a traditional family unit with his mother, while Mathieu adopts Pépinot as his son). Rejecting the high-tech, fast-paced qualities of, for example, Jean-Pierre Jeunet's nostalgically-tinged *Amélie* (2001), *Les Choristes* employs a simple mise-en-scène and editing style reminiscent of the 1950s. The crucial role of music to evoke the spirit of the past in nostalgic cinema, meanwhile, is foregrounded as a central feature of the narrative, and there is scarcely a scene without classical music, whose underlying ideological implications are intimated when Mathieu comments that his fellow teacher is "a regular guy who considers sport and music as the essential motors of national cohesion".[12] The film's focus on classical music is significant to its differentiation (as French) from other films in the "inspirational teacher" genre. As Powrie states, the use of classical music in nostalgia films serves to affirm European culture (1997, 18-19). *Les Choristes'* autobiographical credentials are relevant here: not only is Barratier a trained musician, but he wrote much of the music featured in the film, contributing to his auteur status.

Barratier's inclusion of a contemporary section lends the film the retrospective, autobiographical tone absent from Dréville's original. That he cast his own uncle, Jacques Perrin (notably almost reprising his role from *Cinema Paradiso*), as the adult Morhange further suggests the autobiographical relevance of the flashback structure. On the other hand, Barratier claims that he set the film in an era prior to his own childhood because he wanted "a neutral, universal colour" (une couleur neutre, universelle) and to "put the emphasis on timeless themes of childhood" (mettre l'accent sur des thèmes intemporels de l'enfance) (Baudin 2003). Thus, while Barratier claims his is an autobiographical film, it is also avowedly *impersonal* in its goals of universal accessibility and applicability. The film's indebtedness to *La Cage aux Rossignols*, suggestive of the ambiguous, even debateable, nature of *Les Choristes'* autobiographical qualification, also indicates that conventional, exclusive understandings of personal cinema may be inadequate concerning mainstream works such as this which rely on established codes (or, in this case, on the specific content and style of Dréville's film).

Powrie suggests that the autobiographical credentials of a film are likely to "increase the sense of nostalgia" (1997, 15). As with the previous two films, *Les Choristes* uses personal experience less as its focus than as a means of evoking credibility and enhancing existing generic qualities. The emphasis Barratier places on the personal basis of his film seems designed to assert the authenticity, validity and originality of the story. Powrie notes that the nostalgia filmmaker must at once have the auteur stamp without too individual a style (1997, 20); the autobiographical basis of *Les Choristes* on which Barratier insists, while simultaneously maintaining the "universalism" of the story, can be seen to accommodate these two criteria. This positioning once again suggests that autobiographical credentials are potentially a site of interaction between mainstream and auteur practices.

Conclusions

While the concerns associated with autobiographical identity and expression–such as truth status, the probing of memory, the intersections of personal and collective histories, and the narrative constitution of selfhood–are not those one expects to find articulated in conventional comedy, heritage or nostalgia cinema, films such as *Ma Femme*, *Balzac* and *Les Choristes* demonstrate that autobiographical voices are a genuine presence in mainstream French cinema. Rather than taking the ontological concerns of autobiography as their subject, they employ traits and devices of personal storytelling as means of lending believability and individuality to otherwise generic narratives, and in so doing, they do not compromise the principles of familiarity and accessibility associated with mainstream cinema, and may even contribute to their popularity. As Steve Neale contends, genre categories are characterised by repetition and sameness, but also variation and change (1990, 56), and the use of personal material is arguably one method of achieving originality within conventional modes; rather than contradicting their popularity, autobiographical practices are employed to enhance existing generic requirements and add a personal touch to these formulas.

The presence of autobiographical discourse in popular contemporary French film is worthy of attention for several reasons. It brings into focus many abiding thematic concerns of French cinema old and new, including the representation of identities, and the persistent interest in the past and its memories. It is also indicative of broader cultural movements: the recent proliferation of, for example, first-person documentaries, television docudramas and Weblogs, all point to a culture in which notions of objective truth are increasingly mistrusted, and personal storytelling, testimonial discourse and subjective viewpoints are valued as never before.

Films such as *Les Choristes*, as the highest grossing French feature of 2004, perhaps demonstrate an emerging influence of autobiographical discourse on mainstream cinema. Finally, as I hope these analyses have suggested, such films offer productive sites for reassessing traditional and exclusive definitions and boundaries of various cinematic categories: *personal*, *popular* and *French*.

---

[1] This contrasts with the filmic equivalent of the biography, the "biopic", which was one of the first clearly established popular genres in Hollywood.

[2] "…et maugré la comédie, tout ça est vrai, noute maîtresse; car ils font semblant de faire semblant".

[3] "Je vois beaucoup de choses de moi en voyant le film. Je vois des préoccupations, j'y ai même vu des choses qui m'avaient échappé dans un plan dans un cadre."

[4] In particular, the cinematic medium's supposed lack of a past tense is often cited as a merit by autobiographical film scholars (e.g. Everett 1999, 56) in depicting memory as a phenomenon of the present and the open-ended nature of memory and identity in which the past and present constitute one another–a central facet of autobiographical endeavours.

[5] Frédéric Strauss also notes that this is a recurrent feature of many of the films from *Tous les garçons et les filles de leur age* (1994, 9).

[6] "…la Révolution culturelle est la toile de fond, pas l'objet."

[7] Michelle Bloom notes Sijie's expressed preference for literature over cinema as an art-form (2005, 316), leading one to ponder whether the film adaptation constituted a deliberate act of popularisation, drawing on conventions in the interests of wider accessibility.

[8] When Ma finishes reading *Ursule Mirouet*, he announces "I feel the world has changed"; the villagers love their clothes inspired by *Le Comte de Monte-Cristo*; and French novels are used as valuable currency.

[9] For example, he claims: "It's not really a remake; I bought the rights, so for legal reasons I credit Dréville. I took from his film only the plot about a supervisor who goes to a boarding school to organise a choir. But the two movies are really, really different. All the characters, and a lot of what happens in my movie, are one part autobiographical, the other, my imagination" (Gronval 2005). Elsewhere he states, "Pierre Morhange's story is my story" (Suozzo 2005). Despite these claims, *Les Choristes* can nonetheless clearly be read as a remake (see Vincendeau in the present volume).

[10] As well as *Dead Poets Society*, similar territory has been broached by: *The Corn is Green* (Irving Rapper, 1945), *To Sir With Love* (James Clavell, 1967), *Stand and Deliver* (Ramon Mendéndez, 1988), *Mr. Holland's Opus* (Stephen Herek, 1995), *Music of the Heart* (Wes Craven, 1999), *The Emperor's Club* (Michael Hoffman, 2002) and *Mona Lisa Smile* (Mike Newall, 2003).

[11] Barratier himself states: "[m]y film is autobiographical, but I was more comfortable setting it in the past, so it became a universal fairy tale. I didn't want

to get into issues like housing projects, unemployment or assimilation" (Hoggard 2005).

[12] "…un brave type, qui considère le sport et la musique comme les moteurs essentiels de la cohésion nationale".

CHAPTER SIX

POP-ART FRENCH CINEMA AND VALERIA BRUNI-TEDESCHI'S *IL EST PLUS FACILE POUR UN CHAMEAU…*

TIM PALMER

In contemporary French cinema, the relationship between the mainstream and the art-house manifests itself in arrestingly fractious ways. Take, for instance, the model of popular film set out at the start of Laurent Baffie's *Les Clefs de bagnole* (2003). Baffie, known for cultural satire and candid camera pranks on French television, plays himself, pitching his script to luminaries such as Claude Berri, Dominique Farrugia, and Alain Terzian. As Baffie outlines his premise–one man's search for lost car keys, which ninety minutes later turn out to have been in his left trouser pocket all along–the film's style is deliberately unsophisticated: its focus shifts erratically, a make-up artist wanders in and out of shot, the soundtrack is acoustically uneven, and digital videography makes the image indistinct and overexposed. To emphasise its lowbrow intentions, *Les Clefs de bagnole* also offers ironic juxtapositions of mise-en-scène. Baffie's pitch lurches further into self-parody ("Yes, it's an adventure, it's a quest, his rite of passage, an allegory!"[1]) while the camera lingers on totems of cinematic prestige behind the producers' desks: framed posters of modern auteur classics like Michael Haneke's *La Pianiste* (2001) and David Lynch's *Mulholland Drive* (2001), festival trophies from Europe and North America, Berri's sculpture of a hand-cranked *cinématographe*, and Farrugia's face inserted into a still from *Citizen Kane* (Orson Welles, 1941). Unsurprisingly, Baffie fails to attract the interest of these financiers. When he is also rebuffed by most of France's leading actors, a quip from Jean Rochefort sums up the film's agenda as a self-consciously worthless *divertissement*. Directly to camera, Rochefort rejects Baffie with the line, "I've worked with the greatest, I can't work with the lowest!"[2]

While *Les Clefs de bagnole*'s opening defiantly–gleefully–resists sustained interpretation, it nonetheless invites conclusions about the status of popular French film. This would appear to be an unabashedly scurrilous cinema, lacking any intellectual pretensions. Following Baffie's logic, these are films likely to win audiences but not awards; they are incomprehensible to the critical and professional academy; they are self-evidently artless and ephemeral. Setting up such glaring clashes between low and high culture has, furthermore, become something of a trademark for the mainstream French cinema artisan. Consider the title sequence of Jan Kounen's *Dobermann* (1997), which climaxes as an animated attack dog urinates on the opening credits, before an abrupt cut takes us to a lavish wedding ceremony held in the Notre Dame cathedral. This recent vogue for contrasting the profane with the sacred may well have begun with Jean-Jacques Beineix's operatic thriller *Diva* (1981), and especially *37°2 le matin* (1986), whose notorious opening shot tracks slowly, inexorably, into a close-up of Zorg (Jean-Hugues Anglade) and Betty (Béatrice Dalle) having sex on a bed over which hangs a reproduction of the Mona Lisa. As brash as they are emphatic, Baffie and his like-minded contemporaries make the opposition between low and high French cinema, the popular and the elite, unmistakably blatant.

This chapter will analyse the impact of this low-versus-high paradigm within contemporary French cinema, rethinking the generative force of the dichotomy. Initially, I will explore the increased divergence between recent popular and art-house French filmmaking, the extent to which both forms have become polarised. To do this, I survey a series of production shifts, situating the contemporary proliferation of popular, Hollywood-oriented genre filmmaking–most notably the rise of the twenty-first century French blockbuster–alongside a new radicalisation of art cinema. What has emerged, we will discover, is an accelerated and reinvigorating divide between mass cinema and its specialist counterpart. While the French film mainstream has diversified, become more robustly attuned to transnational styles and conventional tastes, art-house cinema, conversely, is now the domain of experimental, austere practices, akin to an avant-garde.

To contextualise such findings, however, I go on in the second part of this chapter to examine a corollary, more neglected tendency in French filmmaking, in which popular and art cinema exist as a point of productive intersection–collision and confluence–rather than binary division. This pop-art template I define through the case study of Valeria Bruni-Tedeschi's *Il est plus facile pour un chameau...* (2003). Qualifying and in many ways challenging the conventional low-versus-high film/art equation, Bruni-Tedeschi's film emblematises a contemporary French cinema that blurs distinctions between the mass-oriented and the intellectual, drawing from and intermingling the features of both. As a result, *Il est plus facile pour un chameau…* is a representatively hybrid film: in its fluid approach to narrative design, its address to the viewer as a comedic yet staunchly progressive feminist text, its playful use of multi-media, its contradictory political agenda, and its elusive visual style. In broader terms, Bruni-Tedeschi's film not only highlights the pop-art model, but also its viability as a fertile middle ground in the crowded marketplace of French cinema today.

States of the art: from *Brice de Nice* to Claire Denis

Befitting the confidence of Laurent Baffie and his peers, popular cinema in France has indeed enjoyed a recent resurgence. Clearly, the main catalyst for such Hollywood-inspired filmmaking has been Luc Besson. Besson's influential business model, based on an iconoclastic career begun by *cinéma du look* hits like *Subway* (1985) and *Le Grand bleu* (1988), uses an aggressively commercial aesthetic. Almost unique in operating without state subsidies, Besson, who co-founded his transnational EuropaCorp outfit in 2000, produces films that cater to mass, international audiences rather than elitist cinephiles defending the "cultural exception" (Vanderschelden 2007, 43-44). So forceful are Besson's beliefs, and so lucrative the results, that to some eyes his work directly assaults the identity of French cinema itself.[3] Furthermore, as Charlie Michael observes, in Besson's wake has arrived a vigorous series of "popular genre films that feature special effects and glossy production values… [f]or those of us accustomed to thinking of French cinema as a low-budget, philosophical alternative to Hollywood, the past few years might have been a bit disorienting" (Michael 2005, 55).[4] Notable breakthroughs here are action spectaculars like *The Fifth Element* (Besson, 1997), *Le Pacte des loups* (Christophe Gans, 2001), *Les Rivières pourpres* (Mathieu Kassovitz, 2000), *Blueberry* (Kounen, 2004) and the highly successful *Taxi* franchise (Gérard Pirès, 1998; Gérard Krawczyk, 2000; Krawczyk, 2003; Krawczyk, 2007). These blockbusters have found large audiences in France and often abroad, meshing favourably with a new institutional climate in which heightened private investment has disproportionately boosted high-budget French super-productions, generating films that now routinely cost more than 10 million Euros (Michael 2005, 58-60).

    Besides such iconic blockbusters, the proliferation of mass-oriented genre films has also begun apace in middle- to low-tier productions, on a scale arguably unparalleled in French cinema history. The last few years have seen the release of spy thrillers (notably *Agents secrets*, Frédéric Schoendoerffer, 2004), heist and caper movies (*Dobermann*), erotic thrillers (*Déjà mort*, Olivier Dahan, 1997; *Corps à corps*, François Hanss, 2003), martial arts epics (*Le Baiser mortel du dragon/Kiss of the Dragon*, Chris Nahon, 2001), medical conspiracy thrillers (*Qui a tué Bambi?*, Gilles Marchand, 2003), science-fiction (*Immortel (ad vitam)*, Enki Bilal, 2004), and a slew of grisly serial-killer films (*Le Plaisir et ses petits tracas*, Nicolas Boukhrief, 1998; *Cette femme-là*, Guillaume Nicloux, 2003). Proximate to these, and perhaps more peculiar, is the phenomenon of once venerated film categories being–depending on your perspective– repackaged for a broader audience, or, alternatively, vulgarised beyond repair. *Banlieue* cinema provides a vivid example. Carrie Tarr characterises this cycle through its social activism, in which quasi- documentary studies of marginal demographics and urban spaces create "representations of conflict highlighting… individual problems of identity and integration" (2005, 84). But the most high-profile recent *banlieue* film in France is the shamelessly exploitative, science-fiction-martial arts cross-over fantasy *Banlieue 13* (2004), co-written and produced by Besson and directed by his journeyman protégé Pierre Morel. Similarly, the once- renowned heritage genre, hailed by Phil Powrie as "the hegemonic French cinema of the 1990s" (1999, 2), has manifested itself anew in fast-cut, violent, youth-oriented form as the CGI spectacle of Pitof's *Vidocq* (2001), whose success led to its director being hired by Warner Brothers for their comic book spin-off *Catwoman* (2004).

Not all popular French cinema has such transatlantic aspirations. In fact, the backbone of the film market in France remains the performance- or troupe-driven comedy, lesser-known abroad but essential to the national industry retaining its indigenous market share. Since 2000 the French box office has been consolidated by comic stars and the careful development of comedy franchises: most prominently the *Astérix* series (*Astérix et Obélix: Mission Cléopâtre* (Alain Chabat, 2002) is the highest-grossing twenty-first century film in France with over 14.3 million tickets sold[5]), *Les Bronzés 3: Amis pour la vie* (Patrice Leconte, 2006; second with 10.3 million admissions[6]), *La Vérité si je mens! 2* (Thomas Gilou, 2001; eleventh; 7.8 million) and *Brice de Nice* (James Huth, 2005; thirty-eighth; 4.3 million). While such comedy properties are ubiquitous on-screen and in the popular French film press, however, they tend to receive only piecemeal international distribution, and almost never reach the key North American market.[7] Even on DVD, such comedies are typically released without English subtitles, reflecting excessive trade caution about the perceived appeal of lowbrow French slapstick, as well as a self-imposed limit on the transnational circulation of French cinema at its most mainstream.

A solution to this exportability problem has come with a major new French production trend–the horror film. This genre, historically the most denigrated but profitable of all, has inspired a phase of French cinema whose popularity extends far beyond local audiences. Until quite recently, the French horror film had been a marginal format, typified if at all by the classical works of Henri-Georges Clouzot, Georges Franju's *Les Yeux sans visage* (1960), and, less reputably, Jean Rollin's softcore erotica. But in a burst of recent activity a group of young French filmmakers has revived–or in real terms established–what Réné Prédal calls "le cinéma gore" (2002, 97-98).[8] This has led to a series of lower-budget productions that loosely mimic horror sub-genres from Hollywood: slasher films (Lionel Delplanque's *Promenons-nous dans les bois*, 2000; Alexandre Aja's *Haute tension*, 2003), urban vampire thrillers (Antoine de Caunes's *Les Morsures de l'aube*, 2001), tales of the supernatural (Jean-Paul Salomé's *Belphégor, le fantôme du Louvre*, 2001; Eric Valette's *Maléfique*, 2002; Julien Magnat's *Bloody Mallory*, 2002), and macabre suspense films about backwater grotesques (Kim Chapiron's *Sheitan*, 2006; David Moreau and Xavier Palud's *Ils*, 2006). Unlike the traditional French comedy, *le cinéma gore*'s more visceral appeal has translated internationally, culminating in a series of Hollywood horror films directed and largely crewed by French émigrés. Like (less illustrious) echoes of Jacques Tourneur's work for Val Lewton's RKO unit in the 1940s, these Franco-American B-movies include Kassovitz's *Gothika* (2003), Gans's *Silent Hill* (2006), and Aja's remake of Wes Craven's *The Hills Have Eyes* (2006).[9]

This extraordinary wave of popular French cinema, and its clear departure from traditionally refined French film art, has been greeted with palpable agitation within the industry. Predictably, to the intellectual analyst, typified by the enduringly pro-auteur polemicists at *Cahiers du cinéma*, such Franco-Hollywood products reveal a deep-seated artistic banality. To others more sympathetic to the Bessonian approach, particularly in the pragmatic popular press of magazines like *Studio* and *Première*, the films are a welcome sign of French commercial acuity. A more neutral industrial summary has come from David Kessler, director of the Centre National de la Cinématographie (CNC), who in *Libération* offered a tentative redefinition of the national production landscape based upon the impact of *Taxi 2*, *Yamakasi* (Ariel Zeitoun, 2001), *Le Pacte des loups* and the twenty-first century revival of mass French filmmaking.

Kessler declared: "This is a revelation: it demonstrates the popular potential of our national cinema, contrary to the fatalist discourse that we've been hearing for too long... This success shows us the principal force of French cinema: its diversity" (Michael 2005, 61).

Extending Kessler's point about this diversification process, we should note its equal applicability to the auteurist cinema for which France is more traditionally recognised. For as France's popular cinema has broadened its appeal through a profusion of international formulas, the French art-house sector has consolidated its (national) identity by, conversely, specialising so much as to risk alienating even its minority audience. Central to this trend is the rise of the contemporary French *cinéma du corps*, represented by such infamous films as *Sombre* (Philippe Grandrieux, 1998), *Romance* (Catherine Breillat, 1999), *Baise-moi* (Virginie Despentes and Coralie Trinh Thi, 2000), *Intimité (Intimacy)* (Patrice Chéreau, 2001), *demonlover* (Olivier Assayas, 2002), *Irréversible* (Gaspar Noé, 2002), and *Twentynine Palms* (Bruno Dumont, 2003).[10] Radical and uncompromising, the *cinéma du corps* is the most divisive type of French cinema since the New Wave. Its narratives dwell on sexuality and physicality stripped of all romantic connotation, set in atavistic diegetic spaces–frequently the criminal or leisure underworlds of Paris–whose antisocial inhabitants are driven to acts of corporeal rage. *Sombre*, for example, depicts a wandering puppeteer carrying out a series of sexual assaults in rural France; *Intimacy* deconstructs a clinical yet explicitly carnal relationship; and *demonlover* tracks a cyber-pornography network from Paris to Japan. Beyond these challenging subjects, however, it is the stylistic execution of the *cinéma du corps* which even more forcibly affronts its viewers. Emblematised by Claire Denis's recent films–principally her strikingly obscure drama of sexual cannibalism, *Trouble Every Day* (2001), although the impulse persists in *L'Intrus* (2005) –these nihilistic films are often lyrical to the point of abstraction, psychologically opaque, spatially elliptical, lacking stable narrative unities and legible film form. Alongside Denis, the interlinked work of other *cinéma du corps* filmmakers–Marina de Van, Dumont, Noé, Assayas, Grandrieux, as well as a growing list of international directors–galvanises an art cinema whose reputation for severity exceed that of its predecessors.

Throughout France's art-house community, moreover, even in projects less directly confrontational than the *cinéma du corps*, there is often a commitment to self-reflexive, rarefied design. Stylistic experimentation is an increasingly accepted practice among veterans and first-timers alike, while open-ended, puzzle-box narration–the hallmark of 1960s modernism, made famous by Alain Resnais and Michaelangelo

Antonioni–is once again in favour. Consider the openings of two recent debut features, which contrast sharply with our earlier, mainstream examples.[11] Lucile Hadzihalilovic's *Innocence* (2004) fades up to an out-of-focus, fast motion blur of bubbles and dank green organic matter in motion, as a deep rumbling noise reverberates on the soundtrack. The shot's startling effect references the work of avant-garde pioneer Stan Brakhage, especially his studies in cognitive abstraction *Mothlight* (1963), *Dog Star Man* (1961-1964), and *Eye Myth* (1967). Similar in its disorienting approach, albeit with representational images, is Siegrid Alnoy's *Elle est des nôtres* (2003). Her film begins with a clicking sound, never situated, followed by a quote from Dostoyevsky's "The Dreams of a Ridiculous Man," and a medium close-up of a windswept woman's face, neutrally composed. She vanishes, revealing a distant, out-of-focus figure crossing a remote mountainside. Accompanying but not matching the images is a loud clap of thunder and the rasping sound of a woman's gasps for air.

The radicalism of these openings–suggestive of a non-narrative, associative perceptual sampling–is echoed in different ways by Hadzihalilovic and Alnoy's more senior arthouse contemporaries. Reverse storytelling is another anti-mainstream device of choice. In *5x2* (2004), François Ozon uses backwards narration to invert ironically the demise of a couple, beginning with their divorce proceedings and ending on an idyllic yet forlorn long take, shot at sunset, of them walking blissfully out to sea on holiday in Italy. The same effect-and-cause plotting adds bleak poignancy to the rape-revenge course of Noé's *Irréversible*, which climaxes near its start when the wrong culprit is murdered in an underground nightclub. More self-conscious still is Chéreau's *Gabrielle* (2005). Chéreau's film, also about an unravelling marriage and a loveless sexual relationship, adapts a Joseph Conrad novella with Brechtian alienation effects, alternating colour shots with black-and-white, breaking its action into subtitled chapters, and superimposing unspoken lines of dialogue onto the screen. Consistently, the twenty-first-century French art-house attempts these bewildering yet bravura stylistic means. More generally, while the French mainstream is now globalised and attuned to the masses as never before, such practices have been assertively countered by France's auteurist vanguard. Collectively, as one *Cahiers du cinéma* editorial argues emphatically, the French art-house seeks nothing less than "to stake out the contemporary avant-garde" (Joyard 2002, 10).

A camel through the eye of a needle:
French pop-art cinema

As we have seen, French popular and art-house cinemas today stand poised in opposition, differentiated as products in exceptional ways. If, as Susan Hayward and Ginette Vincendeau contend, the "success of the *politique des auteurs*... and the films of the New Wave drove a wedge between '*auteur*' and 'popular' cinema" (2000, 6), then recent French filmmaking makes this division even more antagonistic than the famous 1960s. But this dichotomy is not the whole story. The final section of this essay will explore the largely overlooked tendency of contemporary French pop-art cinema, and a middle course created from connections and citations *between* low and high cinemas. While there is a clear neglect of French popular film *per se*, revision is perhaps more pressingly due with regard to the traditional separation of mainstream and art-house cinema, the long-standing cliché that French films either compete with Hollywood and generate box office revenue, or else win prizes and create auteurist art worthy of scholarship. My–contrary–point of departure is that much recent French cinema derives international visibility, textual charisma, and an appeal to audiences, both specialised and mass, from shifting permutations of the popular and the artistic. What the example of Bruni-Tedeschi's *Il est plus facile pour un chameau...* shows is that high and low French filmmaking can exist profitably, fascinatingly, in a state of cultural flux.

Bruni-Tedeschi's background and professional experiences might make her initially seem predisposed to high art and an auteurist agenda. The daughter of a prominent industrialist and a concert pianist, Bruni-Tedeschi moved to France at the age of nine when her family was targeted by the extreme left Red Brigades in Italy during the early 1970s. Based largely in Paris, Bruni-Tedeschi began what can only be described as a glittering career. She trained as an actor at the prestigious Théâtre Nanterre-Amandiers, working with Patrice Chéreau, who chose her for the lead of his screen adaptation of Chekhov's *Hôtel de France* (1987). Based upon this performance, she went on to collaborate with many of France's leading filmmakers: in Jacques Doillon's *L'Amoureuse* (1987), Diane Kurys's *La Baule-les-Pins* (1990), Laurence Ferreira-Barbosa's *Les Gens normaux n'ont rien d'exceptionnel* (1993) –for which she won the most promising actress *César*–Noémie Lvovsky's *Oublie-moi* (1994), Claire Denis's *Nénette et Boni* (1996), and Claude Chabrol's *Au coeur du mensonge* (1999). After 1998, Bruni-Tedeschi supplemented her acting work with periods of writing, beginning with a series of semi-autobiographical dialogue scenes and narrative fragments. These she read to Lvovsky, who helped her develop the script of what eventually became her debut as co-writer-director.

Il est plus facile pour un chameau…, the resulting film, depicts the fantasies and tribulations of Federica (Bruni-Tedeschi), an émigré Italian and frustrated playwright living in Paris. Federica feels guilty about her inherited wealth, for which she repeatedly seeks counsel from a priest (Pascal Bongard). His advice to her is the biblical adage that it is easier for a camel to pass through the eye of a needle than for a rich man to enter the kingdom of heaven. Romantically, Federica not only lusts after the flustered curate, but is also distractedly torn between three other men. There is her socialist history teacher boyfriend Pierre (Jean-Hugues Anglade) who seeks marriage, her married ex-lover Philippe (Denis Podalydès) who seeks adultery (and who may actually be a figment of Federica's imagination) and an unnamed Man In The Garden (Yvan Attal) who lunches with his son in the park outside her apartment on the rue Renoir. In her family relationships, Federica is also under stress. As her ill father (Roberto Herlizka) begins a terminal decline, Federica falls out with her jealous younger sister Bianca (Chiara Mastroianni), her mother (Marisa Borini, Bruni-Tedeschi's actual mother), and her wayward younger brother Aurelio (Lambert Wilson). Little is resolved in any of these meandering plotlines, and the film ends as the father's body is returned to Italy by plane.

The deliberate dissonance of *Il est plus facile pour un chameau…* was noted by many critics, occupying a range of cultural strata, upon its release in Paris in April, 2003. In *Les Inrockuptibles*, France's leading pop culture magazine, Jean-Baptiste Morain suggested that, "the first film of Valeria Bruni-Tedeschi is at once tender and mean-spirited, serious and light-hearted, balanced and chaotic, just self-deprecating enough not to be antipathetic, just narcissistic enough not to be sympathetic" (2003, 34). In the more venerated *Positif*, Francoise Audé, Philippe Rouyer, and Claire Vassé all concurred with Morain's perspective. Audé noted that Bruni-Tedeschi's "story continues to accumulate contradictions," while Rouyer and Vassé observed how the film strategically "balances different registers… [and] ruptures in tone" (2003, 29). In *Le Point*, Olivier de Bruyn, too, underlined the discordance of *Il est plus facile pour un chameau…*, which he traced to a schizophrenic relationship with the art cinema mode itself. De Bruyn claimed that in form and content Bruni-Tedeschi's film was "triggered by a contemporary French cinema landscape doomed too often to minimalist introspection and existential reasoning… however, the script makes no secret of its connection to the true vocation of the cineaste" (2003, 109).

Building from this critical consensus, we can situate Bruni-Tedeschi's hybrid project more concretely within a pop-art template. David Bordwell offers a salient context, writing about the popularisation of radical technique in contemporary Hong Kong cinema. The resulting mêlée, Bordwell suggests, derives from highly refined, occasionally modernist features that are conscripted into a generic, stylistically engaging cinema. As Bordwell reflects:

> In commercial film, experimentation is usually not anarchic messing about but self-conscious craftmanship... Driven by competition, contrariness, or just the urge not to repeat oneself, the ambitious artisan presses against tradition, testing how far one can go while still playing by the rules of the game. (2000, 261-262)

Ultimately, then, the goal is to render avant-garde idiosyncrasies into legible form, staving off the viewer's consternation while refreshing the materials of mainstream entertainment. A core principle of this pop-art cinema, in France as well as Hong Kong, is the need for its practitioner to sustain commercial viability but also directorial distinctiveness, to synthesise revitalised popular product from the esoteric approaches of the art-house. Distilling low art from high art–or vice versa–the pop-art filmmaker can have it both ways.

In its narrative design, *Il est plus facile pour un chameau...* certainly offers a skittish, yet skilful, mixture of art-house solemnity deflected by mainstream self-mockery. Opening without any exposition or backstory, the film shifts between Federica's pampered childhood in Italy and her present-day worries in Paris, intermingled with comic visions and cartoon skits. Using straight cuts without any temporal or subjective cues like dissolves, Bruni-Tedeschi wanders playfully among her diegetic strands. This creates a stream-of-consciousness cinema, blending moments of youthful nostalgia, present-day malaise, and hypothetical projections of implausible victories, all varying wildly in mood. Significantly, the film also provides a running commentary on its own artistically erratic status. Federica labours over her writing throughout the film, and at one point she attempts to pitch a play to a would-be backer and cultural avatar, just like Baffie in *Les Clefs de bagnole*. The scene in which Federica meets the prominent theatre director here takes place twice, with multiple conclusions. Initially, this pompous figure (who describes airily his season of Brecht, a Kundera adaptation, and an *Uncle Vanya* revival) fervently thanks Federica for existing, then deluges her with praise for her script's popular appeal: "When I read your play I cried twice–*twice*! –and laughed too."[12] Second time around, though, the director now turns on the same material from a mass audience's standpoint, attacking its intellectual pretensions and morose self-involvement: "It's heavy, it's sad… The real problem is that it depresses me; I don't do depressing."[13]

Throughout the narrative, moreover, Bruni-Tedeschi flits between the lowbrow and the highbrow, while plot points accrue whimsically, disrupted by this inconsistent style. Near the opening, diegetic piano music continues as we cut from a cartoon of Federica struggling to push a camel's backside through the eye of a giant needle, to Federica pirouetting at her ballet class, through jump cuts of her silver Jaguar speeding across the centre of Paris. Within scenes, events collide or are interrupted. One apparent flashback even begins with the adult Federica leading herself, as a child, in a stately dance through the Italian family home. Another sequence, more perplexing still, careens from a flashback (the young Federica at the Luna Park fair in Italy), to a possibly imagined recent encounter with Philippe in a café, to a bizarre pop-Freudian fantasy of her dressed as his daughter, climbing nervously into bed with him and his wife. On the one hand, Bruni-Tedeschi embodies here the mainstream director's broad comic sensibility, poking fun at Federica's solipsism and the stunted emotional growth of a poor little rich girl. But on the other hand, Bruni-Tedeschi also creates a complex subjective portrait of a stalled but active protagonist, a feminist deconstruction of a woman in crisis. To do this, moreover, she adopts the experimental instincts of international art cinema. Like Ozu, she elides or subtends pivotal encounters in favor of observational minutiae; like Resnais, she reverses temporal flow and mixes truth with fiction. Jean-Michel Frodon energetically analyses the cinematic mélange that develops, which "takes off from its joyful contempt for the rules of genre… [enjoying] the most invigorating freedom, a madness which unsettles–including those within the drama–all systems of storytelling and description" (2003, 26).

Within such open formal conflicts, *Il est plus facile pour un chameau…* interweaves features of French culture both high and low. In a mainstream vein, the film opens with the seemingly requisite establishing shots that–especially in comedies–showcase on-screen a travelogue iconography of Paris. Under blazing sunshine, we see Federica drive down the Champs-Élysées, towards the Eiffel Tower (under which is superimposed the title caption), alongside the Jardin du Luxembourg on the left bank, and on past tourist landmarks guaranteed to please international audiences. Bruni-Tedeschi also cites a range of performance art forms across a broad cultural spectrum. Federica attends several times a Guignol puppet play, dances an extended accordion polka on a nighttime date with Philippe beside the Seine, takes ballet classes, goes to the opera with Pierre, tumbles through a circus routine ("Je suis la grande trapéziste!") to amuse her hospitalised father, and sits mesmerised through television variety shows as a youngster. At the level of visual style, Bruni-Tedeschi uses multimedia to achieve similar aesthetic diversity. The film's animated asides–Federica grappling with the eponymous camel, a crowd cheering her writing, stars dancing in the night sky while she kisses Philippe–amplify the fantastic aspects of the live action, echoing the devices of both auteurs and mainstream comedians. Federica's cartoon reveries at once mimic the dancing Volvo logo imagined by Claire Denis's traffic-bound protagonist in *Vendredi soir* (2002), as well as the high-speed CGI-animated car chase projected by Baffie in *Les clefs de bagnole*.

More multifarious than mainstream artisans, Bruni-Tedeschi still shares their suspicion of elitist culture and the sacrosanct, which she deflates with earthy wit. Religion is a particular target. While Federica waits for her unwitting priest confidant to finish a traditional baptism ceremony, for example, a voiceover cuts through the service, and his earnest entreaties to avoid sin, with hearty sexual yearnings offered apparently from his perspective. "I want to take you," the curate whispers huskily, "from *behind*" (J'ai envie de te prendre... par derrière). Later on, Federica is urged by Bianca to commit to both Pierre and the institution of marriage, and Bruni-Tedeschi stages the scene with Federica urinating on the toilet, dismissing the idea out of hand as she gets up to wipe herself. In its pop-art approach to politics, *Il est plus facile pour un chameau...* is equally evasive. The uneven tone is set near the start when Bruni-Tedeschi has Pierre bellow socialist anthems and lines from "L'Internationale"–"The world has a new foundation: we were nothing, we shall be all!"–from the window of Federica's luxury car as they pause in traffic near the jewellery district of the Place Vendôme (one passer-by, perhaps an extra, whoops in delight at the sentiments).[14] Yet later, during a lavish tea with Federica's mother, the same character is given a long speech in which he talks movingly of his father, ruined by thirty years of ten-hour days on the production line. Class conflict and political tensions, like gender roles and money, are for Bruni-Tedeschi issues worthy of sympathy and scorn, thoughtful reflection but also satirical contempt. Everything and nothing is sacred.

By way of conclusion, we can consider the professional advantages of the pop-art model. Beyond its obvious capacity for textual flair and stylistic invention, perhaps most crucially it grants opportunities for international distribution and exhibition. In recent years, this type of cinema has become programmed perennially by the expanding range of middle-rank film festivals, such as Moscow, Boston, Stockholm, Chicago,

San Sebastian, Los Angeles, and London. Bruni-Tedeschi, following this trajectory, won at the 2003 Tribeca Film Festival awards for best emerging filmmaker and best actress. Such institutional endorsement also extends to the prestigious North American market. *Il est plus facile pour un chameau...*, in this context, was chosen for the 2005-6 *Tournées*, a package of films offered to American schools and universities by the French American Cultural Exchange (FACE), a partner of the Cultural Services of the French Embassy in the USA, co-sponsored by the CNC and the French Ministry of Foreign Affairs. As an official *Tournées* selection, *Il est plus facile pour un chameau...* was designed to screen as part of locally organised French film festivals. In effect, Bruni-Tedeschi's film was promoted as a culturally appropriate product for subsidised export from France–an artwork too sophisticated for the multiplex, but more palatable for audiences than radical French art-house fare. In this category, Bruni-Tedeschi joins the ranks of contemporary pop-auteurs like Yvan Attal, Jacques Audiard, Christian Carion, Cédric Klapisch, Patrice Leconte, and many others. Raising the profile of French cinema abroad, occupying a dynamic cultural middle ground, this pop-art French cinema combines low art with high art in fresh, original, invigorating ways. Perhaps Bruni-Tedeschi herself sums up this cinematic template, and its diverse appeal, most succinctly. Asked by an interviewer whether *Il est plus facile pour un chameau...* was a mainstream comedy or a lofty tragedy, she replied: "I prefer it when these two elements are put intimately side-by-side: it seems to be me that there's actually nothing stronger than that" (De Bruyn 2003, 109).

---

[1] "Oui, c'est une aventure, c'est une quête, ça part d'une initiative qu'on fait, une allégorie!"

[2] "J'ai tourné avec les plus grands, c'est pas pour tourner avec les plus petits!"

[3] See, for example, Susan Hayward (1998).

[4] The relative failure of Besson's own Angel-A (2005)–with just under 850,000 admissions in France and only a modest release in the UK–after nearly six years away from directing, may indicate that his popular touch is now best suited to the role of financier, writer, and promoter of young talent like Gérard Krawczyk and Pierre Morel.

[5] Sources: www.cinemaffiches.com and the CNC.

[6] *Taxi 2* (2001) completes the top three; French productions occupy half of the twenty-first century's top ten.

[7] Anecdotally, this impression continues in the classroom. When I screened *Brice de Nice* as the finale to a French cinema survey class, one student later confessed: "I didn't know the French made films like that!"

[8] Prédal's term is here taken largely as a point of departure, given that most new French horror films were released after his invaluable volume was published.

[9] The same trend continues beyond the horror genre, as with Jean-François Richet moving from *Ma 6-T va crack-er* (1997) and *De l'amour* (2001) to the Hollywood remake of *Assault on Precinct 13* (2005), and Florent Emilio Siri following *Nid de guêpes* (2002) with the Bruce Willis vehicle *Hostage* (2005).

[10] For an overview of the *cinéma du corps* and its figureheads Claire Denis, Bruno Dumont, and Gaspar Noé, see Palmer (2006a). For a related contextual essay see Palmer (2006b).

[11] One explanation for the experimentation evident among younger and first-time filmmakers comes from the stylistic radicalism encouraged, even mandated, in French film schools. Noémie Lvovsky, who co-wrote *Il est plus facile pour un chameau...* and mentored Bruni-Tedeschi as its director, was, tellingly, a graduate of la Fémis, one of France's most prestigious and exacting film academies. See Palmer (2006b, 173-174) and Prédal (2002, 39).

[12] "En lisant votre pièce j'ai pleuré deux fois—deux fois!—et j'ai ri aussi."

[13] "C'est lourd, c'est triste...Le vrai problème est que ça me déprime; moi, je ne peux pas faire quelque chose qui me déprime."

[14] "Le monde va changer de base: nous ne sommes rien, soyons tout!"

CHAPTER SEVEN

TAUTOLOGICAL USES AND ABUSES IN THE RECENT FILMS OF JEAN-PIERRE JEUNET

MICHELLE SCATTON-TESSIER

In the 1980s Jean-Pierre Jeunet started his cinematic career in short animated films, commercial advertising and music videos whose casts provided him with a great number of secondary actors for his later feature films. His early years in filmmaking coincided with a growing passion for a new aesthetic in popular visual representation on the small and big screens in France, leading to a shift in television advertising from the informative commercial to the *nouvelle publicité* as art form. For the movie-going public and critics alike, this exploration of visual aesthetics and mise-en-scène would come to be recognised as the *cinéma du look* of such advertising directors as Jean-Jacques Annaud, Jean-Jacques Beineix, Luc Besson and Leos Carax among others. Although the worlds of television advertising and feature filmmaking have long been interlinked in France, the sheer quantity of successful films in the 1980s to early 1990s by this band of new directors brought to the surface a fear on the part of film critics of the influence of an *esthétique pub,* associated with the worlds of marketing and sales imposing itself on the "cultural exception" of cinema.[1] Much ink has been spilt over this era of French filmmaking and its now renowned directors; however, little research has been dedicated to popular advertising elements in the cinema of Jean-Pierre Jeunet.

Over the years, Jeunet has worked to promote British Telecom, Lotus, the Banque Nationale de Paris, Électricité de France, Boursin, public service road safety announcements, Peugeot and Renault; some of his best-known videos include those for Julien Clerc's 1984 "La fille aux bas Nylon" and Etienne Daho's 1986 "Tombé pour la France." As of publication, Jeunet has directed *Delicatessen* (co-directed with Marc Caro,

1991), *La cité des enfants perdus* (co-directed with Caro, 1995), *Alien Resurrection* (1997), *Le Fabuleux destin d'Amélie Poulain* (2001) and *Un long dimanche de fiançailles* (2004). He is in the production stages of the film interpretation of Yann Martel's novel *Life of Pi* due out in 2009.

The principal goal of this study is to question the extent to which Jeunet's recent cinematic style has developed out of his initial training as a creator of images for advertising; the following pages thus propose an inquiry into the narrative structures in *Le Fabuleux destin d'Amélie Poulain* and *Un long dimanche de fiançailles* which seduce viewers through the use and abuse of widely-known advertising techniques with the intent of creating identification, complicity and immediate satisfaction on the part of the audience.

Negative criticisms of these two films gravitate around what some have called Jeunet's *esthétique publicitaire*, the techniques and methods used to reach the "minimum viewer", the one who will make the smallest effort to follow the film's narrative, the most passive and least patient viewer imaginable: the ultimate zapper. It is Jeunet's ability to satisfyingly address the average moviegoer that links his seductive cinema to the very definition of *publicité* in which one tries to target the largest group possible: the public, who are thus treated as a homogeneous mass. As Haineault and Roy state in their well-received text on advertising analysis, *Unconscious for Sale:*

> In order to become public, a discourse must in effect gradually get beyond its specificity and win the approval of a broad majority. As a consequence, it can count only on the least emotional or intellectual common denominator of its intended audience. As a result, it will deny itself the human wealth of our profound diversity, all the more so since it will target a wider audience (1993, xxi).

Like television advertising and other popular big-budget films (*films grand public*), *Le Fabuleux destin d'Amélie Poulain* and *Un long dimanche de fiançailles* rally us together around common traits of a defined group. They propose that:

> ...[f]or thirty or sixty seconds we are heroes, famous or renowned, magically able to resolve conflicts that, just a moment before, were driving us crazy... we readily become passionately enamoured of these little moments of *publicity* we are granted. We enjoy these moments because they transform what is everyday into majestic feats. We adulate them because, through them, the child-magician beats all odds (1993, xxi-xxii).

Jeunet's "moments of publicity" promote stereotypes in picturesque and universally recognisable landscapes of France and its regions. Colour schemes are carefully crafted; camera work is well balanced between extreme close-ups of faces or objects and long takes involving intricate camera work (Vincendeau 2001a, 24). Characters are archetypes: in *Le Fabuleux destin d'Amélie Poulain,* the plot follows the daily tasks of the retired widow, the single girl (the child-magician herself), the hypochondriac, the urchin, the jealous ex-boyfriend, the frustrated writer, the invalid and the alcoholic concierge; in *Un long dimanche de fiançailles,* cowards, heroes, cold-blooded killers, vengeful girlfriends and shell-shocked soldiers lead the heroine through a biological and geographical puzzle. Reduced to personality traits, these archetypes reassure the viewer in his or her "mediocrity," securing him or her in the given understanding of individuals, leaving little room for complexity or personal interpretation. Carved out of regional specificity, Mathilde (Audrey Tautou) is perhaps the best crafted of Jeunet's archetypes and comes from the most significant change made to Japrisot's novel in which Manech (Gaspard Ulliel) comes from "Cap-breton, within sight of Biarritz" (1994, 16) and where Mathilde's family has a summer home. For Jeunet, she is the stubborn Breton woman who limps (recalling the popular saying "hard-headed as a Breton" (têtu comme un Breton) as well as a congenital hip disorder common at one time in Brittany); she is the young Bretonne ashamed of appearing as *une bécasse* (a silly goose), as in Bécassine, the famous turn-of-the-century comic-strip Breton maid. [2] Throughout *Un long dimanche de fiançailles,* one finds Jeunet's *chic* in his play on the traditional reputation of Brittany, offering a mythical and exotic version of the region and its crafts to seduce the average French viewer, while calling upon well-known landscapes of Paris for the international audience. Although well anchored in their time period and geographical setting, these people at first appear rather different from the intended viewers; however, they go beyond any type of pure difference to establish a deep resemblance at some level with the spectator, a method of character formulation often used in commercial advertising (Haineault 1993, 103). They call upon universal themes of friendship, love, jealousy, abandonment, mourning, hope and fear, offering something with which almost all individuals in the audience may identify.

Jeunet assumes nothing of his audience; he provides all the details to keep the minimum viewer informed and ensure the story line is understood. A dialogue or voiceover usually explains the image, anticipating a viewer who does not have the necessary code to understand the cultural reference, as exemplified by the introductory scene between

Amélie and her neighbour, Mr. Dufayel, in which Amélie does not
recognise the painting he is reproducing:

> Amélie: I really like this painting.
> Mr. Dufayel: It's the *The Luncheon of the Boating Party* ...
> (Amélie raises her eyebrows in ignorance.)
> Mr. Dufayel: ... by Renoir.[3]

Here, the tautological effect (the painting is shown and accompanied by a
dialogue giving its painter and title) appears necessary: the female
protagonist is missing a cultural reference in order to fully understand Mr.
Dufayel's project. Either the viewer identifies with Amélie and thus feels
reassured because he hadn't recognised the painting and now has the key
information (he experiences embarrassment, then relief) or the viewer
knew the painting and relishes in a moment of self-satisfaction.

Advertisers make extensive use of tautologies, for they are one of the
most bankable means of getting one's point across to the widest audience
and constitute explanation in the very simplest of terms. In television
advertisements, and by extension in *Le Fabuleux destin d'Amélie Poulain*
and *Un long dimanche de fiançailles,* tautology refers to a reiteration of
the voiceover with a visual sequence, which generally works as visual
evidence (*preuve par l'image*), the fetishisation of the image in an ever
more visual society.

Jeunet's *Le Fabuleux destin d'Amélie Poulain* and to a greater extent
Un long dimanche de fiançailles, his first literary adaptation, illustrate the
limits of a coupling of filmic narration and seductive aesthetics. The
difficulty stems from the near-impossible creation of an image, saturated
with visual mastery, which can speak for itself. To avoid misinterpretation
of his graphic illustrations, Jeunet is obliged to amplify each short
sequence by an accompanying leading discourse, which directs the eye
and comments on what the viewer should understand, thus often creating a
somewhat unpleasant tautological effect.

Tautology is one of the most common persuasive mechanisms in
advertising, and it is a narrative trick exploited in *Le Fabuleux destin
d'Amélie Poulain,* but more systematically employed in *Un long dimanche
de fiançailles.* Structurally, tautology implies an unnecessary and
ineffective repetition, usually with words that add nothing new, as in "life
is life," "it's raining or it's not raining," or as exemplified in "Buy my
product, not that of my competitor Mr. Smith. Why? Because his is his
and mine is mine." The very sense of a tautology implies that the
tautologist and the listeners comprehend the same cultural codes: that of X
equals Y. For example, the common French expression, *un sou est un sou*

(a penny is a penny) necessitates that the tautologist and his interlocutor understand that *un sou* (currency) *est un sou* (is a value within a monetary system). Such is also the case for "a woman is a woman", as in Jean-Luc Godard's 1961 film title, where a modern notion of what is a woman also labels a biological female.

Tautologies rely on logical truths; in all their forms, they create statements, necessarily taken as true, because by virtue of their logical forms, they cannot be used to make false assertions. Tautology is a question of semantics and not of logic, as it is all about content and all about authority. As linguist Josette Rey-Debove has explained, "[it] is a proposition that is always true in virtue of its content, independently of the experience" (1978, 319). Tautology is an impasse in which, as Roland Barthes writes in *Mythologies*, "one takes refuge in fear, or anger or sadness, when one is at loss for an explanation" (1957, 240).[4] Tautologies are always true because they permit no ambiguity or personal interpretation; they reformulate a cultural code. They allow for no discussion, no existence of difference, each creating a static system. They are similar to proverbs, dictums and popular sayings, in that even when slightly deformed, the original version remains recognisable by the reader. They are tropes that function well in a period of slogans and of shock statements (*phrases-choc*) in which the first explanation is often that which is adopted. Barthes clarifies:

> It is true that tautology is always aggressive: it signifies a choleric break between intelligence and its object, the arrogant threat of an order in which one would not think. Our tautologies are like masters who pull abruptly on a dog's leash: thought must not range too widely, the world is full of suspicious and vain alibis, one must keep common sense conservative, one must shorten the leash to stay within a tangible reality…. The tautologist cuts with rage everything which grows around him, and that could suffocate him (1957, 97).

This notion of the "master pulling on the dog's leash" recalls Jeunet's over-zealous control of his films' images, prepared first as an intricately-drawn storyboard, in photographs, then filmed, all under his direct supervision, digitally altered, viewed by a sample audience, then touched up for clarity.[5] It is perhaps this mastery that has led film critic Serge Kaganski to comment:

> The snag is that Jeunet is gripped by such a wish to master and absolutely control his images that his films no longer breathe, such that his world appears to be filmed in a bubble. Thus, *Amélie Poulain* makes one think of

those snow globes enclosing the monuments of Paris that one sees in the kitsch souvenir shops. (2001)[6]

Though often carrying negative associations, tautologies and other forms of redundancy, exceeding what is necessary or normal, do have positive connotations: they duplicate the message in variants so as to prevent a failure of an entire system. In advertising, they reinforce the message in order to ultimately persuade the viewer to purchase or to change his behaviour. In normal speech, they help remind the interlocutor of certain facts so that he may better follow the story. Such tropes are especially effective in complex plots like that of *Un long dimanche de fiançailles*. Here, Jeunet and screenwriter Guillaume Laurant chose to periodically replace characters' names or pseudonyms with their professions, "the carpenter" for Bastoche and "the welder" for Six-Sous, as illustrated in the opening sequences. At other times, the region of origin replaces the characters' names: "the Corsican" for Ange or "the farmer from Dordogne" for Notre-Dame. The reiteration of information takes on three distinctive forms in Jeunet's method.

Most commonly, the primary tautological effect appears as a voiceover preceding the image, such as in all the "he likes/he doesn't like" sequences of *Le Fabuleux destin d'Amélie Poulain*, which economically introduce characters' pasts so that we may better understand their present behaviour; this combination of explanatory voiceover and highly-stylised image reappears at each presentation of new major and minor characters. One particular scene best illustrates this model while working as an analogy for the director's relationship with the viewer. Early in her heroic exploits, Amélie chaperones a blind neighbour through the streets, narrating while leading him through a barrage of bustling people, animals and items for sale, eventually leaving him in sheer bliss before the metro entrance. Her narration guides the neighbour and the viewer through the chaotic streets, just as the film's voiceover accompanies Jeunet's often overcharged images. This model of voiceover preceding image also dominates in *Un long dimanche de fiançailles*, particularly during the film's prologue, when the voiceover tells of condemned soldier Bastoche's German boots, as a medium shot frames his feet dredging through the rain and mud, and when we are told Bastoche (Jérôme Kircher) is a carpenter, then see him planing wood in his workshop. Shortly after, the voiceover introduces Six-Sous as a welder; then he is seen welding. Later, soldiers Benjamin Gordes and Célestin Poux tell of their war experiences; then we witness the events about which they were talking. This particular pattern resonates in the majority of the vignettes, or short sequences, functioning as relative clauses or hyper-links in the film's main plot.

Secondly, information is conveyed simultaneously in voiceover and graphic explanation as in the opening sequence of *Amélie,*[7] and in *Un long dimanche de fiançailles,* when the Corsican soldier Ange surrenders, while Manech sleeps with his hand on Mathilde's breast, or as Mathilde reads letters in her search for Célestin Poux and Benjamin Gordes. Lastly, there are vignettes followed by an instructive narrative, as seen in the crucial scene of Notre-Dame's confession to Mathilde in which he describes the explosion of the trapdoor and his survival of the battle at Bingo Crépuscule. Jeunet's use of tautology (visual and verbal redundancy) in both films appears justified differently. In *Le Fabuleux destin d'Amélie Poulain,* they support the playful atmosphere, adding to the game-like quality. In *Un long dimanche de fiançailles,* they guide the viewer through a complex narrative of similar character names, intertwining histories and subplots with tangential biographical sequences.

Reinforcing the dialogue or voiceover with visual evidence implies that there is a latent ambiguity in the processing of information, mistrust on the part of the advertiser or filmmaker in the image itself (lack of clarity, an overload of information) or distrust in the competency of the viewer to understand the image. In the case of Jean-Pierre Jeunet, the question posed is whether Jeunet lacks faith in his images or in the capacity of the viewer to understand them because the latter does not have the sufficient cultural knowledge or experience to decode the message.

Frédéric Bonnaud, writing for *Film Comment,* has touched upon this element of *Le Fabuleux destin d'Amélie Poulain,* as "one of those films that never stops reassuring the audience that it's on their side, taking them firmly by the hand and leading them... well, nowhere really" (2001, 38). "Leading them nowhere" because the redundant structures and vignettes function as a closed system, each hounding the viewer with the same pattern of information with the content slightly transformed. These sequences of voiceover followed by visual evidence establish the model which dominates throughout. Jeunet's tautological clips are short, impressionistic scenes, bearing similar formats, colour schemes and cinematography, such as close-up, medium shot and direct camera address. They focus on one moment or emphasise one aspect of a character, an idea or a setting. They oversimplify and exhaust the idea expressed, while satisfying our inquiry into characters and situations.

As highlighted in the above quotation, the entire structures of both *Le Fabuleux destin d'Amélie Poulain,* and *Un long dimanche de fiançailles* fold back on themselves in action, colour schemas, camera work, cultural references and dialogue. The majority of the themes or elements introduced are somehow reproduced elsewhere in the film, creating a quasi-redundancy and balance: in the opening sequence of *Le Fabuleux destin d'Amélie Poulain*, a fly is crushed by a car; later, Amélie tells the viewers that she seeks the often-overlooked details of films as she points out the stray fly in François Truffaut's *Jules and Jim* (1962); a horse leads the *Tour de France*, and Mme Suzanne was maimed by a horse accident; a bicycle in Bredoteau's memory box recalls a past *Tour de France*, and another more recent *Tour de France* on television is taped by Amélie for Mr. Dufayel; finally, a post card in Bredoteau's memory box reminds him of watching his aunt wash her undergarments, and later Nino interrupts a peep-show striptease at the sex shop where he works; at the end of the film, Lucien spies on Amélie and Nino through Mr. Dufayel's video camera. This structure is recuperated in *Un long dimanche de fiançailles*, in which Mathilde and Mr. Pire's daughter both limp; Mathilde prefers the tuba which echoes the sound of a lighthouse foghorn of the Breton coast; a young Manech comments on an albatross which is then evoked by Célestin Poux in a recitation of verses from "L'albatros" by Charles Baudelaire, and "albatross" is also explained as being the name of a World War I German fighter plane much later in the film. The above examples of recycling and nods to earlier scenes and moments in the film establish a neatly-packaged homogeneous pattern of odd character traits or noticeable references.

It is well known that Jeunet employs repetitive behaviour (even nervous twitches) as comic relief, paying homage to his own cinema at times (*Delicatessen*) and touching on the burlesque *à la* Jacques Tati in *Un long dimanche de fiançailles*. His repetition, in all its forms, creates a certain balance in which references and cinematographic models provide familiar landmarks and eventually closure on a theme.

In Laurant's dialogue for *Un long dimanche de fiançailles*, this redundant or tautological effect comes through in four ways. Firstly, Rouvières and Mathilde's "it was even a sure thing–it was predictable" (C'était tout à fait prévisible–c'était même couru d'avance) creates a dialogue leading to no true exchange and closes the conversation in on itself. Secondly, play-on-words by the same character, such as Célestin Poux's "I didn't see it with my own eyes… In fact, out of the five, I only saw three of them get killed with my own eyes in front of my eyes" (Je l'ai pas vu de visu… En fait, sur les cinq, il y a trois que j'ai vus se faire dézinguer de visu sous mes yeux) reiterate information in different linguistic registers. This type of verbal pun is extended into the visual by two early sequences in which Mathilde quickly repeats "my deceased parents" (feu mes parents), literally "fire, my parents," and sets fire to a photo of her parents. Thirdly, avoidable tautologies of everyday speech rely on the musicality of the words, yet say little, as in uncle Sylvain's advice to Mathilde, "if you can't cry, then talk. If you can't speak, say nothing" (si t'arrives pas à pleurer, tu peux parler. Si tu ne peux pas parler, dis rien). Lastly, lines in both films, such as the Corsican prostitute Tina Lombardi's "...cause louses do lousy things, no need to look any further" (parce que les salopards font des saloperies, il faut pas chercher plus loin) mimic everyday popular language. It is worth noting that Laurant includes the greatest number of tautologies, including the most accepted tautology of common speech, "because that's how it is" (c'est comme ça) in a crucial scene between the speaker of the phrase, Tina Lombardi, and Mathilde. Here, Tina's tautological speech illustrates a rejection or denial of any true inquiry into a social system as she awaits death by guillotine from that very social system. Crammed with recognisable expressions which can be easily memorised, rhymes, repartee, quirky rhythms, puns and slogan-like phrases, the dialogue of both films resembles well-polished renditions of real speech, amusing phonic games to accompany Jeunet and cinematographer Bruno Delbonnel's innovative, highly stylised images.

   This interplay of tradition and innovation has its roots to a great extent in both the visual and verbal aspects of modern advertising (Mieder 1997, 308). Whereas innovation usually comes through in special effects and the use of digital technology, the traditional takes a multiplicity of forms such as the presence of authentic architecture and familiar spaces and places, verbal folklore genres, fairytales, legends, folksongs, riddles, popular sayings and proverbs (1997, 310). As Barthes has noted, proverbs and tautologies rely on a magical quality (1957, 240). They both suppose a cultural knowledge, close upon themselves and allow for little individual interpretation, taking one fact as a basic truth for many. Moreover, both succeed by their cadence and musicality, which promote familiarity and, consequently, frequent use. Tautologies and proverbs (as well as popular sayings) recall the traditional verbal expressions of a culture, and thus can be read as a conservative manoeuvre (or at times laziness) on the speaker's part to avoid debate or more critical thinking.

   In both films analysed here, Jeunet and Laurant balance reference-laden and fragmented narrative with dialogues in which the majority of characters express themselves through whimsical invented sayings, usually leading to a non-developed exchange: "Luck is like the *Tour de France,* one waits for it for a long time and it passes quickly," "At least you don't risk becoming a vegetable because even artichokes have hearts," or the repeated "doggy fart, joy in my heart."[8] The above exemplify the meeting of the proverbial and slogan-like quality in both films, creating a cult film-like dialogue of continuity, memorability and recognisability (Mieder 1997, 310).

Dialogues are also riddled with renditions of proverbs such as Confucius' "when the finger points to the sky, the idiot looks at the finger,"[9] or "a woman without love is like a flower without sun" or "unlucky at cards, lucky in love." Like popular sayings, proverbs reiterate traditional values in short, simple, easily memorised sentences which are identifiable by a given group; they allow for no new information, closing conversation into the complicity between the two interlocutors. They inspire trustworthiness by awakening positive traditional feelings in the viewer (Mieder 1997, 308). They establish authority and give a reassuring sense of community. We see this in the proverb scene between the waitress Gina (Clotilde Mollet), and Nino (Mathieu Kassovitz) in which Jeunet uses proverbs integrated into lively repartee, not only to get the viewers' attention at a crucial part of the film, but to create identification between the intended viewer and Nino.

Gina, possibly from a rural background, has little dialogue in the film, yet holds a key role in the romance plot of the film. Like Madame Suzanne, she is always shown doing something with a goal or a purpose and never demonstrates neurotic behaviour; unlike other developed characters, she moves on (we know that she left Joseph and has a new love interest). She is associated with physical work and human contact; she can identify others' ills and has some knowledge of healing. She is the only recognisably healthy, traditionally respectable character in the film and the most down-to-earth person. For her, words have a practical purpose:

> Amélie: Strange weather today! …
> (Suzanne laughs.)
> −Did I say something wrong?
> Suzanne: No. Everyone gives me the weather forecast.
> Hipolito: Talking about the weather to forget that time goes by.
> Gina: No, to avoid talking nonsense.[10]

Here, Gina proposes language as a vehicle for an exchange of functional information; developed conversation is posited as "nonsense." Language remains redundant, as a verbal commentary on the visual (what the weather looks like). Keeping interactions "light," this exchange limits conversation to a sameness, a commonality of shared weather conditions; any evidence of difference is denied. Through "talking about the weather," conversation stays conservative, recalling Barthes' comment on tautologies, "one must keep common sense conservative, one must shorten the leash to stay within a tangible reality" (1957, 97). Barthes links the use of popular ancestral proverbs and "talking about the weather" to a "(petit-) bourgeois" understanding of the world as object and

> [t]o active speech gradually solidified into reflexive speech, but where reflection is curtailed....The foundation of the bourgeois statement of fact is common sense, that is, truth when it stops on the arbitrary order of him who speaks it (1997, 243).

Given her no-nonsense take on language, it is not surprising that Gina is the one to test Nino on his knowledge of French proverbs. What is questionable, however, is her role as cultural quizzer. The fact that she is presented as the only mainstream character in the film *and* that she questions Nino on his French cultural knowledge can be seen as ideologically problematic.

> Gina: What doesn't a swallow make?
> Nino: A swallow? ... A summer.
> And clothes? ... −The man.
> Tit for? ... −Tat.
> Slow and steady ... −Wins the race.
> A rolling stone ... −Gathers no moss.
> He that will steal a penny... −Will steal a pound.
> Out of sight ... −Out of mind.
> Not bad! ... −Have you got any more?
> In my family, we say that someone who knows his proverbs can't be completely bad.[11]

Proverbs reintroduce tradition in order to establish a complicity between the character and the intended audience; they work to remind each viewer of his place within, or exclusion from, the public targeted by a director like Jeunet or an advertiser. At first glance, Gina's use of proverbs serves not merely to repeat cultural knowledge, but to verify Nino's social integration and, thus, his worthiness and compatibility with Amélie. More importantly, her role is to test the (French) viewer and Nino to know whether or not he shares the same cultural background as the "norm." The key to this scene's success in terms of its being entertaining and consistent to the film narrative is Gina's role as a bastion of practicality and Nino's role as a marginalised eccentric. Nino's successful completion of Gina's proverb game brings him back from the margins of society and establishes him as a properly socialised citizen. By the end of the film, his association with marginalised urban space, the sex shop and the dark carnival ride at the *Foire du Trône,* is replaced by the now well-known steps of Montmartre.[12] Nino's last interaction with the public, then, is in a conventionally socially acceptable space, previously literarily and emotionally marked by Amélie.

As in television advertising, well-placed reference points, tautologies and proverbs in Jeunet's recent cinema comfort the viewer by placing him/her in a privileged position, on the side of the heroine who decodes language (and people's lives) for him/her, consequently implicating the viewer in the narrative through complicity, such is the case in the scene of Mathilde's deciphering of Notre-Dame's letter to his wife in which the second word of each line spells out the letter's true message, in the style of an acrostic poem. [13] As highlighted in Serge Kaganski and Frédéric Bonnaud's film reviews of *Le Fabuleux destin d'Amélie Poulain,* this complicity is reinforced through visual technique: the close-up or medium shot with direct camera address. These frames, which recall *spots publicitaires,* are not unique to Jeunet's cinema; however, the sheer number of such images, and the duration of the shots, bring the advertising technique to our attention.

Building on well-established visual and verbal strategies to seduce the widest spectrum of viewers, *Le Fabuleux destin d'Amélie Poulain* and *Un long dimanche de fiançailles* appeal to younger audiences through innovative cinematographic techniques and the older crowd by evoking the traditional. From the outset, they create an "unwitting complicity of the public" (Bazin 1971, 27), entrapping us in the role of the "minimum viewer" revelling in intricate and fractured narratives in which one need not think too much or for too long. It is perhaps a negative reaction to this imposed role which surfaces in the strong criticisms by certain critics, notably Bonnaud and Kaganski. It is worth considering that these critiques are more than reactions to a single film or director *per se,* but to the very blurring of the domains of art, marketing and sales in popular contemporary French cinema. They are, perhaps, responses to a cinematographic representation of the times: an era of saturation of images and immediate information, wrapped in nostalgic exercises in style of a certain formatted Frenchness targeted for a global market.

---

[1] The term "cultural exception" draws heavily on the notion of an interest in maintaining cultural diversity in order to promote all world cultures in the face of an ever-increasing global market. In the French film context, the cultural exception is a means of acknowledging that certain goods and services, such as books, music, films, multimedia games and other audiovisual creations, are somehow different from other goods and services on the world market and thus should be treated with exception. Considering these types of goods and services as special within the realm of mass consumption highlights their place within cultural or creative

industries as denoted within article IV of the GATT agreement of 1947. http://www.unesco.org/culture/industries/trade/html_eng/question17.shtml. Also see Danan (2000).

[2] The comic-strip turned comic-book (*bande-dessinée*) *Bécassine* first appeared in 1905 as the creation of Joseph Pinchon and Jacqueline Rivière. Bécassine's full name is Annaïck Labornez, literally translating as "Annaïck The Hard-headed", *bornez* sounding like *bornée* in French pronunciation.

[3] "J'aime beaucoup ce tableau... C'est *Le déjeuner des canotiers*... De Renoir."

[4] Translations of all quotations from *Mythologies* are my own.

[5] Jeunet has noted in the DVD film commentary that only one scene in *Un long dimanche de fiançailles* was filmed without his presence.

[6] "Le hic c'est que Jeunet est sous l'emprise d'une telle volonté de maîtrise et de contrôle absolu de ses images que ses films ne respirent plus, que son monde parait être filmé sous cloche. Amélie Poulain fait ainsi penser à ces boules de neige enfermant les monuments de Paris que l'on vend dans les boutiques de souvenir kitch."

[7] Narrations by André Dussollier in *Le Fabuleux destin d'Amélie Poulain* and Florence Thomassin in *Un long dimanche de fiançailles*.

[8] "La chance c'est comme le Tour de France on l'attend longtemps et il passe vite."
"Vous au moins vous ne risquez pas d'être un légume parce que même les artichauts ont un cœur."
"Chien qui pète, joie sur ma tête "

[9] "Quand le doigt montre le ciel, l'imbécile regarde le doigt."

[10] The original French reads: "C'est l'angoisse du temps qui passe qui nous fait tant parler du temps qu'il fait," an exemplary pun creating balance and closure within the sentence structure.

[11] "Qu'est-ce que ne fait pas une hirondelle? ... le printemps. Et L'habit? le moine. A bon chat ? bon rat. Petit à petit? ...l'oiseau fait son nid. Pierre qui roule? ... n'amasse pas mousse. Qui vole un œuf? ... vole un bœuf. Cœur qui soupire... n'a pas ce qu'il désire. Pas mal... Vous en avez d'autres des comme ça? –Dans ma famille, on dit que celui qui connaît bien les proverbes ne peut pas être complètement mauvais."

[12] Montmartre is well known as a bohemian and revolutionary quarter, annexed to the capital in 1860. Evoking Montmartre, as Jeunet does, calls on the reputation of *la butte* as an artistic, working-class neighbourhood as well as a popular tourist area of Paris.

[13] This scene is preceded by another in which a German tourist erases all but the first letters of the words from a blackboard restaurant menu; read in sequence these letters from "M... M... M...," a code for Mathilde to meet her in the ladies' toilets so that they can speak of Manech's last minutes at Bingo Crépuscule. Once again, Jeunet balances his narrative by creating two scenes which depart from a similar syntactic trick.

CHAPTER EIGHT

A (MIDDLE-) CLASS ACT:
TASTE AND OTHERNESS
IN *LE GOÛT DES AUTRES* (JAOUI, 2000)[1]

SARAH LEAHY

Le Goût des autres is undeniably a popular French film: as a comedy it takes its place in the most enduringly popular of French genres; and in terms of box office returns, it was the sixth most successful film at the French box office in 2000, clocking up a record-breaking two million viewers in just three weeks, and gaining just under 3.8 million entries during its first run. It was the second most popular French film of the year, coming after *Taxi 2* (Gérard Krawczyk, 2000), which gained an enormous 10.3 million entries, and was one of only five French films to make the box office top twenty.[2] In the wake of the following year's box office hits, *Le Fabuleux destin d'Amélie Poulain* (Jean-Pierre Jeunet, 2001), *La Vérité si je mens 2* (Thomas Gilou, 2001), *Le Placard* (Francis Veber, 2001), and *Le Pacte des loups* (Christophe Gans, 2001), all of which gained between 5 and 8.6 million spectators, these may seem like modest figures, but in early 2000, French cinema was seen to be floundering in dire straits both financially and artistically, and *Le Goût des autres*–as the first French film of the year to perform decently at the box office–was credited by many with reviving the national industry. According to *Le Film français*, the release of Jaoui's film on 1 March brought the domestic share of the market from 8% to 30%, accounting for a quarter of all cinema entries in its first week (Conter 2001, 25). It is interesting to consider this response to *Le Goût des autres* in relation to that elicited by *Taxi 2*, released on 25 March. In spite of the latter's phenomenal success, achieving 3.5 million spectators in only two weeks, it was not similarly hailed as saving French cinema–and neither did it receive the same level of critical success as Jaoui's film, which was nominated for nine Césars, winning in four different categories (best film, best supporting actor, best supporting actress, best writer), while *Taxi 2* failed to secure a single nomination (Dacbert 2001, 3).

Jaoui's film does not conform to either of the dominant successful genres of late 1990s French film. Its quiet, understated style could not be further from that of action blockbusters such as *Le Cinquième élément* (Luc Besson, 1997), *Taxi 2*, *Jeanne d'Arc* (Luc Besson, 1999), but as a comedy of manners, it is also a problematic fit as a popular French comedy–a genre exemplified in the late 1990s by *Les Visiteurs 2: Les Couloirs du temps* (Jean-Marie Poiré, 1998), *Le Dîner de cons* (Francis Veber, 1999) and *Astérix et Obélix contre César* (Claude Zidi, 1999). *Le Goût des autres* draws more on Woody Allen for inspiration than on the knockabout, often crude French comic tradition of *La Grande vadrouille* (Gérard Oury, 1966) or *Les Visiteurs* (Jean-Marie Poiré, 1993). The paradox is that, in finding its American influence in Allen rather than in the Hollywood blockbuster, Jaoui's film came to be seen by critics as part of a specifically French cinematic tradition in a way in which the French action comedies (*Taxi 2*, *Les Visiteurs 2*) did not.

Le Goût des autres does find common subject matter with *Les Visiteurs*, *Le Dîner de cons* and so on, in sending up the bourgeoisie, but it rejects broad farce and slapstick in favour of observational comedy, highlighting questions of taste and cultural snobbery. Identity in the film is synonymous with cultural consumption and the possession or lack of a certain cultural capital. And yet, far from positioning itself at the high end of culture, the film arguably belongs to a rather middlebrow cinematic tradition–the "quality tradition" of script-led, finely crafted, well-acted films, often with a literary heritage, that has dominated French mainstream cinema in the post-war period. This may be an original script rather than an adaptation, but *Le Goût des autres* nonetheless has literary credentials. It draws on the theatre for its subject matter (the main narrative strand could be said to be constructed around three trips to the theatre) and for its actors (Anne Alvaro and Christiane Millet are both veterans of the stage), while the writing background of Agnès Jaoui and Jean-Pierre Bacri, who are well known in France for their plays *Cuisine et dépendances*, *Un air de famille* (adapted for the screen by Philippe Muyl and Cédric Klapisch respectively), and for their adaptation of Alan Aykbourn's play *Intimate Exchanges* into *Smoking/No Smoking* (Alain Resnais, 1993) is solidly theatre-based.

The critical and popular success of the film is particularly interesting in the way that it can be seen to mirror the film's narrative concerns. If we consider briefly two critical reactions to the film then we can see how the particular French tradition it is seen as belonging to (and in particular the perceived prominence of the scriptwriter as auteur) is regarded from differing cultural perspectives. The first example is taken from *Télérama*, a weekly magazine with a distribution of approximately 650,000 published by the media group Publications de la Vie Catholique (PVC), with a broad cultural remit to cover the visual arts, theatre, music, cinema, television and radio.[3]

> If the Jabacs [Jaoui and Bacri] give the impression of spontaneity, it is because the characters seem as if they might at any moment escape from the actor, to live their strange, slippery, unpredictable lives. (Rémy 2000, 32)[4]

Here, Vincent Rémy implies that Jaoui and Bacri's writing is what rounds out these characters, suggesting situations and lives beyond what we see acted out on the screen. For Rémy, then, it is specifically the quality of the script rather than the acting or the mise en scène that makes these characters so believable (unpredictable and spontaneous). This apparently situates Jaoui and Bacri directly in the French tradition of great scriptwriters for the cinema: Henri Jeanson, Jacques Prévert, Jean Aurenche and Pierre Bost, Michel Audiard.

The second example is taken from *Les Cahiers du cinéma*, which, as a monthly publication with a formidable history as one of the world's foremost "intellectual" cinema journals, has a rather more "refined" distribution figure of approximately 25,000.[5]

> All the characters have the same hang-dog look, adopt the same low profile. What they are living is already a script, nothing but the script. [...] Rarely has the question of the other appeared so theoretical and anaesthetised–so lacking in urgency. Perhaps Jaoui and Bacri will be remembered as those who transformed a simple tendency into *the* genre of French cinema. (Burdeau 2000, 5)[6]

For Emmanuel Burdeau, then, the privileging of the script over the mise en scène (which he sees as "scholarly", "mute" and "remaining at a respectful distance in order to let the script speak") has the opposite effect. Far from being spontaneous, the characters for him are bound by the script, which, however finely wrought, saps their vitality as well as the urgency of the questions the film is addressing. Burdeau's reference to François Truffaut's attack on script-driven cinema of the 1950s (Truffaut 1954), dominated as it was by writers such as Henri Jeanson, Jean Aurenche and Pierre Bost, places his review within a context of elitist film criticism and a philosophy of cinema as an art form that has been developed in the *Cahiers du cinéma* since the post-war years.

The relationship between taste and cultural hierarchies, then, is apparent not only in the narrative of the film but also in its reception. *Le Goût des autres* raises debates that relate very closely to Pierre Bourdieu's definitions of taste and cultural consumption as performing a function of social legitimation (Bourdieu 1984, 7). In this chapter we will explore the film's representation of taste and otherness as an indicator of French culture and social class. The film's focus on the middle class can be seen as a failure to address questions of cultural diversity, treating the question of alterity at a purely individual level. However, the emphasis the film places on the difficulties of integration even within such a restricted social milieu could be seen to offer a critique of the Republican notion of universal values.

Le Goût des autres is an ensemble piece featuring six main characters: Jean-Jacques Castella (Jean-Pierre Bacri), the director of a manufacturing company; his insurance company-imposed bodyguard, Franck (Gérard Lanvin); his chauffeur, Bruno (Alain Chabat); his wife, Angélique (Christiane Millet), an interior designer; Clara Devaux (Anne Alvaro), his English teacher, who is also an actress and with whom he falls in love; and Manie (Agnès Jaoui), Clara's friend who works in a bar, and who, after rekindling a brief fling with Bruno, embarks upon a relationship with Franck. Castella, eager to impress, ingratiates himself with Clara's friends, who are quite willing to take advantage of his money while ridiculing his ignorance of art, theatre, literature and so on. All of the main characters would seem to be alienated in some way: Castella is the victim of his own success–a self-made man, he can no longer mix with those from his own background and yet has nothing in common with those he is now surrounded by; Manie's job clearly offers her neither financial nor professional satisfaction and her emotional life consists of brief affairs with men who do not even remember her (such as Bruno); Clara is depressed–at forty years of age she is single, she has not achieved success on the stage and is obliged to teach English to make ends meet; Bruno is in denial about the fact that he has not heard from his girlfriend–who is working in the States–for three weeks, and manages to be shocked when finally a letter does arrive to tell him she has been sleeping with someone else; Franck and Manie are unable to communicate with each other or reach a compromise that would enable their relationship to work out; and finally Angélique appears to relate more to her little dog than to her husband.

A question of taste

As the film's title suggests, otherness is central to its narrative structure. The expression of taste is seen as constitutive of identity, which is thus determined by acts of cultural consumption. However, the inability of the characters to look beyond their immediate sphere and their own particular tastes means that the other remains unreachable–boundaries between self and other are too clearly marked and too fixed to be easily transgressed. Thus the existence of the "other" does not seem to offer any possibility of blurring the boundaries of identity, but rather serves the purpose of reinforcing those boundaries against any possible encroachment from outside. As a result, the characters' relationships are more easily defined as clashes rather than links or bonds–with the possible exception of Castella, none of the central characters is open to experiences outside of their own cultural sphere. Given the centrality of taste to the construction of identity in the film, it is interesting to consider it in relation to Bourdieu's definition:

> Tastes, (i.e. manifested preferences) are the practical affirmation of an inevitable difference. It is no accident that, when they have to be justified, they are asserted purely negatively, by the refusal of other tastes. In matters of taste, more than anywhere else, all determination is negation; and tastes are perhaps first and foremost distastes, disgust provoked by horror or visceral intolerance (sick-making) of the tastes of others. (Bourdieu 1984, 56)

Two aspects raised here by Bourdieu can be recognised in Clara and her intellectual friends. The first is the definition of tastes through opposition or negation. The hypercritical attitude of Clara and her friends is seen on several occasions: her artist friend Benoît's reaction to the paintings currently on display when he visits a gallery where he plans to exhibit his own work; the group's reaction to a production of *Le Malade imaginaire*; Clara's reaction when Manie points out a man who finds the actress attractive. Indeed, it seems that Clara is always complaining about something, even contradicting herself in her dislikes. For example: she is unhappy when not performing in a play, yet is never pleased with her performances; she complains when she receives attention from a man in the bar and hates the idea of dating, but she is also unhappy being single; she does not want to sign on at the Job Centre, but neither does she want a job teaching Castella English. She also expresses distaste for television, men with moustaches, the paintings in the gallery she visits with Benoît and Antoine, and the production of *Le Malade imaginaire*.

The second aspect is the extraordinary vehemence with which these negative reactions are expressed. Bourdieu mentions "horror" and "visceral intolerance". Dislikes are expressed in the strongest terms–the language of disgust recurs regularly: just to refer to the examples given above, the paintings are "so ugly", the Molière production is "crap" and leaves them feeling "sick" and the man in the bar is "hideous".

For Clara and her friends, then, it would not do to be seen to simply "enjoy" a painting or a theatrical production. Criticism confers cultural superiority: one is no longer merely a passive *consumer* of culture, but an active *participant* in it. So, as another artist, Benoît feels the need to trash the paintings on display, while it is Clara's duty as an actress to put the director of *Le Malade imaginaire* in his place. Thus her reaction appears "intelligent" compared with that of the crass Castella who apparently enjoyed himself immensely, and in spite of being at the theatre and out of his normal cultural sphere, seems to have had a much better evening. But this encounter also reveals that while Castella might be uneducated, at least he is sincere. Clara and her friends on the other hand, quote from the review in *Le Monde*, in a way which suggests that their "intelligent" criticism is playing safe by following an orthodoxy laid down by the Parisian cultural elite.

This hypercritical attitude, then, is perhaps designed to conceal a certain insecurity regarding personal judgement. Jaoui commented on this question of negativity and insecurity in an interview which appeared in *Première*:

> When you're the only one who likes a film, for example, there's a tendency to feel more stupid or weaker, less intelligent. Whereas, if you're the one who doesn't like something, you feel superior… This is the root of lots of misunderstandings because everyone is putting on an act. (Katelan 2000, 85)[7]

Clara and her friends, then, may appear sure of themselves, confident to the point of arrogance, but their need to criticise, and to continually demonstrate their cultural superiority in fact suggests they are constantly in need of reassurance regarding their position as the possessors of what Bourdieu might term "natural" taste:

> The ideology of natural taste owes its plausibility and its efficacy to the fact that, like all the ideological strategies generated in the everyday class struggle, it *naturalizes* real differences, converting differences in the mode of acquisition of culture into differences of nature; it only recognizes as legitimate the relation to culture (or language) which least bears the visible marks of its genesis, which has nothing 'academic', 'scholastic',

'bookish', 'affected' or 'studied' about it, but manifests by its ease and
naturalness that true culture is nature–a new mystery of immaculate
conception. (Bourdieu 1984, 68)

This "immaculate conception" is precisely what these characters do not
achieve–in fact they come across as pretentious, as "working too hard" at
their cultural identities. Far from representing the avant-garde, in fact they
fall into the realm of what Bourdieu (1984, 23) terms "academic capital":
Racine's *Bérénice*, Molière's *Le Malade imaginaire*, Ibsen's *Hedda
Gabler* are the plays performed or viewed, and are, after all, canonical
works. For Bourdieu, success in the educational system–where cultural
values can be inculcated–does not necessarily confer a "cultural
disposition", rather it provides the foundations on which this can be built:

> The full possession of academic culture is the precondition for going
> beyond school culture and acquiring a free culture… a culture that has
> thrown off the shackles of its academic origins and which is regarded by
> the bourgeoisie and the educational system as the highest of values.
> (Bourdieu and Darbel 1966; cited in Rigby 1991, 99)

In spite of their pose, then, Clara and her friends represent a
bourgeois, provincial clique who, notwithstanding a certain amount of
cultural literacy, lack the confidence for true originality and take their lead
in matters of taste from metropolitan gurus (for example, the theatre critic
of *Le Monde*). Interestingly, Benoît complains that no journalists are
coming to his exhibition, as they are only interested in the currently trendy
installation art. And yet, by choosing a medium that is apparently
overlooked because it is no longer fashionable (painting), Benoît sets
himself up as the underdog, thus providing himself with a convenient alibi
for failure before he has even tried. Likewise, Clara's predeliction for
performing in tragedy ensures her a select but perpetually small audience.

Set in opposition to these hypercritical characters is the figure of
Angélique, Castella's wife, an interior designer who "helps out" friends
and family. Angélique is a kind of monster: she suffocates her victims
with frills, chintz and little ornaments. Less a style guru than a design
fascist, she imposes her vision of aesthetic beauty on others: on her
husband, whose lack of interest she has interpreted as tacit appreciation of
their home; and on her sister-in-law, recently moved back to Rouen from
Paris after her husband left and finding herself with a flat in need of
decoration. Angélique constantly criticises her husband, controlling his
eating habits and telling him to dress more like Weber, the Parisian
technocrat Castella has employed for his diplomacy. Quite unlike Clara,
with her need for reassurance, Angélique is completely sure of herself.

She is a strong proponent of what Bourdieu would call the "ideology of natural taste" (1984, 68), as her remarks to Béatrice, who dares to express a preference for a different kind of wallpaper, show:

> There are some things which seem obvious to me that you don't seem to want to understand ... some things go together and others don't, there's a kind of coherence, you know...[8]

These remarks bring us back to Bourdieu's definition of taste:

> Aesthetic intolerance can be terribly violent. Aversion to different lifestyles is perhaps one of the strongest barriers between the classes: class endogamy is evidence of this. The most intolerable thing for those who regard themselves as the possessors of legitimate culture is the sacrilegious reuniting of tastes which taste dictates shall be separated. This means that the games of artists and aesthetes and their struggles for the monopoly of artistic legitimacy are less innocent than they seem. At stake in every struggle over art there is also the imposition of an art of living, that is, the transmutation of an arbitrary way of living into the legitimate way of life which casts every other way of living into arbitrariness. (Bourdieu 1984, 56-57)

The character of Angélique clearly demonstrates this arbitrariness. She is convinced that her taste is right and natural (legitimate) and that she knows "what goes together" and is horrified when others try to overturn her judgement (as when Castella tries to hang one of Benoît's paintings in their sitting room). What is perhaps most astonishing about this character, though, is that even with no one to share her vision, she nonetheless remains utterly secure in her taste, which would seem to be legitimised on one level through her professional status (certainly as far as she is concerned), but which in fact is constantly undermined in the film which presents it as ridiculous and the counterpoint to "good" taste, whatever that may be. Once again, we see how it is much easier to define taste through opposition–to unite the film's spectators in horror of Angélique's style.

Castella, surrounded by all these different tastes, does not appear to have formed any of his own. He is a figure who does not fit in anywhere and seems unable to find a place where he feels at home. He is constantly asking if his presence is required, whether it be at the theatre with his wife, or in meetings with Weber and potential clients. Castella is an *ingénu* faced constantly with new situations, but with no style or tastes of his own he is unable to react in an informed way. His wife's lack of tact reinforces the self-made man's feelings of inferiority faced with the accomplishments of Weber, the product of an elite higher education establishment. If Clara and her friends aspire to the "disposition esthétique" outlined by Bourdieu, Castella embodies its diametric opposite. His reactions to cultural manifestations are almost physical–to the astonishment of Clara and Antoine, he sings along to a tune he recognises as Henri Salvador's 1966 hit, "Juanita Banana", but which they know to be an aria from *Rigoletto*. His initial reaction to Racine is "Oh shit, it's in verse?" (Oh putain, c'est en vers?) Castella is a "barbarian"– concerned solely with *function*, as he makes clear to Clara during a discussion about her acting career when he compares the audiences for *Le Malade imaginaire* with those for *Bérénice*:

> Why don't you do a comic play? That'd be good, 'cos people, they just want to enjoy themselves, to be entertained. They want to forget their worries, they don't want to... Look, look at this evening, for example, it was sold out, but the last time, it was what, not even half full?[9]

Here, it is impossible to argue with his reasoning–it is true that comedies are more popular (in the sense of gaining larger audiences–and the box office figures for contemporary French cinema tell us the same thing), and they would surely provide Clara and her friends with more regular work, saving them their regular trips to the Job Centre. While Clara reacts ironically "Oh, ok then, I'll go into comedy" (Ah oui, d'accord, je vais faire du comique) and ignores Castella's advice, her friend Antoine is quick to profit from his "functional" attitude–proposing that his partner Benoît (whose painting Bourdieu (1984, 30] characterises, along with all post-impressionist painting, as affirming "the *absolute primacy of form over function*" (le *primat absolu de la forme sur la function*)) design a mural to brighten up Castella's factory.

Clara seems to appeal to some kind of existential void in Castella. In spite of his physicality, his desire is not expressed in primarily sexual terms and her rejection of him propels him into a deep depression. It is this manifestation of existential angst that renders Castella endearing in spite of his crassness and he is easily the most sympathetic character in the film. He is infantilised–typifying the male mid-life crisis, he reverts to childlike behaviour. In Castella's case, this is extreme, even to the point of requiring a full-time minder. He appears to be stuck at a pre-Oedipal stage of development: he lacks motor skills (he is clumsy physically as well as socially), he delights in toilet humour, he is in a position of linguistic inferiority to Clara, his English teacher (in the love poem he writes her in the few English words he knows he recycles his weather vocabulary but still gets his tenses mixed up). Thus his behaviour is excused: his frequent faux pas (for example, when he announces to Benoît and Antoine, Clara's gay friends, that journalists are all "pédés" (poofs), or when he insults Weber) are ultimately presented not as stemming from malevolent intentions, but rather as the result of Castella's innocence faced with a more sophisticated world (Burdeau 2000, 4).

However, his wife is not let off the hook so easily. She is the only character who does not command our sympathy in any way, mercilessly played for her comic value. It is arguably here that Jaoui's film reveals its own aesthetic (and moral) positioning. When Angélique visits Béatrice at the end of the film, when this time it is her husband who has left her, we do not feel sorry for her–rather, the implication is that she has got what she deserved. It is this ridiculous character (whose personality is as suffocating as her decorating style) that suggests that the film shares more with Clara and her friends, and that the spectators it addresses are equally "discerning". This is easy comedy–while the other, more nuanced characters demand sympathy as well as derision, Angélique functions as the butt of the film's humour–a self-absorbed, unpleasant and stupid woman upon whom we can heap our disdain. There is a strong element of misogyny in her portrayal that is that of the French "intellectual" – Angélique's tastes are clearly designated as "feminine" (TV mini-series, her little dog, her over-sentimental attitude to animals, her preferences in interior decoration) and are cast as beneath contempt, while her small-minded attitude shows her to be without possibility of redemption. Castella on the other hand, in spite of his misanthropy, is granted this possibility because he not only makes an effort to understand the other (even if his motives are more romantic than cultural) but he also stands up for his own judgement–however uneducated it may be–with the result that the final scene sees the hitherto dour Clara bestowing a radiant smile upon him from the stage.

Otherness is of course, like taste, a relative concept. While *Le Goût des autres* appears to pose the question of the other as central, in fact it deals with a very homogeneous group: all white, all verging on middle age and all more or less middle-class, from *midinette* (Angélique) to bohemian (Manie); from parvenu (Castella) to intellectual (Clara and her friends). Even Bruno and Franck, who work in more blue-collar positions and could thus be designated working-class, are presented as more culturally and socially savvy than their employers, with whom they are contrasted. They certainly integrate more easily with the other characters than either Angélique or her husband. By restricting its horizons in this way, the film remains firmly within the "ordinary", the everyday experience of such characters–there is no question of introducing social marginality as an issue. Even though many of the characters experience financial problems (Clara has to supplement her income with state benefit and gives occasional English lessons; Manie boosts her wage by selling dope under the counter; Castella's sister is obliged to accept handouts from him now that her husband has left her; Franck and Bruno discuss the temptations of corruption for those on relatively low wages such as themselves) the poverty they experience is of the genteel kind, and never seriously encroaches upon their middle-class lifestyles–Clara teaches English to wealthy business executives rather than stacking shelves in a supermarket, for instance. Neither does the film make any attempt to address the question of otherness drawn along lines of what Bourdieu terms "subsidiary characteristics" of class, such as age, ethnicity, or religion (Bourdieu 1984, 102). Given the importance in French public life in the late 1990s of issues relating to these questions of identity and otherness, and the continual prominence in the media if not in the priorities of politicians of the *fracture sociale*–the increasing marginalisation of the *banlieues* and their inhabitants–it is striking that a film apparently so concerned with this question of "the other" should reduce this to the purely personal.[10] By failing to represent the presence of socio-economic and ethnic differences in contemporary France, and by eliding differences of gender and sexuality as manifestations of personal taste, the film avoids any sustained interrogation of Republican "universal" values. By restricting its horizons in terms of class and ethnicity, *Le Goût des autres* does not recognise otherness in terms of *difference*, thus refusing to address the question of the other as a political one.

Brian Rigby offers a succinct definition of the Republican notion of culture: "a unified culture whose values are permanent and universal" (Rigby 1991, 16). It is also linked to the notion of "la francité", or "essential Frenchness"–which implies a belief in the superiority of French culture–art, literature and philosophy–and which can be seen in the French colonial attitude–France's "civilising mission". And what is more, in spite of apparently democratic, Republican associations, French "Culture with a capital C" is closely based on an aristocratic version of "natural taste". As Rigby points out, Bourdieu's aim, in his work *La Distinction* and in his sociological project overall, is to address the relationship between culture and power in France, and more precisely, what he sees as the equation of "unified" Republican culture with aristocratic high culture which is taught to all with greater or lesser success through the education system. As we have seen, for Bourdieu education provides the opportunity to move beyond the barriers of class, and to acquire the "cultural disposition" necessary to hold power. The problem is that for most of the working class, this system fails. The main reason for this, according to Bourdieu, is the location of the working class outside culture–they exist only as the foil against which other classes can measure their own cultural capital. As a result, there is also a lack of aspiration among the working classes–they reject dominant notions of culture and therefore they remain in their position of "barbarians", for whom function must always take precedence over form. However, the adoption of an aristocratic form of culture as "universal" and "natural"–clearly another important reason behind the disadvantaging of the working class in this domain–is not really called into question at all. Bourdieu's concerns are to simply describe what he observes, rather than to change society.

As a result, Bourdieu has been accused of upholding the very cultural values he sets out to analyse and critique (Rigby 1991, 112). As Rigby points out, by designating working-class culture as barbaric, Bourdieu appears to be reasserting the Kantian distinction between a superior, disinterested appreciation or contemplation, and an inferior, interested consumption. And this view would seem to be reinforced when we consider that Bourdieu also argues that the working class are complicit in the domination of their class–that they have internalised the rules of a game in which they will always come out as losers (Rigby 1991, 115-116). The main difficulty that Rigby and others have identified with Bourdieu's work lies with his deterministic view of culture as being ultimately dependent on social class–a view which can leave his reader with the impression that Bourdieu himself shares the idea of working-class culture as non-culture (*l'inculture*).

It would seem that the same deterministic attitude lies at the heart of *Le Goût des autres* which portrays a society just like the one Bourdieu describes, where the definition of identity in terms of taste and cultural expression, far from opening up performative possibilities of mutable identities, instead reinforces these as class-bound and fixed. It would appear to suggest that, in fact, the Republican ideals which have dominated French social, educational and cultural life during the post-war period, through their insistence on universality and integration, far from expanding the understanding of the cultural disposition, are to some extent responsible for this impossibility of *thinking the other*. Rather, this system could be seen as instilling an underlying sense that, since everyone is really the same, there is no need to embrace difference.

This is certainly the key problem for the characters in the film. On the one hand, *Le Goût des autres* offers characters and spectators a point of consensus as we unite against Angélique–the counterpoint to all "thinkable" tastes–the other who reassures us that we are all the same. On the other, it can be seen as rather pessimistic about the possibility of forming relationships across cultural (class) divides. Franck and Manie fail to move beyond their differences, each too set in their ways to find the necessary mutual trust. The "happy end" that sees Clara seeking Castella's approval for her opening night performance as Hedda Gabler is rather contrived, merely eliding the problem of otherness represented as insurmountable elsewhere in the film. And yet, there is hope in the figure of Castella. When Clara confronts him, worried that his interest in Benoît's painting may just be a way to impress her, he mounts a solid defence of his right to express his taste:

> I like his paintings so I buy them–I don't see what the problem is. So why did you think I was buying them? To please you, is that it? To look good? You didn't think for one minute that it might have been because I liked them? Is that your opinion of me?[11]

Thus, Castella stakes a claim to an identity that may not be aristocratic but is nonetheless legitimate–and, even more importantly, demonstrates the benefits of opening up to the taste of others–a benefit that Clara belatedly recognises. Perhaps, then, we should take *Le Goût des autres* as something of a cautionary tale, asking us to learn that, like Castella, we need to acquire a taste for *difference*, and move beyond a model of integration and "universal" cultural values that encourages a homogeneous notion of legitimate (aristocratic) taste. In this way, the film could be seen as truly popular, in the senses not just of box office success or of its generic identity as a comedy following the quality tradition of French cinema, but also in its call to open up to others–and to difference.

---

[1] Thanks are due to Will Higbee and Ginette Vincendeau for their perceptive comments on a version of this paper given as a conference paper at Popular Contemporary French Cinema (Manchester Metropolitan and Manchester Universities, January 2006).

[2] The other three films were: *Les Rivières pourpres* (Kassovitz, 2000) which came ninth, with just under 3.2 million entries; *Jet Set* (Onteniente, 2000) which came seventeenth, with 1.9 million entries; and *Harry, un ami qui vous veut du bien* (Moll, 2000) in twentieth position, with just under 1.9 million entries. See "Focus 2001: Tendances du marché mondial du film".

[3] See "Statistiques générales", *Quid*.

[4] "Si les Jabac donnent l'impression de la spontanéité, c'est qu'à chaque instant un personnage semble en mesure d'échapper à son interprète, de vivre sa vie bizarre, faite de dérapages et d'imprévus." All translations my own unless otherwise stated.

[5] See "Statistiques générales", *Quid*.

[6] "Tous [les personnages] ont le même air de chien battu, le même profil bas. Ce qu'ils vivent, c'est déjà du scénario, rien que du scénario… Rarement la question

de l'autre a paru aussi théorique et anesthésiée; aussi peu pressante… Peut-être se souviendra-t-on de Jaoui et Bacri comme de ceux par qui une simple tendance est devenue *le* genre du cinéma français."

[7] "Quand on est seul à aimer un film par exemple, on a tendance à se sentir plus con ou faible, moins intelligent. Alors que quand on est celui qui n'aime pas, on a un sentiment de supériorité… D'où beaucoup de malentendus parce qu'il y a beaucoup de poses chez les uns et les autres."

[8] "Il y a des choses qui me semblent évidentes et que tu ne veux pas comprendre… il y a des choses qui vont ensemble et des choses qui vont pas ensemble, il y a une cohérence, je sais pas moi…"

[9] "Pourquoi vous faites pas une pièce comique? Ça c'est bien parce que les gens ils veulent qu'une chose, c'est se distraire. Ils veulent oublier leurs soucis, ils ont pas envie de se se… Voyez, regardez ce soir par exemple, c'était plein, alors que la dernière fois il y avait quoi, la moitié de la salle, même pas?"

[10] Prominent issues in the 1990s included the question of parity, the PaCS, debates surrounding immigration and its regulation with repressive legislation on both sides of the political divide (consider the *sans papiers* affair and related legislation: the reform of the Nationality Code in 1993, the Debré law of 24 April 1997 and the Chevènement law of 11 May 1998).

[11] "J'aime ses peintures, je les achète, je vois pas où est le problème. Et vous, vous pensiez que je les achetais pour quoi? Pour vous plaire, c'est ça? Pour me faire bien voir. Vous vous êtes pas imaginé une minute que ça pouvait être par goût. C'est ça l'opinion que vous avez de moi?"

CHAPTER NINE

L'ESQUIVE (KECHICHE, 2004): REASSESSING FRENCH POPULAR CULTURE

CARRIE TARR

L'Esquive, entitled *Games of Love and Chance* in English, is the second film to be directed by Abdellatif Kechiche, a French actor/director of Tunisian descent.[1] Despite the fact that it was made on a tiny budget, written and directed by a *beur* filmmaker, set in a multi-ethnic Parisian *banlieue*, and performed by a (mostly) non-professional cast, a combination of factors which would seem set to deny it popular appeal, it has been surprisingly successful. It initially opened in 2004 in twelve cinemas, to critical acclaim, and went on to achieve 283,578 spectators in its first run, a figure which compares very favourably with the 81,172 spectators achieved for his first film, *La Faute à Voltaire*, in 2001. More astonishingly, it was the winner of four Césars (the French equivalent of the Oscars) in 2005, displacing frontrunners *Les Choristes* (Christophe Barratier) and *Un long dimanche de fiançailles* (Jean-Pierre Jeunet) for the main honours of best film, best director and best screenplay (for Kechiche and Ghalya Lacroix), as well as gaining a most promising actress award for its young female lead, Sara Forestier.[2] Its subsequent re-release on some sixty screens achieved an additional 188,468 spectators and, as the *Cahiers du Cinéma* reviewer put it, "since its release in January, it hasn't stopped being at the centre of debates... For once, a film has provoked discussion: in newspapers, schools, everywhere" (Bégaudeau 2004, 78).[3] Although *L'Esquive* does not compete with its rivals for the Césars in terms of box office success–it was widely rumoured that its selection was motivated by the desire to promote small auteur films rather than big-budget spectaculars–its relative popularity as a *beur*-authored film, and the fact that it became a national talking-point, merit critical attention. In the context of a study of popular French cinema, it is also of interest that contemporary French popular culture–as manifested through the lived experiences and, particularly, the language of its young *banlieue* protagonists–is its primary subject matter.

It is not insignificant that both *Les Choristes* and *Un long dimanche de fiançailles* draw on subject matter set in the past and thereby avoid directly addressing contemporary French popular culture or issues affecting contemporary France. As with Jeunet's earlier smash hit, *Le Fabuleux destin d'Amélie Poulain* (2001), these two films construct a nostalgic vision of an imagined French community from which the challenges to French identity represented by the presence of immigrants and their descendants are largely absent. *L'Esquive*, shot in the *banlieue* housing estate of Franc-Moisin in the "neuf-trois" (the slang term for the department number of Seine-Saint-Denis, to the north-east of Paris), is a more topical film, narrated in an edgy, energetic style, which responds to anxieties about the fractured and multi-ethnic nature of contemporary French society through its focus on the ordinary, everyday lives of young people living on the estate. At the same time, its narrative framework, the staging at the local school of a classic eighteenth-century play, Marivaux's *Le Jeu de l'amour et du hasard* (1730), actually results in a similarity of theme to *Les Choristes*, that is, the creation of community (or an illusion of community) through the successful participation of the underprivileged in a high-art project. In *Les Choristes*, an inspirational teacher tames a class of wayward schoolboys by enlisting them in a choir. In *L'Esquive*, a group of *banlieue* adolescents with an enthusiastic teacher transcend their condition by taking part in the production of a play. The feel-good factor produced by the successful access of young people associated with the popular culture of the *banlieue* to bourgeois high art may in no small measure account for the film's (relative) success, and is certainly one of the factors which distinguishes it from other *beur* and *banlieue* films.

Kechiche, himself a second-generation Tunisian immigrant who grew up in the *banlieue* of Nice, near the Victorine film studios, first found success as an actor, famously playing a young, streetwise Algerian immigrant in Abdelkrim Bahloul's *Le Thé à la menthe* (1985), one of the films to herald the advent of *beur* cinema (see Tarr 2005). In *L'Esquive*, Kechiche deliberately draws on his background as both a *beur* and an actor to counteract negative media representations of adolescents from the *banlieue*, and to show how their preoccupations both transcend and are frustrated by their backgrounds. As he puts it:

> These young people have no place in the audiovisual landscape. There's a lack, and it's a pity because it's an opportunity for [French] culture. I was looking for a more truthful representation. This population is so little represented, and when it is, it's often in a very caricatural way, drawing on

clichés and stereotypes. Representation is important, especially in the way others think about you. The way these young people are represented often feeds the political discourses of the extreme Right. (Cited in Mélinard 2004)[4]

However, in the light of the riots which ravaged *banlieues* the length and breadth of France in October/November 2005 (and in which adolescents played a key role), one has to ask if the relatively gentle, feel-good representation of the *banlieue* offered by this film is one which is actually "more truthful", or whether *L'Esquive*'s success is due to the fact that it dodges the realities of *banlieue* life, rather than illuminating them. To what extent does its novel but apparently unproblematic bringing together of *banlieue* popular culture and bourgeois high culture result in a work which lacks critical edge? I want to suggest that the challenges to conventional representations of the *banlieue* evident in *L'Esquive* are only one facet of what is in fact a multi-faceted text which allows for ambivalent, even contradictory readings. Although its feel-good element may offer comfort to those who maintain, despite the evidence of the October/November riots, that the Republican universalist road to integration for France's ethnic others is still workable, the film deploys strategies which simultaneously disrupt and undermine its vision of integration and community, providing a much more complex, political stance on the *banlieue* than is at first apparent.

Genre hybridity

Popular films are predominantly genre films, which are "strongly anchored, economically and ideologically, in mass culture" (Moine 2005, 7).[5] *L'Esquive* draws on a variety of genres, allowing it to appeal to different audiences rather than simply being branded a *beur* or *banlieue* film, and so enhancing its chances of box office success. A brief plot summary will make this clear. The narrative centres on fifteen-year-old Krimo (Osman Elkharraz), who falls for his classmate Lydia (Sara Forestier), but is unable to articulate his feelings, while Lydia single-mindedly pursues her desire to shine as Lisette in the school play, *Le Jeu de l'amour et du hasard*. Krimo, who never normally reads a book, bribes his classmate Rachid (Rachid Hami) to let him have the role of Arlequin in order to woo Lydia by proxy, but is unable to rise to the occasion. Lydia refuses to commit herself to going out with him, so Krimo's closest friend, Fathi (Hafet Ben-Ahmed), tries to force the situation, also unsuccessfully. Eventually, after the successful performance of the play (in which Rachid resumes the role of Arlequin), Lydia goes to see Krimo, but he refuses to answer her call. The film invites readings as a teen romance, a coming-of-age film, a comedy of manners, a school movie, and a film about putting on a play, as well as a variation on the *beur* and *banlieue* film.

The most popular *beur* and *banlieue* films to date (that is, films which have attracted over a million spectators in France) have been Mathieu Kassovitz's stylish *La Haine* (1995), the *Taxi* trilogy (Gérard Pirès, 1998; Gérard Krawzcyk, 2000; Gérard Krawzcyk, 2003) starring *beur* actor Samy Naceri, and the films by *beur* filmmaker Djamel Bensalah, *Le Ciel, les oiseaux… et ta mère* (1999) starring *beur* comedian Jamel Debbouze, followed by *Le Raïd* (2002) and (with 876,855 spectators) *Il était une fois dans l'Oued (La légende de Johnny Bachir)* (2005), both of which star actors who made their name thanks to *Le Ciel, les oiseaux…* The success of *La Haine* promulgated the notion of the *banlieue* film as a vital, new, contemporary genre, while the *Taxi* trilogy and Bensalah's films have demonstrated that action and social comedies featuring multi-ethnic casts can also attract large audiences. What these films have in common, however, is their address to a young multi-ethnic youth market through their function as male buddy movies, drawing on popular *banlieue* language, humour and culture at the same time as they explore the (problematic) place of black-blanc-beur *banlieue* males in France.[6]

The subject matter and setting of *L'Esquive*–the lives of adolescents in the *banlieue*–certainly mark it, ten years after *La Haine*, as one of the latest avatars of the *beur/banlieue* strands of New French Cinema, albeit one in which many of the features of the most popular *banlieue* films are marginalised. Its low budget and "new realist" style (shot with a digital handheld camera and drawing on mostly non-professional actors resident in the estate where it was filmed) locate it within the series of almost artisanal films made by *beur* filmmakers, from Malik Chibane's *Hexagone* (1994) and Zaïda Ghorab-Volta's *Souviens-toi de moi* (1996) to Rabah Ameur-Zaïmèche's *Wesh wesh, qu'est-ce qui se passe?* (2002). These films, made in the interstices of the French film industry, took many years to reach the screen and attracted only a limited audience. They all tend to emphasise everyday life in the *banlieue* for young men and/or young women of Maghrebi descent rather than engaging in dramatic, action-driven plotlines. Kechiche himself had harboured the project for *L'Esquive* for over ten years before eventually finding a producer (Jacques Ouaniche) ready to invest in it, following the critical success of *La Faute à Voltaire*.[7] However, whereas *Hexagone* and *Wesh wesh*, like *La Haine*, draw in their own way on what have become identified as clichés of the genre, i.e. the oppressive mise-en-scène of the concrete blocks of flats in the *banlieue* and the themes of unemployment, drug-dealing and violence among young working-class *banlieue* males, Kechiche employs a number of devices which enable *L'Esquive* to spin off into new ground and attract new audiences.

First, the film focuses on adolescents and their vulnerability, rather than on the older youths who inhabit the majority of *banlieue* films, and so is more able to avoid (dodge?) issues related to male unemployment, frustration and criminality.[8] Secondly, its narrative structure is centred on the production of a school play, and a Marivaux play at that, thus shifting generic aspirations towards the teen comedy and the school film on the one hand, and the literary adaptation on the other. Its incorporation of the teaching and performance of a Marivaux text guarantees its appeal for academics and more middle-class spectators generally, inviting intertextual readings based on the choice of play within the film and the ways in which it relates to the relationships between the contemporary protagonists, as well as on the juxtaposition of the language of *marivaudage* with that of the *banlieue*. And thirdly, by foregrounding the interactions between male and female protagonists, and in the process giving adolescent girls equal, if not more dominant roles to play in the diegesis, it opens up the *banlieue* film to romance and the comedy of manners, as well as offering an internal commentary on gender difference and appealing to a more female audience.[9] As a result, the film offers a very different purchase on the *banlieue* from the majority of *beur/banlieue* films.

A universal story?

L'Esquive's originality lies in part in its introduction of a Marivaux text into a *banlieue* setting and its consequent juxtaposition of high and popular culture, literary and popular language. It thus begs analysis in terms of its ability to marry the two, and the ideological effects of such a marriage. For a number of French critics, however, the use of the Marivaux text serves mainly to underline the fact that the storyline could apply to any group of adolescents (as the film's English title indicates). For example, Jean-Philippe Tessé notes that, while Kechiche might have been expected to make a film about the *banlieue*, "his film is above all about adolescence" (Tessé 2004, 52).[10] The film's narrative structure cleverly uses scenes from the Marivaux play, intercalated with and enlivened by the reactions and comments of Krimo's and Lydia's peer groups, in order to highlight the unspoken feelings and desires of its principal *banlieue* protagonists: Krimo is only able to try wooing Lydia by disguising himself as Arlequin, Lydia uses her role as Lisette in order to prevaricate. The delicate handling of feelings of desire, jealousy and humiliation afforded by this approach extends to the treatment of the other major characters–Frida (Sabrina Ouazani), who plays Lisette's mistress Sylvie, Magali (Aurélie Ganito), Krimo's erstwhile girlfriend, and Fathi, the male friend who is concerned that Krimo should not lose face–and gives their interactions a universal appeal. From this perspective, the ideological significance of the film's choice of *banlieue* setting is a humanistic one–*banlieue* adolescents, whatever their ethnic origins, have feelings like anybody else, feelings which are universal rather than particular.

Perhaps in order to underline the universal dimension of the narrative, but also in line with the generic demands of the teen romance and comedy of manners, *L'Esquive* offers an imaginative reworking of the masculinised spaces typical of other contemporary *banlieue* films. The film begins by plunging the spectator into a vociferous (though barely comprehensible) debate taking place between a multi-ethnic group of adolescent youths gathered on the estate, reacting aggressively to an affront to their masculine honour in a way typical of the *banlieue* film; it then swiftly dodges away from the direction this suggests (male buddy violence) and instead follows Krimo into a series of more feminised spaces: the staircase outside Magali's flat where she reluctantly ends her relationship with him; his own flat where he has a conversation with his mother; and the Chinese dressmaker's shop on the ground floor where he first sees Lydia proudly wearing the dress she has had made for the part of Lisette when she plays at being the mistress. This feminisation of space subsequently extends to the open-air spaces outside and between the blocks of flats where, unusually, the young women, not just the young men, congregate to chat ("thatche"). The apparent self-confidence of this chorus of young women of (predominantly) Maghrebi descent contrasts with dominant media representations of young *banlieue* women as victims of Arab fundamentalism and/or of gang rapes. At the same time, thanks to the film's tight framing of the adolescents' faces and its focus on human interactions, the ever-present blocks of flats do not block the horizon as they do in *Wesh wesh*, suggesting that the *banlieue* is, or can be, a place of opportunity, open to alternative ways of being.[11]

The outdoor spaces of the *banlieue*, already defamiliarised by the presence of young women and the lack of older, unemployed youths, are further opened up and transformed by the introduction of theatrical elements, notably the informal play rehearsals held in the open-air amphitheatre, and the spectacle of Lydia flaunting her costume and fluttering her fan, and of Rachid sporting his Arlequin costume. But a key space for testing out the ability of the *banlieue* to represent universal values is that of the school, where the (white, female) French teacher (Carole Franck) enthusiastically rehearses her (unrealistically) docile class for their end-of-year production. The school is significant as the site of France's supposedly secular education system which, according to Republican universalist values, opens up the possibility of integration for its ethnic others. *L'Esquive* seems to embrace this possibility when, at its conclusion, first a mixed class of primary-school-age children, then the mixed group of adolescents, successfully perform together for a multi-ethnic audience, a moment of celebration of community.[12]

If the use of space in the film challenges the sense of exclusion which is conventionally associated with the specificity of the *banlieue* experience, it might be thought that its incorporation of *banlieue* slang would be a constant reminder. *Banlieue* slang is a form of non-standard popular French which is often denigrated because of its hybridity and its association with marginalised multi-ethnic populations. Arguably, however, the adolescents' use of slang is the most exciting, entertaining and even poetic aspect of the film. Even more difficult for the non-*banlieue* spectator to understand than in *La Haine*, and without any accompanying glossary or subtitles, it explodes in repetitive torrents of *verlan*, Arabisms, neologisms and insults. It is particularly innovative coming from the mouths of the young women, who address each other as "brother" (frère), and talk about having "balls" (couilles), appropriating the masculinism of popular French for their own purposes. More importantly, however, it is juxtaposed in a non-judgmental way with Marivaux's elegant eighteenth-century turns of phrase. The juxtaposition highlights the fact that in both types of language, speech functions in a similar way: both are performative and theatrical, and, crucially, both demonstrate that there is a difference between what is said and what is meant. The film thus works to suggest that both types of language are equally valid, or even, through its energetic delivery, that the hybrid language of the *banlieue* is actually more alive and colourful. Although the ability to shift from one mode of language to another is what marks out the most able characters–at several points it is made clear that the adolescents adjust their language to talk to adults, be it in class or in conversation with Krimo's mother–the film revalues the popular language of the *banlieue* in and of itself, offering it up as a bearer of universal meanings, rather than as the impenetrable speech of a marginalised minority.

It is possible, then, to read the film positively, either as a universal story about the delicate relationships between teenagers which simply draws on a *banlieue* setting and *banlieue* language, or as a film which revalues and gives universal meaning to the culture of the *banlieue* through a dramatisation of its hybrid language and its ability to infuse the production of a Marivaux text with its energy and theatricality. However, there are equally pressing signs pointing to the specificities of the *banlieue* situation, which militate against such positive readings.

Or a tale of exclusion?

While the mise-en-scène of *L'Esquive* minimises the oppressiveness of the *banlieue* setting, it is notable that, like other *beur/banlieue* films, it makes no other spaces available for its *banlieue* protagonists. The young people never leave the estate, and their only excursion to its periphery, when Fathi drives Krimo (in what is probably a stolen car) to an encounter he has engineered with Lydia and friends (with a view to getting Lydia to make a decision as to whether she will go out with Krimo or not), leads to a brutal confrontation with the police. Described by many critics as an unfortunate recourse to a cliché of the *banlieue* film, the sequence is actually an important reminder of the power of the state and the institutionalised racism of the police, which keeps these adolescents where they belong, away from the city centre and the life of the nation, and which drives the sort of protests which took place in France in October/November 2005. The police gratuitously subject the adolescents, girls included, to an extended and unnecessarily violent stop-and-search routine, in the course of which Frida's copy of the Marivaux text is first assumed to contain illegal substances and then used to hit her. The sequence, which ends ironically with a close-up of the battered book, is in vivid contrast with the ensuing performance sequence, showing how the legitimacy of the adolescents' attempt to access bourgeois culture is denied in the wider world. Furthermore, the lack of access to spaces outside the *banlieue* is not compensated for by reference to other geographic spaces. The parents' former homelands do not figure at all as part of the film's imaginary, and the only space to be mentioned outside the estate is the prison of Fresnes, where Krimo's absent father is imprisoned, shortly to be joined by Fathi's brother-in-law. Krimo may hang paintings of boats on his bedroom wall, sent to him by his father, but they represent a fantasy space with no basis in reality.

The difficulties faced by these adolescents in transcending the confines of the estate are also signalled in a key classroom scene in which the teacher explains the meaning of the Marivaux text to her charges, who are arguing about Frida's performance of Lisette's mistress in her disguise as a servant. The teacher points out that in *Le Jeu de l'amour et du hasard* there is no such thing as chance: despite their disguises, servants and masters recognise each other because they are, and will remain, prisoners of their origins. This view of society, which the teacher does not question, and therefore appears to endorse, is potentially shocking. It implies that her young *banlieue* pupils, despite imaginatively inhabiting other roles and being given centre stage by their performances, are equally prisoners of their origins, in this case their ethnic background as well as their class. It also seems to run counter to the teacher's own obvious belief in her mission to help her students better themselves by understanding and appreciating classical French culture, not to mention Kechiche's (correct) assumption that participation in the making of the film might help the young *banlieue* actors acquire "an awareness of their own artistic potential and thus claim the means of expression" (cited in Mélinard 2004).[13] Yet the teacher herself does not pick up on the contradiction or invite reflections on the Marivaux model from her students. Indeed, it is notable that, in this representation of the French education system, little attempt is made to capitalise on the creative energies arising from the cultural differences of the students, evident elsewhere in their use of language. The one-way cultural traffic imposed by a curriculum which has no interest in bringing into play the students' cultures of origin is a clear sign of the limits of the school as the site of integration (though it is up to the spectator to perceive this, rather than it being spelt out within the film). However, the choice of the Marivaux text is peculiarly apt in demonstrating that class (and other) differences are not to be willed away, and that the transformations which the performance of the text have afforded are not for real.

In fact, in line with conventional Republican universalist lines of argument, the film does not openly admit that ethnic difference is an issue. Because the group of young people stopped by the police includes a white adolescent as well as adolescents of Maghrebi descent (the majority), police violence can be seen as directed against *banlieue* youths as a class rather than because of their ethnicity. In addition, one of the policemen is black, one a white woman. However, by casting a white actress in the role of Lydia, Kechiche (perhaps inadvertently) clearly establishes the possibility of ethnic difference as a factor in Krimo's aspirations and failure. The difference between inarticulate Krimo, who cannot act, and over-articulate Lydia, who moves with ease between languages and roles, is intensified by the exhilarating, energetic performance of blue-eyed blonde-haired Sara Forestier, who differs from her peers in that she is not from the *banlieue* and was already a professional actor when she attracted

Kechiche's attention. Her star appeal for majority white, mainstream audiences has since been confirmed by her award of a César and numerous screen roles, including in Michel Deville's adaptation of Feydeau's *Un fil à la patte* (2005). In her performance as Lisette, and in the way in which she is shot and lit, Forestier's Lydia outshines Frida as Sylvia, as well as Krimo as Arlequin (and although Rachid manages the part well, he is marginal to the diegesis as a whole). The film thus not only runs the danger of allowing a white professional actress to outperform the non-professional *beur* actors, but also sets up white Lydia as an unattainable object of desire for *beur* Krimo.

The difference between the genders is also significant. With the exception of Rachid, Krimo's male friends are completely dismissive of any interest in theatre (though they are present at the final performance). They also remain inarticulate compared with the girls. Although Fathi is able momentarily to disempower Frida through brute force when he needs her to help him put pressure on Lydia (the violence with which he confiscates her mobile phone provides a reminder of the brutality to which young ethnic minority women are subjected in other *banlieue* films), he is unable to match her verbally, and it is through their verbal skills that the girls not only gain the spectator's attention but also show that they may be able to better themselves. While the boys talk about watching hardcore porn and avenging slights to their honour, the girls discuss their aspirations for the future; and it is the girls who dominate the final stage production (which includes a black girl in the role of the master, Dorante). The film thus suggests that gender as well as ethnicity may be a determining influence in social mobility (or the lack of it).

The film's double-edged ending underlines the different ways in which it can be read. On the one hand, the performance of the school play is a triumph, uniting students and parents, adolescents and adults, people of different ethnicities and different generations, showing that the multi-ethnic *banlieue* kids can do it too. On the other hand, it also highlights Krimo's isolation. Having walked out when the teacher tried to coerce him into injecting some life into the role of Arlequin, he becomes an outsider, gazing in longingly at the performance from outside the school building, humiliated by his failure. If the Marivaux play gives some individuals a voice, then, it also separates out those who can and those who cannot appropriate it. Whereas *Le Jeu de l'amour et du hasard* ends happily with the formation of the two couples, masters and servants, *L'Esquive* ends less happily with the breakdown of communication between the (passive, male) *beur* and the (active, female) white adolescent and thus the failure of their incipient romance. But if the Marivaux play ends on the restoration of a rigid, hierarchical social order, so, arguably, does *L'Esquive*, albeit one based on ethnic and gender difference as much as class.

Conclusion

Taking for granted the pleasures afforded by *L'Esquive*'s exciting cinematography, excellent performances, and clever and imaginative script, this analysis of the film's hybridity and its consequent ideological contradictions enables one to see why it has enjoyed both critical and (relatively speaking) box office success. Its complex, innovative and productive combination of popular and high cultural references raises key issues with regard to the incorporation of the multi-ethnic *banlieue* into the identity of the nation while producing potentially different meanings for different audiences. The film can be read as an optimistic vision of the potential for assimilation into the community of *banlieue* adolescents, or even of the acceptance of their hybrid identity; but it can also be seen as a realistic depiction of continuing divisions and inequalities which have a particularly negative impact on *banlieue* males, and which demonstrate the difficulty, if not the impossibility, of integration. By virtue of its contradictions, in true Brechtian fashion, it invites spectators aware of its ambivalence to debate the issues further.

---

[1] A direct translation of "l'esquive", a term used in fencing, is "the dodge".

[2] It has since become accessible to a much wider audience through its DVD release (at a tantalisingly low price) and its screenings on Canal+.

[3] "Depuis sa sortie en janvier... il n'a pas cessé d'occuper le centre du débat... Pour une fois, un film fait parler: dans les journaux, à l'école, partout."

[4] "Cette jeunesse n'a pas de place dans le paysage audiovisuel. Il y a un manque et c'est dommage parce que c'est une chance pour la culture. J'avais envie d'une représentation plus juste. C'est une population très peu représentée et quand elle l'est, c'est souvent d'une façon très caricaturale avec des clichés, des poncifs. La représentation a une importance même dans l'idée que l'autre se fait de vous. Souvent, la façon dont on les caricature alimente les discours politiques de l'extrême droite."

[5] "...leur fort ancrage, économique et idéologique, dans la culture de masse".

[6] *Indigènes* (2006), by veteran *beur* director Rachid Bouchareb, has since achieved well over three millions spectators in France, making it the most popular *beur*-authored film to date. The film explores the "hidden history" of Franco-Algerian relations, in this case through the experiences of four Maghrebi soldiers fighting to liberate France at the end of WW2, It won the best actor award at Cannes for its ensemble male cast.

[7] *La Faute à Voltaire*, which addresses the plight of a Tunisian immigrant in Paris, won the Golden Lion in Venice for best first film.

[8] Jacques Doillon made a similar choice in using children in *Petits frères* (1999), a study of the multi-ethnic *banlieue* seen mostly through the eyes of a young white Parisian girl who has run away from home.

[9] Other representations of adolescent girls from the *banlieue* are more problematic: *La Squale* (Fabrice Génestal, 2000) suggests that the principal protagonist is almost as violent as her male peers, while *Samia* (Philippe Faucon, 2001) foregrounds Samia's spirited rebellion against the strictures of Maghrebi family life.

[10] "[Kechiche] filme avant tout l'adolescence."

[11] The multi-layered nature of the *banlieue* is a feature of Zaïda Ghorab-Volta's 2002 film, *Jeunesse dorée* (see Tarr 2005, 182-5).

[12] The film's representation of the school is in dramatic contrast with the way it is represented as the site of violence, conflict and exclusion in the opening sequence of Jean-François Richet's *Ma 6-T va crack-er* (1997), for example.

[13] "…une conscience de leur propre potentiel artistique, et par conséquent, une revendication des moyens d'expressions". Rachid Hami, for example, has had a starring role in the TV film *Pour l'amour de Dieu* by Zakia and Ahmed Bouchaala (2006), as well as directing his own short film *Point d'effet sans cause* (2005).

CHAPTER TEN

"COMMENT PEUT-ON ÊTRE FRANÇAIS?": IMAGINING ALTERNATIVE IDENTITIES/FUTURES IN COLINE SERREAU'S *CHAOS* (2001) AND JULIE BERTUCELLI'S *DEPUIS QU'OTAR EST PARTI* (2003)[1]

BINITA MEHTA

In a 1992 essay, cultural critic Stuart Hall discussed the notion of European identity, claiming that the "crumbling of the east-west frontier" has not made for a unified Europe. On the contrary, according to Hall, it has created so much "nationalism, ethnic absolutism, religious bigotry and economic backwardness" that "western Europeans are beginning to talk about Russians, Poles, Bulgarians, Hungarians, Romanians and Albanians in the same language they used to reserve for North Africans, Arabs and Turks" (1992, 46). Moreover, Hall adds that, "in the age of global production and capital flows and liberalised markets and information systems… we are all 'economic migrants' now. The barbarians are already within the gate" (1992, 47). Hall's point made fifteen years ago is still valid today. The riots of October/November 2005 in the suburbs of large metropolitan cities of France, inhabited predominantly by first and second-generation African and Maghrebi immigrants, are proof that the French Republican ideals of *liberté, égalité, fraternité* are not attainable for all its citizens. Thus, in our global world of "dissolving national boundaries… borderlines" (1992, 47), the idea of who is French, what is Europe, who is a European, needs to be redefined and negotiated and that is what both Coline Serreau and Julie Bertucelli do in their films *Chaos* (2001) and *Depuis qu'Otar est parti* (2003) respectively. This chapter will explore the place of marginal female characters from differing ethnic backgrounds in contemporary popular French cinema as portrayed by two women directors. Overcoming obstacles within their own families and wider

French society, these characters create a separate space and identity of their own.

Chaos and *Depuis qu'Otar est parti* can be considered popular films, albeit in distinct ways. *Chaos* uses comedy, while weaving other "popular" genres into its narrative structure. *Depuis qu'Otar est parti* represents the perspectives of ordinary people whose lives are forever altered by their socio-economic status and tough immigration laws. In the introduction to *France on Film: Reflections on Popular French Cinema*, Lucy Mazdon questions the use of the term "popular" to encompass the diversity of contemporary popular French cinema, especially since, as she observes, the perception of an "'art' film or a 'popular' film depends as much upon the particular context of reception as upon the identity of the film itself" (2001, 5). According to Mazdon, films that are not successful at the box office can still be popular if they contain a "linear narrative trajectory" and "familiar themes" and if they "focus on the lived realities of protagonists in recognisable communities" because these features "render [such films] thoroughly accessible" (2001, 6). The plotlines of Coline Serreau's films (including her biggest successes *Trois hommes et un couffin* (1985) and *Romuald et Juliette* (1989)), tend to be linear and chronological, and this is likely to have contributed to the success of *Chaos* at the box office in France, with 1.33 million tickets sold. To add credence to *Chaos*'s status as a popular film, Guy Austin asserts that French filmmakers Diane Kurys and Coline Serreau "took women's film-making into the popular mainstream" in the mid-1980s and that in their films they manage to "explore personal concerns with issues of gender and sexuality... while at the same time addressing millions of spectators" (1996, 87). Adding to its mainstream appeal, *Chaos* was nominated for four awards at the 2002 César Awards, winning one, that of most promising actress for the newcomer Rachida Brakni, the actress who plays Noémie/Malika, one of the lead roles in the film.

Depuis qu'Otar est parti is a more intimate film whose subject matter deals with the status of an ex-Soviet republic within the new Europe. One of the film's characters, the Otar of the title, a native of the former Soviet Republic of Georgia whom we never meet, is working illegally in France. What makes *Otar* a popular film is that it portrays the lives of ordinary people driven by extraordinary circumstances to search for a better life through a plot-line that tackles the current debate pertaining to undocumented workers ("*sans-papiers*") in France, "the lived realities of protagonists in recognisable communities", to use Mazdon's words. *Depuis qu'Otar est parti* won the Grand Prix at the Cannes Film Festival in 2003 and the best first fiction film for its writer-director Julie Bertucelli at the 2004 César Awards.

The female protagonists of *Chaos* and *Depuis qu'Otar est parti* come to understand their identity as women in relation to their society as determined by family and nation. Serreau and Bertucelli propose alternative views of France and what it means to be French in a postcolonial, post-communist, post-Cold War Europe, in the aftermath of the fall of the Berlin Wall in 1989 and the break-up of the Soviet Union in 1991. *Chaos* studies contemporary France from the inside, as experienced by the children of immigrants from the former French colony of Algeria through the lens of gender and sexuality. *Depuis qu'Otar est parti* examines France through the imagined perspective of an outsider living in the Republic of Georgia. *Chaos* questions what it means to be French within multi-ethnic French society while *Depuis qu'Otar est parti* ruminates on the place of France and French culture within an ever-evolving Europe *sans frontières*. As Duncan Petrie states in the introduction to the book *Screening Europe: Image and Identity in Contemporary European Cinema*, cinema not only reflects reality, but serves as a catalyst "in the actual construction of realities" (1992, 3). This is indeed the case for the two films we will study. We will examine how the films' protagonists imagine alternative identities and futures for themselves in a multi-ethnic and multi-religious France of the twenty-first century.

Both films comment on the complexities of contemporary French society in what Carrie Tarr, in her introduction to *Reframing difference: Beur and banlieue filmmaking in France*, has identified as the emergence in the 1980s and the 1990s of two popular genres of filmmaking: the *cinéma beur*, [2] made by second-generation immigrants of Maghrebi descent (an early example of which is Mehdi Charef's *Le Thé au harem d'Archimède* (1985)), and the *cinéma de banlieue*, representing life in the *banlieue*, or suburbs, of large metropolitan cities in France. One of the first films to explore issues of the *banlieue* was Mathieu Kassovitz's *La Haine* (1995) (Tarr 2005, 2-3). Although made twelve years ago, the film's theme of disgruntled youth living in the *cités*, or housing projects, outside Paris and their often contentious relationship with the police bears an eerie resemblance to the *banlieue* youth depicted in television images of the riots that rocked the suburbs of major French cities in October and November 2005. Both *Le Thé au harem d'Archimède* and *La Haine* were well-received by the public. The popularity of *beur* and *banlieue* cinema continued with Philippe Faucon's telefilm *Samia* (2000), whose protagonist is a young *beur* girl (*beurette*) who lives in the *banlieue* and

Abdellatif Kechiche's recent *L'Esquive* (2004) (see Tarr in this volume). The latter won Best Film, Best Director, and Most Promising Actress at the 2005 César Awards. In her analysis of *beur* and *banlieue* film, Tarr elucidates that both categories overlap each other. For example, *banlieue* films are made by *beur* and white filmmakers. What they share is "a concern with the place and identity of the marginal and excluded in France" (2005, 3).[3]

Since one group of the "marginal" and "excluded" is youth from various ethnic groups, often the descendants of first-generation immigrants who live in the crime-ridden *cités*, we need to analyze *Chaos* and *Depuis qu'Otar est parti* within the context of changes in French immigration policies of the past decade. Increasing hostility towards non-European immigrants in France led to the passage of tougher immigration laws in the1990s (Tarr 2005, 4-7). The *loi Pasqua* of 1993, named after the then French interior minister Charles Pasqua, tried to put a check on legal immigration by prohibiting foreign graduates from accepting job offers by French employers, by increasing the waiting period for family reunification from one to two years, and by denying residency permits to foreign spouses who had been in the country illegally prior to marrying. The *loi Pasqua* also retracted the law that gave automatic citizenship to the children of immigrants. These children can now apply for citizenship between the ages of 16-18. Another immigration law–*la loi Chevènement*– passed in 1998 created a special status for scholars and scientists (Guiraudon 2002). In 1996, Jean-Louis Debré, who became the French interior minister after Charles Pasqua, proposed *la loi Debré*, an immigration law of which Article 1 made it a requirement for anyone housing a foreigner to report to the authorities. Protests against the proposed law led to the occupation of the Eglise Saint-Bernard by a few hundred *sans-papiers*. The immigration question continues to play a defining role within the French social and political landscape. In April 2006, President Nicolas Sarkozy, then French interior minister in Jacques Chirac's cabinet, passed even stricter immigration laws. On 24 July 2006, faced with growing criticism of his policies, Sarkozy decided to give 6000 residency permits (*cartes de séjour*) to families of undocumented workers with school-age children based on a programme launched on 13 June 2006. The immigration issue is therefore crucial to understanding the behaviour and actions of the central characters in *Chaos* and *Depuis qu'Otar est parti*. The challenges faced by second-generation Maghrebi immigrants both from the French state and from within their own families is an important subtext for understanding Noémie/Malika's actions in *Chaos*, while the plight of the *sans-papiers* in contemporary French

society, exacerbated by changing borders within Europe, lies at the
narrative centre of *Depuis qu'Otar est parti*.

A combination of comedy, thriller, and buddy movie,[4] Serreau's *Chaos*
focuses on gender relations, on how old identities are reshaped and new
ones invented through the portrayal of a friendship between two women
from very different walks of life, a white lawyer Hélène (Catherine Frot)
and a young *beur* prostitute Noémie/Malika (Brakni).[5] The film criticises
patriarchal structures within Algerian, Islamic, as well as white, bourgeois
culture. The electrifying, fast-paced opening scene instantly plunges the
viewer into questions of identity by bringing together two "French"
families whose paths might otherwise never have crossed. The scene also
reveals the shallowness of Hélène's life and her sense of isolation in her
marriage when she and her husband Paul (Vincent Lindon) witness a
prostitute being pursued and brutally beaten by three pimps. Despite her
pleas for help, Paul rolls up the car windows and drives away to the
nearest carwash to wipe the blood stains off the windscreen. Hélène, on
the other hand, who is unable to ignore what has happened, locates the
hospital where the woman has been taken and helps her through a difficult
recovery. Brought together by this chance encounter the two women form
a strong bond that slowly develops into friendship and becomes a catalyst
of change in both their lives. Despite their different socio-economic and
ethnic backgrounds, they share some similarities in their often complicated
relationships with their husbands, fathers, brothers, and sons. Hélène's
relationship with her husband Paul is cold and distant and closely
resembles Paul's relationship with his mother Mamie (Line Renaud).
Mirroring Paul's treatment of his mother, Hélène's son Fabrice (Aurélien
Wiik) also takes his mother for granted. Yet, Hélène's mistreatment at the
hands of her egotistical husband and self-absorbed son does not quite
match Noémie/Malika's predicament and the oppressive nature of her
patriarchal Maghrebi family.

Noémie/Malika's story, told in a long flashback, a film within a film, is
more poignant. Escaping her domineering father, who had arranged for her
to marry an older man in Algeria in exchange for a sum of money, she
ends up on the streets, a drug-addicted prostitute. Without the knowledge
of her pimps, and with the aim of getting out of a life of prostitution, she
manages to save money, investing it wisely in the stock market. She is
also left a large sum of money from a client, a wealthy Swiss
businessman. When her employers find out about it, they try to get her to
sign the money over to them. She manages to escape. It is this flight from
violence that begins the film.

Once fully recovered from her injuries, Noémie/Malika takes charge in a series of actions that constitute a Molièresque farce. She lays a clever trap for her pimps and the entire prostitution ring and has them arrested. At the same time she cleans up the loose ends of Hélène's life and even manages to reconcile an emotional Paul with Mamie. In the superheroine mode of an action film, Noémie/Malika turns her attention to her own family. She buys the affection of her father and brothers with expensive gifts and offers her sister Zora (Hajar Nouma) the gift of freedom from a forced marriage. In the film's dénouement, Serreau envisions the possibility of connections between women across boundaries of ethnicity, class, and generation.[6] With her money Noémie/Malika buys a large house overlooking the ocean. In the closing shot of the film, calm and serene as opposed to the drama of the opening, the four women, Noémie/Malika, Hélène, Zora, and Mamie sit silently side by side on a bench in the garden of the house, gazing at the ocean. A close-up of their faces reveals varied expressions: Noémie/Malika's is grim, Hélène's dreamy, Zora's anxious. The final freeze frame rests on Mamie's serene, smiling face.

As she does in her earlier films such as *Romuald and Juliette* (1989) and *La Crise* (1992), in which she confronts stereotypes of race and class only to reverse them, in *Chaos* Serreau uses the technique of paralleling and stereotyping to make the broader point of gender inequalities that cut across class and ethnic lines.[7] This technique of paralleling and stereotyping is often found in her popular comedies. Serreau perpetuates and reverses stereotypes to critique the patriarchal nature of contemporary French society and to point to the stabilising role women play within their family units. In an impassioned, didactic speech to Zora conducted in their housing estate compound, with her brothers riding around on new motorcycles, Noémie/Malika makes a powerful critique of her father and three brothers who are only interested in material goods, obedient mothers, wives, and daughters. She does not shower her sister with gifts like she does her brothers. Instead she offers her the opportunity to escape the inevitability of an arranged marriage, to pass the *baccalauréat* exam, and to make something of her life. Noémie/Malika tells Zora:

> But open your eyes. You want to be a slave? Do you see how they speak to you? Zora do this, Zora do that. That is exactly how your husband will speak to you for all your life and you will have no rights any more. Is that what you want? But look at our brothers? Look at these assholes on their motorcycles. All that they want in life is that, motorcycles, mobile phones, easy money, women who obey.[8]

Noémie/Malika's use of language shows that she moves from discussing the specific situation of her brothers to more general statements about young Maghrebi males, thus stereotyping them as lazy good-for-nothings who have little respect for women. Interestingly enough, Zora's reaction to Noémie/Malika's tirade is "You are full of hate" (Tu as la haine). She refuses to believe her and accuses her of behaving just as authoritatively as their father. However, a few shots later, we see that Noémie/Malika's fears are justified. The camera cuts to the scene showing Zora in their apartment in the *cité* studying for her *baccalauréat*. Her brothers order her to cook them dinner and when she refuses they start beating her. Her father intervenes to stop the fight, but only prevents the brothers from striking her face, an important asset for potential suitors. Zora is now certain of her fate. Noémie/Malika pays special attention to her sister because the women in their community, more than the men, are harbingers of change. Passing the *baccalauréat* is a step towards gaining entry into the cultural and economic mainstream.

Serreau is also severe in her critique of humanitarian organisations such as *SOS Racisme*, an organisation founded in 1984 to fight racial discrimination, and accuses them of sexism. At one point in *Chaos*, Noémie/Malika appeals to *SOS Racisme* for help. When she tells her story to an elderly Maghrebi man working in the office he orders her to leave, stating that the organisation was in the business of fighting racism, not helping women who had dishonoured their religion and community. The patriarchal structures that bind society are strong and oppress all women, regardless of class and ethnicity. Although arranged marriages still exist within the Maghrebi community in France, in recent years *beur* women have united to assert their rights and have protested against arranged and forced marriages as well as other oppressive customs perpetuated by family patriarchs–fathers, husbands, brothers and sons (Tarr 2005, 7-8).

Carrie Tarr suggests that Serreau redeems the white male protagonist Paul (he is permitted to shed a few tears when Noémie/Malika reconciles him with his mother) while condemning Noémie/Malika's Algerian father, offering him no chance of redemption. Serreau is indeed harsh on first- and second-generation Maghrebi men in the film, but with the sole purpose of pointing out traditions within Maghrebi, Islamic culture that oppress women. It is also true, as Tarr asserts, that "eurocentric representations of minority women" play into a "reactionary agenda through the vilification of ethnic minority men" (2005, 157). However, the alternative is far worse. By ignoring customs that are oppressive to women one encourages their continued practice. And herein lies the paradox. By damning Noémie/Malika's Algerian father, Serreau underscores the fact that forced marriage of young *beur* women is more egregious a crime than Paul's self-indulgence and his indifference towards his wife Hélène and mother Mamie. Serreau may portray stereotypes, but it is important to note her purpose in employing them. She stereotypes Maghrebi men to draw attention to patriarchal traditions that repress women. Through Noémie/Malika's long tirade against Maghrebi, Muslim males, Serreau dispels the potentially dangerous quality of the stereotype by articulating it, suggesting that repressing such stereotypical views has the potential to be more harmful. She draws attention to the problem of forced marriages of young *beur* women in contemporary France while addressing gender relations in French society in general. Tarr also argues that although the film portrays "cross-cultural inter-ethnic sisterhood" (2005, 154), it "still privileges the white woman's perspective" (2005, 161). This is true to the extent that Noémie/Malika's story and subsequent actions force Hélène to look more closely at the problems in her own life. Hélène does indeed dominate the first third of the film. Yet, the rest of the film clearly belongs to the *beur* heroine. She is the one who makes changes within Hélène's family and not the other way around. In fact, Hélène never meets Noémie/Malika's family except in the final scene of the film (a repeat of an earlier scene, recounted in the flashback, in which Noémie/Malika flees her father) when she accompanies Noémie/Malika in her capacity as a lawyer to the port of Marseille as her father is about to board the boat to Algiers with Zora.

In *Chaos*, Noémie/Malika's body becomes a site for negotiating identity. She slowly takes charge of her own body, abused first by her father, who tried to sell her into marriage, then by her pimps who raped and addicted her to drugs, and finally by her customers who used it for pleasure. Through sheer enterprise, intelligence, and grit, Noémie/Malika goes through a difficult process of detoxification, then convinces her pimps to get her off the streets. As a high-class call girl, she chooses her clients and develops a foolproof strategy for seducing them. Later, she uses the same set of practised moves to seduce then abandon Hélène's husband Paul and son Fabrice. In the end, Noémie/Malika with her newly-acquired wealth does enter the ranks of the bourgeoisie, but she does it on her own terms. Her employers teach her to trade on the stock market, but she turns the tables on them by excelling at it, surpassing them and making a great deal of money. In her critique of *Chaos*, Tarr suggests that Noémie/Malika is forced to "reject her Algerian background and culture in order to be free" (2005, 164). I argue, however, that she rejects nothing but adds to her already hybrid identity formed by her Algerian background and her French upbringing, negotiating a space for herself outside of both communities. The house she buys becomes an ambiguous "third space," as defined by Homi Bhabha in conjunction with his notion of hybridity:

> [F]or me, the importance of hybridity is not to be able to trace two original moments from which the third emerges, rather hybridity to me is the "third space" which enables other positions to emerge. This third space displaces the histories that constitute it, and sets up new structures of authority, new political initiatives, which are inadequately understood through received wisdom. (Rutherford 1990, 211)

This adoption of a "third space" suggests a hopeful reading, but not necessarily the only reading of the ending. Is this a space of freedom or of further repression? Is it within mainstream culture or outside it? Hélène befriends Noémie/Malika, but will French society as a whole accept her? Addressing questions of acceptance and the integration of immigrants, the critic Mireille Rosello states that it is not a question of whether *beurs* "will achieve integration but how a French society, in which they are already active participants, describes them" (1996, 157). How will Noémie/Malika be "described" by French society now that she is wealthy? Is capitalist society colour-blind? Will class win out over ethnicity? Whatever the outcome, Serreau offers a cinematic solution to the problems encountered by the other in contemporary French society, allowing Noémie/Malika the possibility of creating her own future on her own terms. Serreau leaves the fairy tale-like ending ambivalent enough to leave it to the viewers to envision their own future for Noémie/Malika and the other women.

Serreau's *beur* heroine challenges the contexts established for her by others and reclaims control of her life. Passing the *baccalauréat*, that ultimate signifier of French identity, will give her and her sister an entry into the cultural and economic mainstream. Serreau is less concerned with the differences than with the similarities between her female white and *beur* protagonists, and her focus is on the big picture of the challenges faced by a heterogeneous and diverse French society in its bid to attain some kind of "universal" notion of Frenchness. Noémie/Malika is not the "westernised fantasy figure" or "*alter-ego*" of the white protagonist, as Tarr suggests (2005, 165). On the contrary, she is a catalyst who forces the white protagonist Hélène to focus on her own needs and desires rather than catering to those of her husband and son. Thus, Serreau urges the viewer to move "beyond ethnicity" and to accept the protagonist for who she is–French of Algerian background. Noémie/Malika appears to demonstrate to the dominant white culture as well as to the Maghrebi community that she is a hybrid, both Algerian and French.

Thus, in *Chaos*, Serreau does not portray differences between French and non-French cultures. She offers, in fact, different definitions of Frenchness within a diverse, multicultural France. Noémie/Malika is both an insider and an outsider. She is French in that she is born in France, but, as the daughter of immigrants, she understands the immigrant mind-frame and the desire to hold onto cultural traditions, one of which she makes it her mission to fight throughout the film. Serreau condemns oppression where she sees it and is not afraid to be politically incorrect by critiquing the patriarchal influences in Noémie/Malika's life–her father, her brothers, her pimps, her customers. She is equally unafraid of criticising women's oppression regardless of colour or ethnicity. Yes, she does redeem the white male character Paul at the end of the film, but for the "lesser" crime of taking his wife and mother for granted. In Serreau's view, it seems, Noémie/Malika's father has arguably committed the graver crime by not allowing her to take the *baccalauréat* and for forcibly trying to marry her off to an older man in Algeria. There is no redemption for such an act in Serreau's view.

While men are omnipresent in *Chaos*, they are conspicuously either absent or dead in Julie Bertucelli's *Depuis qu'Otar est parti*, although they continue to guide the lives of three generations of women. The matriarch Eka (Esther Gorintin), a widow whose son Otar, a trainee doctor, is working illegally on a construction site in Paris, shares a run-down apartment with her daughter Marina (Nino Khomassourdize), and her grandaughter Ada (Dinara Droukarova) in the decaying city of Tbilisi, the capital of the independent republic of Georgia, part of the former Soviet Union, where unemployment is rampant and power outages and water shortages daily occurrences. Marina, part of the "lost generation" of Russians who came of age during the Communist era, is an engineer by training, but sells junk in a flea market. Her husband died in the Soviet Union's war in Afghanistan and she has a boyfriend and lover whom she keeps at a safe emotional distance. Eka has a contentious relationship with her daughter (in one scene they quarrel about Stalin, who is adored by her mother but condemned as a murderer by Marina), but shares a special bond with Ada that transcends their difference in age. They also share another passion, a love for the French language, its literature, and culture.

France and the French language play a crucial role in their lives. For Eka it is a way of recapturing the Francophile family's past, a past in which Marina's grandfather had volumes of books of French literature shipped over to Russia from France which have been in the family ever since, carefully hidden away from the Bolsheviks for whom France (and the West) represented decadent capitalist culture. These books now line the shelves of Eka's apartment. The three women often converse in French. Eka talks to her son Otar on the phone in French and Ada reads Otar's letters aloud to her grandmother in French along with passages of Marcel Proust's *A la Recherche du temps perdu*. Ada's relationship with the French language is reinforced through the letters she continues to write to her grandmother after Otar's death in Paris. She takes on the identity of the dead Otar in these letters as she imagines herself in various Parisian neighborhoods. Marina's relationship with the French language is more ambivalent. Her mother is critical of her accent and prefers to be read to by her granddaughter. Marina would rather sell the French books for the money the family so desperately needs. In fact, without her mother's knowledge, she does indeed sell the family's volumes of Jean-Jacques Rousseau's writings. Ironically, it is Eka herself who sells all her French books in order to buy tickets to Paris so that the three women could pay a surprise visit to her son. Daughter and granddaughter had been unable to break the terrible news of his death to her. The sale of the French books depicts the transformation of France from imagined space into real space.

The last twenty minutes of the film take place in Paris. Eka, Marina and Ada arrive in the city on a rainy night and take a "Taxi Parisien" to their modest hotel. Eka finally learns about her son's death from his Maghrebi neighbour. The camera follows her as she painfully makes her way back to the hotel, occasionally glancing at her last letter to Otar. When she meets an anxious Marina and Ada, she very deliberately perpetuates the lie. She informs them that Otar, tired of waiting for his French papers to come through, had left for the United States: "It was his dream to leave for America… It is said to be a paradise for people with the entrepreneurial spirit. That everything is possible there."[9] Is Eka's reaction a form self-deception, however, or is she deceiving Marina and Ada in return as well? Is she trumping them and deluding herself at the same time? It is perhaps a fusion of the two since they are equally mechanisms for survival. Eka proves that she is much stronger than Marina and Ada had given her credit for. Now that the imagined space (France) has become a reality, it has to be moved elsewhere, i.e. the United States. Bertucelli may have another reason for deciding to situate Otar in the United States. The United States was a place where everything was possible, because unlike Europe, where one lives in history, Americans pretend to have "overcome" history.

Depuis qu'Otar est parti deals with how France and French culture are perceived in an educated middle-class milieu looking through the lens of a prior era and the magical kaleidoscope of literature. It also provides a portrait of contemporary Europe and the divisions between countries in

Eastern and Western Europe. Asked why she picked Georgia as a locale for her film, Julie Bertucelli says that after having spent six months in Georgia, she had fallen in love with this country that was "a crossroads between Europe and Asia, with Caucasian and Russian and European and Middle Eastern influences." (2004). Bertucelli reveals the remnants of the old-style Soviet bureaucracy in modern-day Tbilisi in the long second scene of the film that takes place in a post office. The postal workers, mainly women, take their time sorting through the mail with outdated machines gossiping as they work. In order to pick up Otar's letter at the post office, Ada has to show two identity cards, her own and her grandmother's.

As a French filmmaker, Bertucelli had a specific motive for picking Georgia as the locale for her film. She claims that through her film, she "wanted to say something about France–not France seen from the inside, France seen from elsewhere" (2004). Moreover, she adds, France's ties with Georgia go back many years and that "Georgians are fascinated by French culture" (2004). As a filmmaker, Bertucelli is less interested in "talking about France" (2004) than she is in showing how "one comes to fall in love with a foreign land one knows only from one's imagination, with all the potential for disillusionment that that contains" (2004). Although Eka's image of France was clearly not the one she encounters during her visit, she is not disillusioned. Even after she learns that Paris has claimed her beloved Otar's life, she still wants to tour the city of her dreams. She tells Ada and Marina: "And now, I want to see Paris" (Et maintenant je veux voir Paris). The Paris that she visits is indeed the city of the Champs-Elysées, the Arc de Triomphe, the cafés and bakeries, and the grand department stores. However, it is no longer the rarefied France of Proust and Rousseau, but a diverse country of communities and immigrants whose origins stem from what used to be its colonies–the black African taxi driver who picks them up at the airport and the North Africans who were her son's neighbours. During her brief stay, the women meet no members of France's white population.

Like *Chaos*, *Depuis qu'Otar est parti* has a quixotic ending. As a way of coping with Otar's death, Eka creates the fantasy of his second migration to the United States. But the film ends with another surprising twist. Ada decides not to return to Tbilisi with her family but to remain in Paris. As they say their silent goodbyes through the glass doors that separate them, Marina and Eka board the plane and Ada takes the escalator down to begin her new, albeit uncertain life as an illegal immigrant in Paris. Ada too must revise her views of France. Her life there will not be easy. The country she will encounter as a *sans-papiers* is not the France of its classic poetry, cinema, and cafes, not the literary, bookish Paris she had recreated in the letters she wrote and read aloud to her grandmother after Otar's death. With Ada now in France, the immigrant story will be replayed. Eka will continue to have ties with France, but they will be based more on reality this time around, even though her reading of Proust and French literature will always mediate this so-called reality. The fanciful finales of both films place them squarely in the realm of the popular, urging the spectator to root for both protagonists, Ada in *Depuis qu'Otar est parti* and Noémie/Malika in *Chaos*. Both have broken free of their pasts–Noémie/Malika from her pimps and her authoritarian father and Ada from the desolation of her life in Georgia.

The whimsical dénouements of both films are open to interpretation, however. While Ada in *Depuis qu'Otar est parti* is a new immigrant who is starting out with nothing, Noémie/Malika of *Chaos* has "made it," at least in the capitalistic sense of the term. Will Ada "make it" too? Will Noémie/Malika face less discrimination than Ada because she is rich? Is money the ultimate equaliser? Noémie/Malika is oppressed by the patriarchal structures within her own family as well as within a consumerist society. To her credit, she takes advantage of the very system that had exploited her to buy a home and to put herself in a position of strength. But, the space she creates for herself is an ambiguous one. Both Noémie/Malika and Ada share a kind of American, Californian desire to remake themselves, to imagine other lifestyles. It is not clear what their futures will bring, but they have shown feminist agency by breaking away from the familiar and the known. By having no strong or positive male characters in their films, both Serreau and Bertucelli make the broader points about the necessity for gender equality within a diverse, multicultural French society, as well as in a Europe whose borders have been modified in the past ten years as the signing of treaties has changed the dynamic between European nations, especially between Eastern and Western Europe. Just as Noémie/Malika, the protagonist of *Chaos*, creates her own hybrid identity, so too Eka, the Francophile matriarch in Bertucelli's *Depuis qu'Otar est parti*, creates a fiction to cope with her only son Otar's death while her granddaughter Ada decides to invent a new identity and future for herself in France. The central characters of both films challenge the status quo by proposing alternative ways of envisioning their futures. Yet, the status quo is as much a fiction as a reimagined identity. The endings of both films are ambiguous because inventing alternative, hybrid identities could mean condemning oneself to fantasy. And yet fantasy is crucial for reaching out to the future, which is, by definition, to come, *à venir*, and therefore unknowable.

The directors of *Chaos* and *Depuis qu'Otar est parti* opt for popular forms of filmmaking to convey ideas that are normally addressed by politically-committed cinema. Both films address social and political issues confronting contemporary France, among them, immigration, the plight of undocumented workers within France and a changing Europe, and the challenges of integrating second-generation immigrants, both men and women, especially of Maghrebi, Muslim origin, into French society. Finally, both offer popular representations of French identity from the perspective of ordinary people.

---

[1] I would like to thank the editors of this volume, Dr. Isabelle Vanderschelden and Dr. Darren Waldron, for their helpful suggestions with earlier drafts of this chapter. Many thanks also to Lauren Kozol for reading and commenting on a very early draft. Finally, many thanks to Gary Paul Gilbert for his support, his keen intelligence, and his insightful comments that helped me delve deeper into this subject.

[2] This term, a distortion of the word "arabe," is used for children of immigrants of North African origin. For a more nuanced analysis of the political implications of the term *beur* today, see Tarr (2005, 3-4).

[3] In addition to Kassovitz's *La Haine*, other important white-authored *banlieue* films of the 1990s include Thomas Gilou's *Raï* (1995) Jean-François Richet's *Etat des Lieux* (1995) and Jean-François Richet's *Ma 6-T va crack-er* (1997). Significant *banlieue* films made by filmmakers of Maghrebi origin during the same period include Karim Dridi's *Bye Bye* (1995), Ahmed Bouchaala's *Krim* (1995) and Malik Chabane's *Douce France* (1995) and *Hexagone* (1994).

[4] Several critics in their reviews of the film have compared it to the darker, more violent Hollywood version of the female buddy film, Ridley Scott's *Thelma and Louise* (1990).

[5] Noémie is her professional "French" name, while Malika is her given, Algerian name. The film does not establish whether Noémie is a name she picked herself or whether it has been given to her by her pimps. To insist on her cross-cultural background, I will use both names in my paper.

[6] In her analysis of *Chaos*, Françoise Lionnet focuses on Serreau's portrayal of "feminine solidarity" within the film that transcends national boundaries. Lionnet states: "Serreau's film provides a 'transnational' feminist perspective by dealing humorously with serious questions of women's rights" (2005, 262).

[7] For a fuller discussion of *Romuald et Juliette*, see Dina Sherzer's article "Comedy and Interracial Relationships: *Romuald et Juliette* (Serreau, 1987) and *Métisse* (Kassovitz, 1993)," in Powrie (1999). For more on stereotypes in Serreau's *La Crise*, see the pertinent chapter in Rosello (1998).

[8] "Mais ouvre tes yeux. Tu veux être une esclave? Tu vois comment ils te parlent? Zora fait ci, Zora fait ça. C'est comme ça que ton mari te parlera dans quinze jours et pour toute ta vie. Tes enfants, il te les volera et tu n'auras plus aucun droit. C'est

ça ce que tu veux? Mais regarde tes frères. Regarde ces connards sur leurs motos. Tout ce qu'ils veulent dans la vie c'est ça, les motos, les téléphones portables, l'argent facile, et des meufs qui obéissent. "

[9] "C'était son rêve de partir en Amérique…On dit que c'est le paradis pour les gens entreprenants. Que tout y est possible…."

CHAPTER ELEVEN

MATHIEU KASSOVITZ: REFRAMING THE POPULAR IN CONTEMPORARY FRENCH CINEMA[1]

WILL HIGBEE

In September 2001, the French cinema journal *Positif* published an editorial entitled "Le Renouveau du cinéma français?" (Ciment 2001, 1). The editorial suggested that the significant rise in French cinema audiences since the late 1990s did not merely reflect increasing numbers of spectators attracted to newly-opened multiplex cinemas to view the latest Hollywood imports on offer. Rather, what these box office figures reflected was the "renewal" or "rejuvenation" of French "popular" cinema. Evidence for this tentative shift away from Hollywood came from the fact that, in the first six months of 2001, French films took 51% of the domestic box office (compared with 28% for the same period in 2000) and that four of the five top box office draws during this period were French, namely *Le Placard* (Francis Veber, 2001), *Le Pacte de loups* (Christophe Gans, 2001; *Le Fabuleux destin d'Amélie Poulain* (Jean-Pierre Jeunet, 2001); *La Vérité si je mens! 2* (Thomas Gilou, 2001)–while Mathieu Kassovitz's *Les Rivières pourpres*, released in late 2000, would eventually attract three million spectators over the course of 2000-01. French director Francis Veber, who had been responsible for two of the most successful French popular comedies of this period (*Le Dîner de cons* (1998) and *Le Placard*) declared:

> A new generation of producers and directors is emerging... social and dark cinema has produced many films, but few of them are good... Directors now seek to please audiences. (Ciment 2001, 1)[2]

Although the more recent revival of the French film industry's fortunes has been largely attributed to the seemingly unstoppable rise of the multiplex, it must also, therefore, be understood in the context of the success, particularly since the late-1990s, of French mainstream genre cinema–spectacular action films, heritage cinema and comedy–that refuses the intimate autobiographical or psychological concerns traditionally associated with auteur cinema. Broadly speaking, popular or mainstream genre cinema since the early 1990s has developed to challenge the hegemony of Hollywood at the French box office in two distinct ways. Firstly, through the resurgence of a *cinéma des producteurs*: big-budget films with high production values that are script-led and often function as star vehicles. These films are characterised by continuity; either because of their reliance on tried and tested generic formulas such as comedy, or else through their association with the lavish spectacle and high production values of the *tradition de qualité* (most obviously reflected in the heritage film). The second, and quite distinct, development in mainstream cinema has been that of the *film d'action* or the spectacular genre film such as the *Taxi* series, *Le Pacte des loups* and *Les Rivières pourpres*.[3] Unlike the heritage film, whose identifiably French cultural and historical focus attempts a clear differentiation from Hollywood, the spectacular genre film–a mixture of action and comedy, accompanied by spectacular set-pieces and stunning visual effects–unashamedly takes many of its cues from American cinema (and thus problematises the notion of a French national cinema that has traditionally defined itself *against* Hollywood).

As the director of *Les Rivières pourpres*, and in his starring role as the quirky love interest to Audrey Tautou's Amélie in Jeunet's *Le Fabuleux destin d'Amélie Poulain*, Mathieu Kassovitz cannot be dissociated from the success of popular French cinema in the early 2000s. Like Jeunet and (to a lesser extent) Luc Besson, Kassovitz's particular brand of popular cinema is not one that shies away from its relationship to American cinema. Indeed, he has always expressed his admiration for American directors such as Steven Spielberg, George Lucas, Martin Scorsese and Spike Lee, while simultaneously speaking out against what he perceives as the insularity and pseudo-intellectual elitism of much auteur-led independent French film production–arguably one of the reasons why, post-*La Haine* (1995) there has been sustained hostility towards Kassovitz from certain sectors of the French film industry and critical press.[4]

The aim of this chapter is not, then, to offer a detailed analysis of individual films as such, but rather to consider the ways in which the influences that have informed Kassovitz (as a director) reflect a significant shift that has taken place in relation to our understanding of the popular in French culture, and in particular a certain section of contemporary French popular cinema (namely the *film d'action*, or what I term spectacular genre cinema). It will address the effects of the shifting configurations of French popular culture that began in the 1980s under the auspices of socialist Minister of Culture Jack Lang's policy of *le tout culturel*, which saw the legitimising of mass cultural forms such as television, advertising and pop music (Dauncey 2003, 12-14). This, in turn, has led to an increasingly prominent place being accorded to an Americanised, multi-ethnic youth culture in France, which forms a central reference point for Kassovitz's cinema. The article will also argue that the cultural myth of Hollywood finds increasing resonance and immediacy with contemporary French audiences and a new generation of post-look filmmakers, such as Kassovitz, to the extent that, for this new generation of French spectators and a certain group of filmmakers, Hollywood is now, for better or worse, an identifiable element *within* French popular cinema.

Locating "youth" in French popular cinema

As a director, Kassovitz has remained faithful to the films and filmmakers that so attracted him as an adolescent—in particular directors of the *cinéma du look* such as Besson and Jean-Jacques Beineix but, equally, American filmmakers such as Spielberg, Scorsese, and Sam Raimi. His predilection for the popular (both in terms of cinema but also the broader cultural references in his films to hip-hop, advertising and music video), itself based as much in American mass popular culture as in French popular culture, has emerged as a key characteristic in Kassovitz's work. In more general terms, his films also point towards important cultural shifts taking place in France during the 1980s and 1990s: firstly, the legitimising of American-influenced mass cultural forms—TV, pop music, fashion—within the sphere of the popular through Lang's policy of the so-called *tout culturel*. And secondly, the reconfiguring of youth, rather than the working class, at the centre of French popular culture: a process that had been underway at least since the 1960s but which, as Brian Rigby suggests, had been largely denied by French intellectuals and politicians, through a refusal to accept mass cultural forms and youth culture in particular as anything other than superficial reflections of an American-influenced materialist, consumer culture (1991, 159-62). Two other key conditions that have arguably placed youth at the centre of the popular in France since the 1990s have been, on the one hand, an emphasis on technologies (and in particular audiovisual technologies) at the heart of popular culture, and on the other the fact that a youth-centred popular culture in France seems more willing to embrace the increasing fluidity and difference (in particular ethnic difference) that comes about as transnational or global cultural forms (particularly the audiovisual) acquire an increasing resonance within local or national cultural configurations and identities. French hip-hop is a prime example here–and it is no coincidence that hip-hop attitude and iconography heavily influences Kassovitz's first two features *Métisse* (1993) and *La Haine*. Clearly, then, popular culture can no longer be contained within national boundaries. Instead, it is increasingly predicated on the shifting configurations of the global and the local–something that is readily apparent in Kassovitz's films.

Viewed more negatively, such cultural shifts have facilitated a form of global mass culture dominated by the image that offers an essentially Americanised conception of the world (Hall 1995, 29): broadening our horizons only to limit and homogenise the scope of the popular. In the context of Kassovitz's cinema, a number of critics have thus dismissed his films as a poor imitation of Hollywood (Bonnaud 2000; Blumenfeld 2000).[5] Although Kassovitz's affiliation to Hollywood seems to manifest itself most directly in his two most recent features, the mainstream French thriller *Les Rivières pourpres* and the American horror movie *Gothika* (2003), the influence of American cinema–both popular mainstream Hollywood and American independent exploitation cinema–can also be found in his earlier social films (*Métisse*, *La Haine* and *Assassin(s)* (1997)). In this context, if Spielberg provides a technical and stylistic reference point for Kassovitz, above all through his use of highly controlled mise en scène and the way in which the camera is often seen to navigate on-screen space alongside the other protagonists, then Scorsese has influenced the pessimistic worldview found in his films and their focus on male-centred violence and alienation. However, Kassovitz's approach to the "business" of selling and promoting his (often) controversial films connects the director to African-American director Spike Lee.

While Kassovitz's links to Scorsese (as cinephile, auteur and Hollywood maverick) and Spike Lee (whose films also provided Kassovitz with narrative inspiration for *Métisse* and to a lesser extent *La Haine*) are more easily accepted by French critics from journals such as *Cahiers* and *Positif*, his admiration for Spielberg is altogether more problematic.[6] The director's vocal and apparently unswerving loyalty to Spielberg is viewed disparagingly in certain sectors of the French film industry, where the sentimentality, populism (verging on demagogy) and blatant commercialism of Spielberg's cinema are anathema to the perceived artistic merit and cultural worth of cinema as the "seventh art" in France. Let us not forget that at the height of the culture wars between

France and the US (Hollywood) in the buildup to the GATT negotiations of December 1993, it was Spielberg's *Jurassic Park* (1993) that went head to head at the French box office with heritage super-production *Germinal* (Berri, 1993).

Despite such barely-disguised hostility from within the industry, Kassovitz has repeatedly affirmed in interviews (Aubel 2003; Tirard 2000) his admiration for Spielberg as an auteur. In 2001, the director publicly defended Spielberg against criticism from none other than Jean-Luc Godard, dismissing his disparaging remarks concerning Spielberg's worth as a filmmaker as "typical of the insularity and pseudo-intellectualism of French cinema culture" (Jeffries 2001). There is a certain irony to this exchange in that, by valorising a popular Hollywood director over a type of French cinema which he sees as reactionary and out of touch with the realities of modern France, Kassovitz is effectively adopting a position not dissimilar to that taken five decades earlier by the very director he aims to criticise (Godard) along with Truffaut, Rohmer and others in the pages of *Cahiers du cinéma*. More pertinently, however, the position occupied by Kassovitz apparently points to a seemingly unbridgeable divide for the director in contemporary French cinema culture between the auteur-led independent sector and mainstream commercial cinema–which, in many respects, was what prevented many French critics taking Kassovitz seriously as a popular auteur in a film such as *Assassin(s)*.

Embracing Hollywood as popular "French" cinema?

Kassovitz in fact emerged in the 1980s and 1990s from a new generation of French cultural consumers and a growing number of popular French filmmakers for whom Americanised popular culture (and in particular cinema) is not viewed as a foreign influence, or suspect cultural import, but is instead accepted as an integral and established part of contemporary French culture. The idea of Americanised popular culture emerging as a "natural" element within contemporary popular culture in France is important in relation to Kassovitz's cinema and also the polemical response generated by his films among French critics and audiences. It is also key to understanding the films of a wave of exclusively male filmmakers (Jeunet, Kassovitz, Gans, Jan Kounen) and the reasons behind the phenomenal success with (mostly young) popular French audiences of certain of their films. In the section that follows, I want to consider how this change might have come about–and why it is possible for us to argue that Hollywood now constitutes, for a significant proportion of French audiences and some French directors, an integral part of contemporary popular French cinema.

Firstly, Hollywood's growing share of the French box office in the 1980s and 1990s—which, according to CNC figures, rose from 30% of audience share in 1980 to a high of 63% in 1998[7]—has undoubtedly encouraged a greater identification amongst contemporary French audiences with the iconography, stars and genres of American cinema. When statistics referring to the sale of video and DVD titles in France during 2000 are consulted, this preference for American cinema rises further still: 71% for Hollywood and 20% for French films (Montebello 2005, 185). Similarly, though French television stations (in particular Canal+) may be legally required to buy and screen a higher proportion of French films, Hollywood blockbusters still tend to dominate the prime-time viewing schedules (Ganne 1998, 15-16).

Further evidence of this affinity with Hollywood can be seen in the results of a survey carried out in 1994 by *Première* to establish a "best of all time" film list in which thirty-six of the top forty films selected by those questioned were American (Frodon 1995, 693). Admittedly, this survey is somewhat self-selecting, given that the readers of a magazine such as *Première* are mostly young and inclined towards Hollywood and mainstream French cinema. Nevertheless, its findings support the idea of this shift for many younger spectators towards identifying with American cinema over French films reflected in the other audience figures quoted above.

In contrast to the economic protectionism practised by Hollywood in the American market, in Europe, Hollywood studios argue for the withdrawal of quotas and the free circulation of audiovisual products. Hollywood thus employs its superior economic power to aggressively pursue audiences in foreign markets; a situation motivated largely by the fact that, since most Hollywood films recuperate production costs in the American market, revenues generated from foreign box offices and related products (DVD sales, merchandising, television rights) provide a much higher profit margin. In the mid 1990s, the Hollywood majors thus forged alliances with French distributors and exhibitors, investing considerable sums in marketing and promotion to ensure maximum exposure for their films at the box office. This arrangement has had a particularly damaging effect on smaller, independent French productions, which are denied the opportunity to establish themselves in cinemas and build audiences via word of mouth.[8] Viewing these various developments as a whole, it is therefore possible to argue that, in terms of market share, box office success and media exposure, American cinema has, since at least the late

1980s, usurped French production for a younger generation as the dominant mainstream cinema in France.

The phenomenal success of Hollywood films with foreign audiences cannot be accounted for by economic power alone. It has also been explained by their ability to seem at once instantly familiar but also specifically "other"; allowing for the transmission of what appear to be universal values and shared aesthetics, which are then customised and reinterpreted by local audiences (O'Regan 1992, 332-33). Of course, French audiences' fascination with Hollywood is not a new phenomenon, and is almost as old as cinema itself. However, for a younger generation of French spectators (and popular youth-oriented filmmakers such as Kassovitz) who have grown up with Hollywood as arguably the dominant cinema in terms of screen exposure (in both cinemas and on television) and market share, American cinema appears less and less as the exotic "other". Recent technological advances in global communications (beginning in the 1980s, but which have had a more profound impact since the 1990s) and the increasing prominence of transnational, multi-media corporations, have further eroded the geographical, temporal and cultural markers of national boundaries. They can thus help explain this subtle but significant shift, whereby the ubiquity and immediacy of Hollywood, its films, stars and iconography, has made American cinema more familiar than ever before to contemporary French audiovisual consumers. This is not to suggest that French spectators perceive Hollywood stars as any less glamorous or their films any less spectacular than before; rather that our ability as consumers to access all forms of Hollywood "product" has rendered them less exotic in terms of their distance from our everyday lives and their cultural difference.

Central to this transformation of Hollywood's place within French audiovisual culture in the 1990s and 2000s is the fact that technological advances have introduced modes of reception that further familiarise foreign audiences with Hollywood. Until the arrival of home video and the deregulation of French television in the mid 1980s, previous generations of spectators would have viewed Hollywood films exclusively in cinemas—a collective, semi-public experience which necessarily removes the individual from the familiar surroundings of their domestic environment and transports them to another (fictional) world on-screen. Today, audiences are just as likely to watch/consume Hollywood in the intimate surroundings of their own home, through terrestrial and satellite television, DVD home cinema and even downloaded from the internet.

Previously, going to see a Hollywood film was conceived almost exclusively in terms of an excursion or social outing (the audience seeking out Hollywood as the distant and exotic "other" culture). Now, in addition to the traditional cinema-going experience, Hollywood "comes to us"; it is transmitted directly into our homes, onto laptops and portable DVD players as never before, permeating more deeply the experiences and cultural practices of our everyday lives as a result. Kassovitz's own comments in interviews regarding his exposure to American cinema provides anecdotal evidence of this shift in cinematic consumption–for while he speaks of returning to the same Parisian cinema for almost year to watch repeated screenings of *American graffiti* (Lucas, 1973) in the early 1980s, he also comments on how he has "learnt" from American cinema through repeated home viewings on laser disc, video and, more recently, DVD (Kassovitz 1998).

The reality, then, that these American cultural influences are now, for better or worse, embedded within French national cinema and, more generally, into what Hall refers to as "global mass culture" (1995, 29). As Tom O'Regan notes, Hollywood has become less an American property on loan to the rest of the world, more a shared transnational cultural resource that is customised or re-coded by local audiences and incorporated into the national cinematic idiom by local filmmakers (1992, 336).

One further point to add here is that, despite the inequalities of power that exist between French cinema and Hollywood, France is, of course, not powerless to resist. Indeed, for many filmmakers of Kassovitz's generation, such as Erick Zonca and Laetitia Masson, who identify themselves unambiguously with the auteur tradition, French cinema defines itself precisely *against* the Hollywood "other" (Ferenczi *et al.* 1999, 18-21). Further resistance to this perceived American "coca-colonisation" of French national cinema can be seen in Lang's policies during the 1980s, which attempted to introduce a whole raft of reforms relating to production, distribution and exhibition that would allow a clearly identified French national cinema to compete with Hollywood for popular audiences and thus retain the dominant share of the domestic box office. The fact that Lang's initiatives largely failed–by the beginning of the 1990s, Hollywood had in fact increased its share of French audiences, who only returned in the late 1990s with the arrival of a number of new French youth-orientated blockbusters influenced in no small part by the genres and production practices of Hollywood–is proof that cultural policy cannot necessarily determine audience tastes, and further evidence of the affinity amongst a new generation of French cultural consumers and practitioners with Hollywood.

Of course, France's ambivalent relationship with American culture–of which cinema has served as the most prominent example–characterised by fascination and appropriation, on the one hand, and hostility and resistance to the American "invasion" on the other, has persisted since at least the early twentieth century (Vincendeau 1992, 51-57). However, in a transnational media age where images of Americanised popular culture permeate national cultural borders more easily, carry an increasing weight within popular youth cultures throughout the world, and are more accessible than ever before, American popular culture (including cinema), now forms an identifiable part of French popular culture beyond any mere influence or imported trend.

Thus, in the context of Kassovitz's cinema–and, indeed, for an increasing number of young French directors–to speak of cross-cultural "exchange" between American and French cinema or an imitation of Hollywood is something of a misnomer. Firstly because, as has already been highlighted, the relationship between French and American cinema is anything but equal. But also because the references to Hollywood and American cinema that appear in the films of directors such as Kassovitz, Gans, Kounen and Pitof are not borrowed or imported as such but rather constitute elements that have been assimilated for some time and are now embedded in French film culture (it is, after all, hard to import something that, to varying degrees, you already possess). Just as in *La Haine* Vinz (Vincent Cassel) stares into the bathroom mirror and aggressively appropriates Robert De Niro's "you talking to me" speech from *Taxi Driver* (Scorsese, 1976) as a means of articulating (in crude French) the frustration, anger and ultimate powerlessness felt by the alienated male youth of the run-down working-class estates of the *banlieue*, so Kassovitz has consistently internalised and appropriated the influence of American cinema into his own brand of French popular cinema.

Les Rivières pourpres: interfacing with Hollywood

If, in *La Haine*, French critics were largely positive about Kassovitz's re-appropriation of American cinematic influences within a specifically French socio-cultural context, they have been less generous with later work, in particular *Les Rivières pourpres*. A crime thriller adapted from the best-selling French novel of the same name by Jean-Christophe Grangé,[9] *Les Rivières pourpres* was intended by Kassovitz to be a French version of contemporary American psychological thrillers such as *Seven* (David Fincher, 1995) and *Silence of the Lambs* (Jonathan Demme, 1991) (cited in Dupy and Guillomeau 2000). The director's first French blockbuster established a new alliance with the French mainstream (producer Alain Goldman and French major Gaumont) and a budget of 100 million francs (15 million euros) as well as the opportunity to work with one of France's biggest stars (Jean Reno).

With its emphasis on serial killers and explosive action sequences, *Les Rivières pourpres* seems more in keeping with American thrillers than the traditional conventions and concerns of the French crime film (the *policier* or *polar*). The post-war *policier* has traditionally functioned as a vehicle for articulating France's fascination with American culture and seduction by American-style consumerism, as well as a means of expressing equally strong feelings of hostility and ambivalence towards the increasing influence of American cultural and economic power over contemporary French culture and society (see Forbes 1992, 47-53; Vincendeau 1992, 50-80). In this respect, the *policier* seems the natural genre for Kassovitz to explore his own fascination with American cinema and popular culture more generally.

While *Les Rivières pourpres* undoubtedly maintains this generic "dialogue" with Hollywood, it also needs to be understood in the context of the decline in popularity of the *policier* in the 1990s, which inevitably forced the genre in new directions in order to survive. Though widely regarded as a staple genre of French popular cinema since the 1940s, by the late 1990s, when Kassovitz commenced production on *Les Rivières pourpres*, the *policier* was in decline as a result of changes in audience tastes and production trends in French cinema. On the one hand, the *policier*'s function as a means for articulating social concerns was usurped in the 1990s by the more direct engagement with political and social issues found in the work of a disparate wave of independent filmmakers under the loosely defined rubric of New Realism or the *retour du politique*. On the other, in terms of popular genre cinema, a more mature, middle-class French audience was displaying an increasing preference for the heritage film, while younger audiences were opting for the visual pleasures of big-budget, spectacular action films such as the *Taxi* series, *Le Pacte des loups* and *Le Cinquième élément* (Besson, 1997).

Kassovitz was astute enough to realise that by 2000 the *policier* no longer held the same attraction for French audiences; *Les Rivières pourpres* thus distances itself quite clearly from many (though not all) of the traditional codes and conventions of the French crime film, taking its cue much more directly from American cinema. Most obviously, the film dispenses with the *policier*'s traditional emphasis on the nature of crime and its repression, an approach that attempts a psychological exploration of either the criminal or law enforcer and an emphasis on reflection over action.

Kassovitz has spoken of how this decision to prioritise energy and movement in *Les Rivières pourpres*–not simply in terms of action on screen, but also narrative structure and editing style–was largely dictated by the constraints of the genre; by which he means the American crime thriller rather than the French *policier* (Dupy and Guillomeau 2000). As at least one reviewer (Péron 2000) pointed out, the chase scenes in *Les Rivières pourpres* identify Kassovitz as one of the few contemporary French directors capable of competing with Hollywood in this type of kinetic, action-suspense sequence.

And yet, even if Kassovitz borrows extensively from the American crime thriller in terms of a reliance on the buddy cop duo and a fast-paced, action-led narrative, he nonetheless uses these elements to adapt a best-selling *roman policier* in a decidedly French setting. Moreover, at key points in the film, Kassovitz deliberately distances the narrative from the American action-film model; for example, Niémans (the world-weary detective) and Fanny (a local alpine guide and suspect in the case) are taken by helicopter to the glacier in search of clues that will lead them to the next body. Whereas the American action/spectacle film moves us relentlessly from one thrill to the next, in *Les Rivières pourpres* the glacier sequence functions almost as a moment of retreat and reflection. As if to highlight this point, it is the more cerebral and physically unconditioned Niémans who ventures in to the Alps with Fanny, not the young, athletic Cassel (the star body who, more in keeping with Hollywood action heroes such as Tom Cruise and Bruce Willis, would have propelled the narrative forward, as he does elsewhere in the film). This foregrounding of spectacle over narrative provides a link to the French *cinéma du look* of the 1980s: Kassovitz's filming of the Alps could be compared to Besson's use of the ocean environment as spectacle in *Le Grand bleu* (1988). Moreover, Kassovitz's use of mountain scenery as a means of establishing the foreboding and oppressive mood of the film is, equally, consistent with the classic French *policiers* of the 1950s in which, unlike the American crime film were "also concerned with atmospheric scenes which do not advance the plot to any extent" (Vincendeau 1992, 72).

If *Les Rivières pourpres* does indeed maintain continuity with the traditional post-war *policier*, it is largely through the genre's function as a means of exploring the relationship between French and American cinema/culture. Unlike the French crime films of the 1940s and 1950s, *Les Rivières pourpres* does not speak of a fear or ambivalence but, rather a fascination with Americanisation (or we might even say the dangers of an *excessive* fascination with the Americanisation that is now embedded in French popular culture). Moreover, this dialogue with America is posited on a specifically cinematic (as opposed to sociological) level and is indicative of a broader shift in French production practices of the 1990s and 2000s as they attempt to win back popular audiences from Hollywood. However, in *Les Rivières pourpres*, Kassovitz's reverence for contemporary American cinema ultimately proves a restrictive rather than liberating influence. Rather than transposing American influences into a specifically French context as he had done so successfully in both *Métisse* and *La Haine*, in *Les Rivières pourpres* Kassovitz attempts to forge an uncomfortable alliance between American and French/European production practices, narrative modes and film style. Consequently, the film appears to collapse under the weight of its ultra-codified references to the action film and American crime thriller, which sit incongruously with the more French and European influences in the film.

Conclusion: "using Hollywood"

In spite of a poor reception from the critics, the success of Kassovitz's two most recent features, *Gothika* and *Les Rivières pourpres*, with a popular youth audience in France supports the argument advanced in this chapter that an affinity and familiarity with Hollywood is now (for better or worse) firmly embedded within French popular film culture. Though certainly not the first French director to engage with Hollywood in this way, in a national cinema that has made strategic use of the auteur's cultural cachet in order to mark its difference from Hollywood (Powrie 1999, 8), Kassovitz is seen by many to side more closely with the American "invaders" than the defenders of French cultural exception.

As O'Regan reminds us, Hollywood's international appeal creates a kind of common mythological space (as powerful as it is problematic) which functions as an agent for the re-stratification of national cultural commodities. In doing so, Hollywood "separates the elite from mass or popular taste and threatens the cultural hegemony enjoyed by national cultural elites" (1992, 334). Kassovitz's films, and in particular his two most recent features address this issue of how national cinema in France is to be defined and promoted. What is more, they reveal the refusal within certain areas of the French film industry to acknowledge either that this cultural resonance with Hollywood (especially among youth audiences and certain filmmakers) contributes to the identity of French cinema in the 2000s, or that a popular youth-orientated cinema such as that produced by Kassovitz, Besson, Kounen and others may in fact occupy a legitimate space within French national cinema alongside the more established and "accepted" practices of the auteur film and popular genres such as comedy and the heritage film.

In contrast to widespread ambivalence towards Hollywood, Kassovitz embraces these transnational influences as a potential source of enrichment in his cinema. And yet, although his films display an obvious passion for American cinema, Hollywood does not remain Kassovitz's sole point of reference. Nor, indeed, are these influences from American cinema limited to the mainstream; alongside Spielberg, Kassovitz draws on the work of directors such as Scorsese and Spike Lee–filmmakers who occupy an uncertain position in relation to the Hollywood mainstream–as well as the mavericks of low-budget exploitation cinema such as George A. Romero and Sam Raimi (Higbee 2006, 9, 22). *Les Rivières pourpres*, equally, owes a debt to European directors such as Dario Argento and Besson.[10]

Similarly, while Kassovitz understands the "business" of American cinema, his relationship to Hollywood is not necessarily one of subservience and unquestioning loyalty that rejects the production practices and difference of French cinema. In fact, he has criticised Hollywood for its fetishisation of the star (resulting in over-inflated salaries for often mediocre actors) and its obsession with marketing and promotion–claiming that a film such as *Gothika* could have been made in France for half the cost of its $40 million budget (Aubel 2003, 24). Rather than becoming an exiled mercenary in Hollywood following *Gothika*, Kassovitz has, instead, expressed a desire to alternate between big-budget (internationally funded) genre cinema–such as his current science-fiction project *Babylon AD* (for which shooting commenced in late 2006)–and a more personal, experimental and even oppositional cinema produced mainly in France (Jeffries 2001). Evidence that the militant edge to Kassovitz's film practice has not been blunted by successive collaborations with Gaumont and Warner Brothers can be found in his role as co-producer (via Kasso Inc) of *Neg'Marron* (Jean-Claude Flamand-Barny, 2005) a low-budget feature foregrounding the experiences of disenfranchised island youth in Guadeloupe and one of the few films since Euzhan Palcy's *Rue Cases-Nègres* (1983) to give a voice to a director of French-Caribbean origin.

Rather than offering an empty imitation of Hollywood, Kassovitz thus "uses" American cinema: as an important (though, as the earlier example of *Les Rivières pourpres* shows, not unproblematic) cinematic reference point, but also as an economic and industrial resource that will permit him in the future to make more ambitious, more personal films. This approach displays a keen understanding of what Maltby refers to as Hollywood's "commercial aesthetic" (2003, 7-14), a symbiotic relationship between "art" and "business" that is essentially opportunistic in its economic practices, and one which Kassovitz hopes will allow him to realise his global ambitions as a filmmaker.

---

[1] This chapter is a version of a larger study of Kassovitz's work by the author. See Higbee (2006).

[2] Une nouvelle génération de producteurs et de réalisateurs arrive...le cinéma social et sombre a donné beaucoup de films, peu de bons... Le réalisateur cherche désormais à plaire à son public.

[3] For further discussion of these films see Moine and Molia in this volume.

[4] For details of the critical response to Kassovitz's output post-*La Haine*, see Higbee (2006, 111-114, 130, 146).

[5] While acknowledging the failings and limitations of these later films, I have argued elsewhere (Higbee 2006, 127-61) against this idea of simply rejecting *Les Rivières pourpres* and *Gothika* as poor imitations of Hollywood.

[6] See, for example, Bourguignon and Tobin (1995, 8-13) in which interviewers from *Positif* are happy discussing the influence of Lee and Scorsese on *La Haine*, though appear more reluctant to engage with Kassovitz's enthusiasm for Spielberg's influence on his filmmaking style.

[7] To give an indication of trends since the mid 1990s, between 1995 and 2004 Hollywood commanded an average of approximately 53% of French cinema audiences, compared to that of 35% for French productions. All figures available online at www.cnc.fr (accessed 7 July 2005).

[8] In the past, a film such as *Diva* (Beineix, 1981) produced on a relatively modest budget with no recognisable stars and by a then-unknown director, took more than a year to establish itself in independent French cinemas before winning awards at the French Césars and then crossing over to a mainstream audience. This situation would be almost impossible in France today where, with fewer independent and art-house cinemas, films are withdrawn from the screens of larger exhibitors if they fail to make a substantial return within the first few weeks.

[9] Jean-Christophe Grangé, *Les Rivières pourpres* (Paris: Albin Michel, 1998).

[10] For a more detailed discussion of "European" influences in *Les Rivières pourpres*, see Higbee (2006, 154-6, 162).

CHAPTER TWELVE

HAVING THE LAST LAUGH: REPRESENTATIONS OF JEWISHNESS IN THOMAS GILOU'S *LA VÉRITÉ SI JE MENS!* (1997) AND *LA VÉRITÉ SI JE MENS! 2* (2001)

JOSEPH MCGONAGLE

A surprise hit of 1997, Thomas Gilou's *La Vérité si je mens!* was a major blockbuster in France; attracting a million cinemagoers in its opening fortnight despite stiff competition from Luc Besson's eagerly-awaited *Le Cinquième élément* (1997) (Blumenfeld 1997, 29). Easily Gilou's most successful film thus far, it became one of the big hits in France that year, with over 4.8 million viewers (Grassin 2001, 52-53).

Clearly, *La Vérité si je mens!* resonated with French audiences and it is intriguing to ponder why a film with an explicit focus upon a minority culture met with such widespread success. The representation of minority groups within popular comedies is not uncommon and French audiences' penchant for popular comedy as a genre has already been noted (Hayward 1993, 10; Harris 2000, 217). Indeed critics cited the film's humour, ensemble cast and dialogue as significant factors behind its popularity (Anon. 1997, 4; Coppermann 1997). It also benefited from a particularly effective marketing campaign, which allowed it to tour the provinces before general release, where preview screenings in a dozen towns and cities attracted 15,000 viewers. In addition, it was widely promoted on French television.

The subject of Jewishness has featured repeatedly in French cinema, and other films since the 1970s (particularly comedies) have also explored contemporary Jewish experience within France, examples being: Gérard Oury's *Les Aventures de Rabbi Jacob* (1973) and *Lévy et Goliath* (1987); Mathieu Kassovitz's *Métisse* (1993); Ariel Zeïtoun's *XXL* (1997); Jean-Jacques Zilbermann's *L'Homme est une femme comme les autres* (1998);

Pascale Bailly's *Dieu est grand, je suis toute petite* (2001); and Roschdy Zem's *Mauvaise Foi* (2006). Beyond comedy, Jewishness features as a prominent theme in Martine Dugowson's *Mina Tannenbaum* (1994); Mathieu Kassovitz's *La Haine* (1995); Renaud Cohen's *Quand on sera grand* (2001); and Karin Albou's *La Petite Jérusalem* (2005). A pertinent comparative example from Belgium is Sam Garbarski's *Le Tango des Rashevski* (2003). However, the remarkable success of *La Vérité si je mens 1* and *2* render the films particularly pertinent for academic investigation.

This chapter will therefore look at how Gilou portrays Jewishness and ethnic difference through popular comedy, a highly successful genre in France in which any challenge to social order is set against the need to attract large audiences. It will begin by analysing the characteristics of the–largely Sephardic–Jewish community Gilou's first film creates. This will lead to a discussion of its use of stereotyping and the significance of its ending for its meaning as a whole. It will also argue that, if the ethnicity of some of the actors who make up this community is considered, the question of authenticity is raised. The sequel, *La Vérité si je mens! 2* (2001) will then be addressed, assessing how Gilou's earlier depiction of a French Jewish community comes to symbolise France as a nation and its resistance to globalisation.

La Vérité si je mens! (1997)

The device Gilou uses in order to introduce viewers to his Jewish community is far from novel: as in his previous works, one's entry is gained via an outsider who manages to penetrate the group in question, here the Gentile Eddie Vuibert, who pretends to be Jewish. This narrative strategy is not uncommon in other French films that focus on Jewishness, which have also created comedy from Jews trying to pass as Gentiles, and Gentiles trying to pass as Jews.[1]

Gilou represents Jewishness in a number of ways. First and foremost, Jewish characters are shown to be a close-knit community. Benzakem's act of benevolence towards the destitute Eddie is the first of a series of actions that asserts that the characters, despite disagreements, function as a group. This spirit of togetherness is such that even when Eddie and his former boss become rivals, their mutual respect for one another remains intact.

An early scene in a nightclub, where Dov introduces Eddie to many members of this community, conveniently presents them to viewers and simultaneously reasserts that everyone there who belongs to this social grouping knows one another. As this group is so tight-knit, their keenness to establish the origins of any newcomers seems scarcely surprising: witness the constant quizzing Eddie faces about his own background and the scene at Dov's mother's house during Sabbath where he clumsily explains his name and family's origins. Any doubts are ultimately smoothed over when, despite her family appearing unconvinced, Dov's mother brings the matter to a close by insisting that if Eddie says he is Jewish then his word will do. This community seems, therefore, more based on consensus than conflict, in keeping with conventions of comedy and popular cinema.

Its bonds are not solely fraternal but also linguistic. Jewish expressions, such as the title uttered by Serge, recur throughout but tellingly the words "pathos" and "goy" (both synonyms for "Gentile") are the ones heard most frequently, revealing the group's preoccupation with ethnic origins. Moreover, there are repeated warnings that this Jewish community can be less than tolerant towards outsiders. When Eddie asks Dov how many non-Jews live in the Sentier (the main Jewish *quartier* in Paris), Dov replies that they would last no longer than two months there, but fails to elaborate why. He does know an Armenian man who lives there–whom, coincidentally, everyone also assumes is Jewish–and adds that, after all, "he hasn't got the word 'Gentile' written on his forehead" (ce n'est pas marqué sur son front qu'il est goy): an acknowledgement that Jewishness (or gentile origins) is not in fact necessarily or immediately visible. This might explain why Eddie's origins attract such scrutiny, for if Jewishness were readily identifiable, no questions would need to be asked. As will become clear, this preoccupation is also linked to this group's insistence upon endogamy.

Given the plot, another characteristic of this community is its focus on business. Set in the textile industry of Le Sentier, several storylines revolve around business deals and Serge and Patrick frequently discuss money matters, at times appearing solely motivated by them. Such an emphasis automatically risks courting certain stereotypes, which will be addressed shortly. This world of business is also one run by men and the main action centres upon them. Women are only seen in the context of their relationships with men, have little else to occupy their lives and are not well-rounded characters. Although more prominent towards the end– as Eddie and Sandra prepare for marriage and Dov is reunited with Karine–women are often merely objects of the male, heterosexual gaze; from the dancing women on television at Dov's house to the scantily-clad Karine and Muriel who join Dov in Patrick's swimming pool. The only strong female characters belong to an older generation: Dov's and

Sandra's mothers are more powerful figures but conform to the stereotype of the interfering and inquisitive Jewish mother, interrogating Eddie on his family background and marital availability, and only appear briefly.

Certain Jewish religious practices also feature frequently, asserting the centrality of Judaism within the lives of those who belong to this group. At the start, Victor finds a Magen David (or Star of David) on the floor beside Eddie, which Victor presumes is his and then serves as Eddie's gateway into that community. Furthermore, characters are specifically established as religious: before handing Eddie the Magen David, Victor kisses it and tells him "don't lose it again; it's a sin" (la perd plus: c'est péché), and the ensuing scene humorously shows its distraught former owner frantically searching the pavement. Equally, Eddie's mistake in turning up to work on Saturday serves as a pretext to show the Sabbath as a day of rest. Religious customs are glimpsed throughout: no more so than when Dov invites Eddie to share the Sabbath with his family. The subsequent scene effectively functions as an introduction to Jewish religious practice on that day, and shows Eddie unwittingly breaking many of its rules, such as drinking all the ceremonial wine the family should share and talking when supposed to remain silent. Further customs are flouted whilst Eddie and Sandra prepare for marriage: during their visit to a synagogue, Eddie repeatedly calls their rabbi "Father" (mon père) and tries to brush over religious protocol–even offering a financial incentive to the rabbi to do so.

Jokes aside, perhaps the strongest aspect of Judaism evoked is the characters' recurrent insistence on endogamy, another reason why Eddie's origins preoccupy so many. Many groups within Judaism–and particularly Orthodox ones–have traditionally discouraged exogamy, although attitudes are changing within certain communities (de Lange 2000, 113-14). Here this tradition seems secure: Sandra's mother beseeches Eddie never to marry a "pathos"; Dov's sister pities Eddie after deducing that his father could not have been Jewish; and before marrying Sandra, Dov seeks Eddie's reassurance that he really is a Jew. The disbelief of Serge–the film's clown–when Patrick insists that he does indeed intend to marry the non-Jew, Effi, proves this point forcefully.

Yet, when it becomes clear that Eddie is not in fact Jewish, an exception is suddenly made to this rule. Significantly, it is the older generation that first seem prepared to relent, with Benzakem telling his wife and friends that Sandra will marry whoever she wants and that such a marriage is not uncommon. Endogamy is clearly negotiable here and, just as Eddie appeared to convince Patrick that his fiancée need not convert to Judaism, the film's message becomes that love conquers all: after a year apart, Sandra and Eddie are finally reconciled, with her, appropriately enough, reciting to him the words he once told her, that "nothing is stronger [than love]" (il n'y a rien de plus fort). The final shots reaffirm this as, to the cheers of watching friends, the two kiss and walk away hand-in-hand before embracing by the Eiffel Tower; this iconic symbol of Paris–a city often connoted as romantic–effectively blessing their union. With such a fairytale ending–its neat resolution another hallmark of popular cinema–*La Vérité si je mens!* asserts that this Jewish community can tolerate difference and accept non-Jews within it, and the location suggests a wider resonance: people, whoever and wherever they are, can overcome their differences. This is how Aïssa Djabri, one of the film's producers, would have it, stating that "the film's raison d'être is an instance of integration" (la raison d'être du film est un phénomène d'intégration) (Blumenfeld 1997, 29).

Such an ending in fact goes against the grain of preceding events as it is the first and only time that this near self-contained community is identified within a larger national space. Excepting Eddie and Effi, no other main characters are identified as non-Jews. There is almost no interaction outside this grouping and the focus remains steadfastly within it. Gilou did, however, deliberately cast actors of differing ethnic origin in order to increase the diversity within this Jewish community, which although largely connoted as Sephardic contains glimpses of Ashkenazi Jews.[2]

Nevertheless, the opening scenes provide an omen of this community's relative lack of porosity. When Eddie stumbles into the courtyard outside Benzakem's company, he passes below a sign that reveals its name to viewers: "American Dream". France's ambivalent relationship with the US aside, this name is all the more ironic, given that, arguably, the community in question resembles the communitarianism often branded in France as "American" or "Anglo-Saxon" and routinely lambasted in French politics and media.[3]

As will have become clear, in many ways *La Vérité si je mens!* incorporates a number of stereotypes about Jews. However, during an interview, its scriptwriters–Michel Munz and Gérard Bitton–seemed attentive to Jewish sensibilities, stating that the members of the general Jewish community they consulted were "sceptical at first. Talking about Jews in terms of sex and money, and no longer broaching the Holocaust were three complete taboos. Nevertheless, it worked and helped the film be a success" (Anon. 2001).[4] If these are taboos then they were certainly flouted. The film's stereotypes include the Jewish mother as matriarch and matchmaker, whilst the decision to base it in the Sentier verges on caricature given that several other films have also been set there, which effectively connotes the area as *the* centre of Jewish experience in France. This has the effect of grounding the group territorially, despite their excursions elsewhere.

Whilst it appears that the filmmakers received help and support from local residents whilst filming in the Sentier (Théate 1997, 34), one may wonder how Jewish groups and people responded to the film, especially given that its promotional campaign explicitly targeted the "Jewish community" in France (Blumenfeld 1997, 29). [5] The director and scriptwriters claimed that *La Vérité si je mens!* had received a favourable response from most Jewish viewers, but not all: it reportedly angered one critic on the newspaper *Tribune juive*; but this was not enough to prevent the newspaper's editors from promoting it (Waintrop 1997, 4).

Yet there is a twist in the tale: the actor who plays Eddie, the *goy* pretending to be a Jew, is in fact Jewish. Once describing himself in an interview as "Jewish, born to Jewish parents in an Italian-Moroccan family", Richard Anconina has played diverse roles throughout his career, for example a young man of North African origin in Claude Berri's *Tchao Pantin* (1983) and a young Catholic in Claude Lelouch's *Partir revenir* (1985) (Hammer 1986, 82).[6] He also memorably played an Orthodox Jew in Gérard Oury's *Lévy et Goliath* (1987) –an intriguing precursor to *La Vérité si je mens!*–where his character, Moïse Lévy, must remove all signs of his religious belief in order to escape from the criminal gang pursuing him. A certain irony results, therefore, from the fact that here Anconina is the only non-Jew played by an actor of Jewish origins. Taking into account the ethnicity of actors runs the risk of (overly) judging their performance according to whether they share the same heritage or belief as the characters they play. Whilst it might seem more "authentic" for an actor of Jewish origin to play a Jewish character, non-Jewish actors might just as ably play such roles: to argue otherwise would equal essentialism and leads to the pigeonholing many actors strive to escape.[7]

In a film where one of the main structuring motifs revolves around Eddie's dissimulation of his gentile origins from Jewish friends and colleagues, the knowledge that Anconina himself is Jewish does alter Eddie's alterity. No longer such an outsider from the outset, knowing viewers will have to suspend their disbelief twice: once that an outsider can successfully pass himself off as Jewish and again that Anconina is a non-Jew forced to pretend he is Jewish. This could have the reverse effect from the one Gilou intended, lessening any sense of interaction between Jews and those outside their community and reinforcing the idea that its doors largely remain closed. Such a reading, however, assumes that

Anconina's ethnicity is already known to the spectator: *La Vérité si je mens!* was seen as Anconina's comeback after his success in the 1980s, so younger audiences might in fact have been less familiar with him and assumed he is *goy* too. This aspect aroused little media attention; neither did the ethnicity of any of Anconina's fellow actors who played Jews.[8] Consider for instance the actor who plays Serge, José Garcia, a non-Jew born in Paris but whose parents hail from Galicia (Baudin 2001, 30). As Garcia's presence indicates, an actor of non-Jewish origin could have played Eddie and undoubtedly met with similar success, but given Anconina's own ethnicity and film career, his presence in this role foregrounds the importance of authenticity in the representation of ethnicity.[9]

La Vérité si je mens! 2 (2001)

After the success of *La Vérité si je mens!*, a sequel seemed inevitable: *La Vérité si je mens!* 2 was duly released in 2001. Despite a few minor changes–most notably Gad Elmaleh replacing Vincent Elbaz as Dov–the main cast remained the same, but the budget more than tripled, increasing from 25 to 82 million francs, therefore allowing shooting in several national and international locations, more elaborate sets and a greater cast (Grassin 2001, 52-53). The film's financiers clearly hoped it would emulate the success of its predecessor and their investment was rewarded, as more than 7.7 million viewers went to watch the sequel.[10]

Many of the original elements were retained: Gilou's humorous focus on the trials and tribulations of the now familiar group of Jewish friends remained but his formula had slightly, but significantly, changed. Although ostensibly still centred on Eddie, this time his fellow characters became more important. With the Jewishness of Eddie–or lack of it– seemingly no longer an issue, the sequel's narrative instead revolves around a business deal of Eddie's that turns sour and derives much of its comedy from Serge, rather than Eddie, having to keep up a pretence.

Like its predecessor, the sequel emphasises a strong sense of community, and the group remain as fraternal as ever. Still very much a team, their mutual efforts are ultimately rewarded when they succeed in duping Eurodiscount (which, as will be explained, serves as a metaphor for international big business) and more than recoup their losses. The film even ends with the five main male friends alone, frolicking on the beach together after Serge's wedding to Chochana.

Nonetheless, their success does not disguise the fact that this is, again, more a community of men than of men and women and that those women who do appear are just as–if not more–problematic than in the first film. Gilou's rather unsubtle representation of women is signalled at the start by Patrick's deployment of a young, attractive woman to lure Serge to the surprise birthday party he has thrown for him. Although the decoy proves a good actress and the joke is on Serge–his rampant lust makes him stumble naked into a room of waiting guests–her body serves, predictably, as little more than bait, even if Serge is made to look ridiculous. The main female stars fare little better, with several gratuitous shots of Karine and Chochana in various states of undress; at one point Karine even begins pole dancing in a nightclub. Generally in the background, and mostly given two-dimensional roles, women only appear as mothers, devoted wives or temptresses. Little wonder that one critic described Gilou's representation of Jewish women as stereotypical, appearing as "randy, capricious and hysterical" (chaudes, capricieuses et hystériques) (Konopnicki 2001). The philandering Dov and Patrick treat them as little else and conversation between men revolves repeatedly around previous and future female sexual conquests.

Like women, religion is also largely sidelined, as although some scenes contain references to Judaism, its importance within the narrative is greatly diminished. Furthermore, the previous film's preoccupation with Eddie's Jewishness has evaporated by the sequel and no reference is made to it. Eddie appears at ease uttering Jewish expressions like his friends and also wears a skullcap at Serge's wedding; he now appears to have been completely accepted–as the original film's ending suggested–but the question of whether Eddie has converted to Judaism remains elided.

In place of religion, the worship of money holds sway: signifiers of wealth recur frequently, from Patrick's convertible Rolls-Royce to the large houses and elite locations the characters frequent. Ostentation rather than discretion is *de rigueur* and is symbolised by Yvan and Eddie's transformation of the Charles Aznavour song *La bohème* into "Ma BM", a French expression for a BMW car (Attali 2001a). Even more than ever, Gilou risks reproducing stereotypical representations of Jews: none more so than the common myth that dictates that they are money-motivated and obsessed by business. Moreover, the main storyline again pivots around financial deals:

> In *La Vérité si je mens! 2*, pied-noir Jews smoke cigars, drive convertibles, wear loudly-coloured shirts and are champions at golf. They talk loudly, are always telling jokes, bribe the rabbi, own a beach in Saint-Tropez called Benhamou Beach, and end up earning a fortune. Their wealth constitutes their identity; another cliché, and one you are allowed not to laugh at. (Blumenfeld 2001, 32)[11]

Such criticism is all too true: on many levels the depiction of Jewishness in *La Vérité si je mens! 2* remains facile and cliché-ridden. Nevertheless, what is intriguing is how this group of characters now come to symbolise the French nation at large. The sequel taps into contemporary French discourses on anti-globalisation and criticism of multinational companies, both of which allow this group of friends to remain Jewish but also to become national heroes.[12]

Whereas the opening credits of the original film situated very clearly where the action was to take place–showing a series of objects evoking the Sentier and its textile industry–the second film starts rather differently. It parodies the famous opening credits of James Bond films, replete with dancing women and dramatic theme tune. Patrick even poses as 007, thereby suggesting that he and his friends now rival Anglo-American superheroes. This transformation augurs further changes: as the plot makes clear, the characters have now outgrown the Sentier and consequently are no longer so tied to Paris, returning to Deauville but now also visiting St Tropez, Tunisia and even Los Angeles.

It is their battle with the multinational hypermarket chain Euro Discount–described as the second biggest retailer of its kind in Europe–that ultimately helps associate the group as both Jewish and French. The etymology of their rivals' names undoubtedly helps, as the word *euro* conjures up the threat of European homogeneity, *discount* a lack of quality, and the surname of its senior buyer, Vierhouten, sounds decidedly non-Gallic. The logo of the company incorporates a large euro symbol (€) too, perhaps signalling covert criticism of European monetary union, if not the EU itself. It is clear that Euro Discount's practices also allow the film to demonise big business and it is no coincidence that the European giant with which they are about to merge is called Kommercia–a near-homonym for *commerce*, a French term for business.

When Eddie subsequently delivers a batch of clothes to Euro Discount, he falls into their trap: Vierhouten claims that Eddie's products are undersized and tells him: "We're not in the Sentier here: there are rules that must be followed".[13] Vierhouten implies that the quality of Eddie's products does not meet Euro Discount's standards but in fact it is the Sentier's standards that come to symbolise those of the French nation at large. Forced to bring expensive legal proceedings, Eddie is literally pushed out onto the streets and has to set up a market stall in order to raise funds for their court case. The diminutiveness of their enterprise reinforces the disparity between them and the hypermarket chain. Through their ingenuity, they outfox the wily Vierhouten with an elaborate ruse. By getting Vierhouten to sign a contract for an order whose measurements were in millimetres, not centimetres, Eddie and friends manage to extract 65 million francs from the retail company, a sum tellingly not quoted in euros and thereby further disassociating them from the European company. The victory of the small Frenchman over the large foreign multinational is complete.

Such David versus Goliath symbolism did not escape critics and was highlighted in several reviews (Deymard 2001, 59; Mury 2001, 45; Konopnicki 2001). *La Vérité si je mens! 2* was even linked to the perennial opposition drawn up between French and Hollywood films: its success, following the release of French blockbusters such as *Le Placard* (Francis Véber, 2001) and *Le Pacte des loups* (Christophe Gans, 2001), seen as a rare victory for French national cinema (connoted as David) against America (inevitably Goliath) (Lalanne 2001, 36). The scriptwriters themselves affirmed this and even linked the characters to the French national hero Astérix, claiming that the group have become "Gallic heroes... The Sentier, it's Astérix's village versus the Roman Emperor, epitomised by mass-market retail" (Attali 2001b).[14] They undoubtedly have a vested interest in suggesting as much, but what is significant is that the sequel permits the successful transition of Eddie and his friends from the streets of the Sentier to further afield. The group's struggle against a European hypermarket chain symbolises many current French attitudes towards the dominance of large multinational companies and their Jewishness–ever-present even if Judaism is less so–does not prevent them from symbolically spearheading this national struggle. No longer confined to Paris, this Jewish community becomes a national signifier for French business, which takes on Europe and wins.

In conclusion, Jewishness within Gilou's films is represented in several striking ways. Both films carefully construct a sense of community by foregrounding social gatherings and celebrations and suggesting togetherness throughout. Both notably feature families, which is hardly surprising given the traditional prominence both of the family and the community within Jewish societies (de Lange 2000, 84). Yet ironically, despite the start of Gilou's first film–with Eddie as an outsider to the Jewish community constructed–little interaction is shown outside this grouping between Jews and non-Jews. It is profoundly endogamous: Eddie is accepted as a Jew from the start–and only because of this. Quite clear rules are in operation and, perhaps, as Dov says in the first film, the essential problem is that "it [Jewishness] is not visible" (ça se voit pas): Jewishness here is not readily identifiable, hence the constant questioning that Eddie faces. This reinforces the group's insistence upon endogamy and the fact that the actor who plays Eddie is of Jewish origin too only increases it. The Jewish community that Gilou creates may, as a result, appear less inclusive.

Nevertheless, in many ways, the genre Gilou's films adopt proves enabling precisely because the comedy that results from Eddie and his friends' trials and tribulations is centred around the experience of a significant minority group within France and permits a sustained focus upon their Jewish community. Furthermore, the phenomenal success and popularity of the first film arguably allow this group of Jewish friends to symbolise the French nation in the sequel–acquiring near-superhero status in their battle against a foreign multinational–a transformation facilitated by the films' comic genre. By having a Gentile try to pass as a Jew, the film also disrupts further conventions (Rollet 1998, 99); reversing expectations by having a member of an ethnic majority in France placed in a subordinate and, at times, precarious position compared to an ethnic minority. However, the way in which the Jewish community Eddie tries to penetrate is constructed relies upon another staple of comedy: ethnic, sexual and national stereotyping (Rollet 1998, 120). The convenient short cuts it provides confirm conventions rather than challenge them, and the fact both films end so happily is also typical of the resolution that popular cinema often requires.

This need for resolution may partially explain why the comedies avoid areas that might threaten it. The sequel elides the question of whether Eddie converted to Judaism and while Jewish characters constitute the majority group on-screen, the films' largely inward focus and use of comedy offer limited insight into Jewishness in France as a minority-group experience. This is especially so given the prevalence of anti-Semitism in France, instances of which have been regularly reported over the last decade but to which no reference is ever made. Furthermore, although the first film accords a significant place to Judaism, it is telling that its presence is noticeably diminished come the sequel, as the plot adopts a story of greater national resonance. Ultimately, then, viewers may be encouraged to laugh with and not at Gilou's Jewish characters, and the group's triumph over Euro Discount in the sequel ensures that Eddie and friends do have the last laugh, but the stereotyped and idealised vision of French Jewishness that seals it arguably means that that their laughter may well ring hollow.

[1] Two examples are Gérard Oury's *Les Aventures de Rabbi Jacob* (1973) and *Lévy et Goliath* (1987). Jean-Jacques Zilbermann's *L'Homme est une femme comme les autres* (1998) should also be cited given the near-miraculous conversion of Simon, the gay hedonistic non-practising Jew, into a religious married man. Indeed, passing may be a more general trope common to the representation of Jewishness in other national cinemas: with reference to the US, see Stratton 2001, 142-66.

[2] Although originally populated by Ashkenazi Jews, the Sentier is today dominated by Sephardim. See Baudin (1997, 31).

[3] It is worth noting that when American Jewish characters appear in Gérard Oury's *Les Aventures de Rabbi Jacob* (1973), Ariel Zeïtoun's *XXL* (1997) and Jean-Jacques Zilbermann's *L'Homme est une femme comme les autres* (1998) they too conform to this stereotype and are characterised as separatist Orthodox communities whereas France is depicted as a more open and liberal space. No such parallels are drawn in Gilou's film but it is telling that the French Jewish community he depicts is flexible enough to allow Eddie to remain.

[4] "Sceptique[s] au départ. Parler de sexe et d'argent chez les juifs, ne plus aborder l'Holocauste, c'était trois tabous inacceptables. Pourtant, elle [sic] a marché et permis le succès du film".

[5] Gilou claimed it even brought an economic boost to the Sentier.

[6] "Juif, né de parents juifs au sein d'une famille italo-marocaine". Although connoted throughout *Tchao Pantin* as being of North African origin, Anconina's character Bensoussan qualifies his own ethnicity within the film. He explains that, whilst his adoptive parents and biological mother were "Arabes", his biological father was Jewish.

[7] See for example the comments of Isaac Sharry, an actor of North African origin who stars in *La Vérité si je mens! 2* and has criticised the prevalence of typecasting in French cinema: "I've never seen a film in France where a *pied-noir* doesn't play a *pied-noir*, where a black actor isn't given the role of a black character. I was discussing this again with my agent, who explained to me that people only want me for either Arab or pied-noir characters. So I can't play someone called Jean-François. I'm forced to play the same role my whole life" (Je n'ai jamais vu en France de film où un pied-noir ne joue pas un pied-noir, où un Noir n'hérite pas d'un rôle de Noir. J'en parlais encore avec mon agent qui m'expliquait qu'on me voulait soit pour des rôles d'Arabe, soit pour des rôles de pied-noir. Je ne peux donc pas jouer quelqu'un qui se prénomme Jean-François. Je suis condamné à jouer toute ma vie le même personnage) (Blumenfeld 2000, 31). Ownership of experience nonetheless remains an important principle within cinema and helps avoid the appropriation of the experience of traditionally marginalised groups.

[8] To my knowledge, only one critic remarked upon it: see Richou 1997, 76.

[9] One might similarly wish to interrogate the ethnicities of the scriptwriters and director. All three are in fact of Jewish origins, though none hail from the Sentier. Whether this permits or excuses the way Jews are represented in their film remains a moot point. See Deymard 2001, 59, Attali 2001b and Anon. 2001.

---

[10] Source: <http://www.bifi.fr> (accessed 23 February 2007). When screened on French terrestrial television in 2003 it also attracted the highest number of viewers for a feature-length film that year (Mermet 2004, 425).

[11] "Dans *La Vérité si je mens!* 2, les juifs pieds-noirs fument le cigare, roulent dans des décapotables, portent des chemises aux couleurs criardes et sont des champions de golf. Ils parlent fort, blaguent en permanence, soudoient le rabbin, possèdent une plage à Saint-Tropez baptisée Benhamou Beach, et finissent par gagner des fortunes. Leur opulence devient le ciment de leur identité. Un autre cliché, auquel il est permis de ne pas rire."

[12] The sequel's marketing campaign suggested this too by linking one of the first film's catch phrases ("*champion du monde*") with the French national football team's 1998 World Cup win: one advertisement showed the backs of five French football team shirts with the main actors' names printed across them. One scene is even shot during an international football match at the Stade de France, the venue of France's 1998 World Cup-final victory.

[13] "On n'est pas dans le Sentier ici: il y a des règles à respecter."

[14] "Des héros gaulois…Le Sentier, c'est le village d'Astérix face à l'empereur romain que symbolise la grande distribution."

CHAPTER THIRTEEN

POPULAR CINEMA AND CRITICAL RECEPTION:
BOUDU, A MISUNDERSTANDING

JACQUELINE NACACHE

Within French cinema, as it is currently configured, there are some films which are marketed as popular and others which actually are popular. While these two categories do not overlap completely, the films contained within them are made with a certain number of similar intentions. These shared characteristics are evident both at a textual and a commercial level. Such films adopt "catchy" subject matter and cast well-known actors, as well as re-appropriating conventions of past box office successes, and their release is preceded by expensive marketing campaigns. However, their success can best be assessed in the light of critical reception, audience responses, box office receipts at home and abroad and sales to television networks, as well as through more informal channels such as message postings and discussions on Web forums and blogs. This article focuses on the area of critical reception and, in particular, on the notion that negative reviews by revered critics condition the way French popular cinema is defined. Such a view, which sees the tastes of the critic as being by definition set against the tastes of the public, is not a new one; it has been central to so-called art criticism more broadly since the nineteenth century, a literary illustration of which would be the character of the dandy-aesthete in decadent novels, such as Des Esseintes in Huysmans's *À rebours* (1884).

The elitism of taste has already formed a central focus of sociological studies–as the object of criticism such as in Pierre Bourdieu's work (1979), as part of an attempt to rehabilitate notions of the natural diversity of taste (Lahire 2004), and as an example of the ability of the ordinary viewer to make his/her own judgement (Leveratto 2000 and 2006). Nonetheless, art criticism's rejection of the works which appeal most to the general public is not a constant, rather a phenomenon that is tightly bound up with the specific culture and period in which it occurs, and is dependent on aesthetic issues within a given society. In France over the last fifteen years, two key developments have framed critical debates, the "crisis of contemporary art" (Michaud 1997) and the heated dispute between critics and filmmakers in 1999. The former, the most recent major controversy to affect the French art world in the twentieth century, reformulated the terms of aesthetic discussion in a manner that has ramifications for all artistic fields. This chapter probes these two crucial debates, using *Boudu* (Gérard Jugnot, 2005). It provides an illustration of the very type of popular cinema that has traditionally been frowned upon by so-called educated critics, who are suspicious of remakes of established classics combining a desire for artistic expression and large audiences.

Critics Vs filmmakers: the dispute of 1999

The dispute of 1999 began with the publication of a private letter written by Patrice Leconte, intended for his colleagues in the ARP (Société des Auteurs, Réalisateurs, Producteurs), which quickly found its way into various press outlets, and opened in the following manner:

> For some time now I have been frightened by the attitude of critics towards French cinema. I do not feel that I am more of a target than anyone else (rather less so, in fact), but I simply read what is being written here and there about our films. Some of the pages I have read, which resemble premeditated assassinations, have sent shivers down my spine, as if their authors had all conspired to kill French commercial cinema, France's popular, mass-market cinema. (Leconte 1999)[1]

Leconte's last point quite explicitly articulates his complaint as being directed not at film criticism in general, but at the treatment meted out to popular cinema specifically. But this fact was quickly forgotten, and the centre of gravity of the debate duly shifted towards the relationship between critics and filmmakers more generally, without distinguishing between popular and auteur filmmakers. This reaction can be put down partly to the treatment of the issue by the media, but more particularly to the rather confused defensive responses which came from certain filmmakers–Bertrand Tavernier in particular, who saw the situation as an opportunity to carry out a large-scale settling of accounts with the critics in general. The directors' self-pitying, recriminatory attitude doomed them to failure in a tradition of French aesthetic debate which grants more sympathy to the figure of the impertinent critic than it does to the mistreated artist demanding retribution. Retribution was, predictably, not obtained, and French cinema as a whole has continued to provoke sharp reactions in the wake of the anthology of picturesque, highly idiomatic insults that blossomed during the 1999 controversy.[2] Popular cinema became the principal focus of the strong negative views expressed in this debate, as was notably visible in the very cool reception given in some publications to *Les Choristes* (Christophe Barratier, 2004). These views contrasted with the unexpected public success of Barratier's film, which many critics tried to explain retrospectively by appropriating a sociological discourse.[3]

In fact, its success is probably more attributable to its adoption of classic dramatisation lines, colourful characters and a familiar historical setting–the post-war period. *Boudu* is particularly interesting in this context because it provides a kind of symmetry with *Les Choristes*: Jugnot was cast in the main role in both films and his performances placed him in the position of the most "bankable" French actor of the time (Mélinard 2005).

Renoir's legacy

By contrast to *Les Choristes*, which came as a surprise box office hit, *Boudu* is one of those French films which are made expressly to attract a wide popular audience, because it contains all the elements that the general public expects. Added to this is its cultural legitimacy as a remake of a recognised masterpiece of classical French cinema, *Boudu sauvé des eaux* (1932), made by one of the most prestigious French directors of the time, Jean Renoir. *Boudu sauvé des eaux* had originally been written as a play for theatre in 1919 by author-actor René Fauchois, and features a beggar (Boudu) saved from drowning against his will by a well-intentioned Parisian bookseller. Boudu's libertarian philosophies disturb the routine of the bourgeois family who take him in. Renoir saw a performance of the play starring Michel Simon in the role of Boudu in 1925, and it was the prospect of directing Simon that led him to envisage its adaptation. Simon's name was also a driving force in attracting money for the production of the film.

The character of Boudu has accrued an autonomy that exists beyond the original and, as a consequence, has inspired more recent films, for example, the American remake *Down and out in Beverly Hills* (Paul Mazursky, 1986). Jugnot's 2005 production provides the latest screen incarnation of Boudu, but the director insisted that his intention was to return to the original play, therefore diverging from the 1930s classic. However, this objective appears to have been significantly undermined by the casting of Gérard Depardieu in the main role of Boudu. Throughout the 1990s, Depardieu repeatedly set out to show that he had matured as an actor by seeking strong roles in film and on television (D'Artagnan, Jean Valjean, Monte Cristo, Bérurier in *San Antonio* (Frédéric Auburtin, 2004),[4] thereby underlining the versatility of his star persona. By taking on Simon's role, Depardieu emulates and competes with his illustrious predecessor. Consequently, despite Jugnot's remarks, it is clear that his *Boudu* owes more to Renoir's film than he would like to suggest.

The critical establishment in pieces

Boudu's association with Renoir probably explains the particularly aggressive reception it generated among the very same critics who had earlier been accused by Leconte of wanting to kill off French popular cinema (and I shall return to this later). Philippe Azoury's review in *Libération*, for example, is unusually violent:

> This is France in March 2005, and we would like to be able to have the fresh perspective and time difference (not to mention the sick bag) enjoyed by a foreign film buff who has been in France for the last two weeks and who has had the chance to witness what is inflicted upon us day in, day out. (Azoury 2005)[5]

In a rare move, Azoury then addresses the filmmaker personally:

> Oh, Saint Jugnot, actor and martyr, filmmaker and martyr, the chattering classes don't like you (chattering classes? Stick it up yer arses!), but then they don't like anybody. But judging from the way you look at people, you don't like anybody either: the bourgeoisie, the rich, they're bastards wallowing in the filth of their pathetic desires. Southerners are clowns. Working-class people are all Spaniards. So, all you're left with is Boudu (Boudu's handy like that, he's just passing through). (Azoury 2005)[6]

Vincent Ostria, writing in *Les Inrockuptibles*, adopts a near-identical register, talking of a "revolting remake... pathetically vulgar... super-cheesy" with "stereotypical Provençal sets in shades of puke yellow" (Ostria 2005).[7] In this instance, *Boudu* is described by Ostria as "even worse" than Mazursky's Hollywood remake of Renoir's film. In the light of the often disdainful reception among European critics of American-style remakes, there could be no harsher insult (see Forrest and Koos 2001, 29). Allusions to vomiting and denunciations of vulgarity equally contaminate newspapers that usually employ a more moderate tone: "Depardieu shows off his flab and vulgarity to nauseating effect. A remake we really could have done without" declared *La Tribune* (Anon.

2005),[8] rehashing the cliché of the "pointless remake", a ritualistic element of the critical establishment. In his conclusion to a very serious comparison of the evolution of the character of Boudu from Renoir's version to Jugnot's in *Le Monde*, Jean-Luc Douin cannot resist a snide and rather laboured play on words: *"Boudu* is Jugnot saved from clowning" (*Boudu*, c'est Jugnot sauvé des veaux) (Douin 2005). Similarly, in *L'Humanité*, after having first conscientiously applied conventional analytical criteria, Mélinard concludes that "it's all a bit flimsy for cinema, but quite sufficient for prime-time broadcasting on the sort of terrestrial channel the film was made for" (Mélinard 2005).[9] Beyond expressing disdain for the television-viewing public, this observation serves as a reminder that, long after it has finished playing in cinemas, a film's "popular" status is decided by its crossover to television, where social, financial and geographical barriers disappear (Mélinard 2005).[10]

Clichéd identities

Cinema is not, of course, the only field to give rise to this kind of critical attitude, and two key elements need to be taken into account in this respect. The first of these are stereotypical critical reactions which reject with disgust any works considered offensive to "good taste", however this term is construed. The second is the traditionally acerbic written style of a certain form of Parisian criticism, encouraged by a readership who finds this insolence entertaining. The debate mentioned above between the *Libération* critics and Tavernier saw some of the journalists digging in on their position in defence of the unmistakable style of the newspaper (wordplay, inside jokes, etc.), a style which many reviewers from other newspapers tried to emulate. Tavernier's reply, given without any serious hope of its being heard, was that "[i]f everybody is imitating the *style Libé*, you need to change it!" (Armanet and Vallaeys 1999).

Yet, style cannot explain everything. It would appear that the rejection of French popular cinema expressed in these disputes has certain specific characteristics and should not, therefore, be confused with other, associated forms of critical intolerance. It would also seem that a principal element in justifying the virulence of these attacks is the stereotypical Frenchness of the films in question, and the political dimension that the attacks thus inevitably take on. Elitist criticism, which sees itself as the natural heir to Enlightenment universalism, is notably characterised by its rejection of what it views as clichéd identities, and this undermines its perception of art as a supra-national phenomenon. Rarely, then, does such criticism miss a chance to label "popular" forms as politically reactionary.

Serge Kaganski's famous reaction to *Le Fabuleux destin d'Amélie Poulain* was not the first to accuse a film of exhibiting a Frenchness deemed overly exaggerated or representing a "low-fat Petainism" (pétainisme light) (Kaganski 2001). Critics have also accused the 1973 film *La Nuit américaine* (François Truffaut) of being "sentimental pap" (bouillie sentimentale) and an "almost Petainist idealisation of the minor professions of the cinema" (Anon. 1999). [11] Similarly, in 1999, Jean Becker, director of *Les Enfants du Marais,* was also referred to as a "Vichyist filmmaker" (cinéaste vichyste) (Anon. 1999). As far as *Boudu* is concerned, these accusations are put less forcefully, but their implications are nonetheless evident. Ostria compares the film to *Boeing-Boeing* (a very successful boulevard play by Camoletti which enjoyed an uninterrupted run from 1960 to 2004) and links Depardieu's performance in *Boudu* to his incarnation of Obélix. Such references to box office successes are typical of a certain type of film criticism which seeks to denigrate French popular culture as being too conservative.

Admittedly, it is not always easy to point precisely to what it is in these films that could justify such critical viewpoints. What is beyond doubt is that these comments are based on a very loose use of the terms "Vichyist" or "Petainist" (with any serious historical reference removed). These remarks are often reduced to the equivalent of the label *"franchouillard"* (salt-of-the-earth French) as applied to films which bring together in too obvious a fashion the stereotypical indicators of French identity, or more generally to a subgenre of French popular cinema (Nacache 2005). This accusation of *"franchouillardise"* is understood primarily in terms of a film's reception, that is, based on a shared understanding of the local cultural systems and values mobilised in the films. Some critics and spectators use *"franchouillard"* as a term of scorn and prejudice against popular films, and this is precisely what happened in the case of *Boudu.* The film's clichéd identity, therefore, is articulated through its cast, with three actors, Jugnot, Depardieu and Catherine Frot, whose names were already linked to major national film successes. In addition, the film's register, which is at once realist and stylised, a feature common to comedy in France, could be read as another characteristic of its grassroots Frenchness. The story is set geographically in a southern French town filmed like a brightly-coloured theatre set. Moreover, the film is full of the sociological goodwill common to comedies, notably the desire to treat a serious social issue lightly–here homelessness.

Criticism made superfluous

Boudu is a new version, then, of a recognised masterpiece of French cinema. This explains why, especially in the left-wing reviews which are culturally more aggressive, such as those in *Libération* and *Les Inrockuptibles*, a feeling of anger emerges when the critics notice that their status is being gradually undermined. In addition, their function as aesthetic mediators is reduced to a minimum.

French cinema criticism has never been under any illusions about its capacity to dictate economic concerns. Ever since it began to ponder its own existence (a self-reflective impulse that began very early on), it has not only never denied its lack of economic clout, but has in fact held this up as a guarantee of its aesthetic independence. By thus dissociating itself from the cinema industry, French criticism has come to resemble the image of the artistic institution to which it aspires, and is able to declare that it works first and foremost in the symbolic sphere, creating an artistic aura, lending support to ambitious cinematographic projects, and finally acting as an enlightened guide able to inform the tastes of cinemagoers. This, then, is a declaration both of criticism's right to exist and, following the precedent of art criticism since the eighteenth century, of its status as an indispensable body of authority once a certain stage in the democratisation of art has been reached. Once art is no longer just the preserve of an elite, the emergence of a class of experts which takes on the responsibility of evaluating artistic production develops its own momentum, and no longer has to justify its existence any more than does the artist himself.

The evolution of French popular cinema challenges the symbolic function of art criticism, and this is exemplified by *Boudu*. The status of remake conditions the reception of the "popular": while, on the one hand, the reference to a great film of the past assigns *Boudu* to a patrimonial role, on the other, it clearly seeks to transfer a film belonging to what is already seen as classic culture into the realm of pure entertainment. The process of creating the remake thus sets up a situation of *de facto* competition between filmmaker and critic, each of whom carries out his own specific mediating task: the former by translating the content of an old film into a language accessible to a wider public, the latter by doing precisely the opposite, that is to say by exercising what I have previously termed the "duty of memory" of the expert critic, who comes clothed in memories and references, and has the job of inscribing the new film within an artistic genealogy (Nacache 1999).

The mediating role of the filmmaker is in profound contradiction with the objectives of the critic-historian. The latter opposes the actions necessary within the re-reading and rewriting of an original film, that is to say changes to the setting, period and tone, as well as the adaptation of the script to suit the personalities of contemporary actors. One merely has to look at how Ostria piles up his references to Renoir, and how scandalised Azoury is by the fact that Jugnot, in an interview given to *Télérama,* had dared to consider *Boudu sauvé des eaux* as being a "minor Renoir" (2005). The remake is thus perceived by the critic as being a potential danger to cinema, but it is in fact easy to see that it poses a much greater danger to the role of criticism itself, a function whose usefulness it compromises. Indeed, in this specific case, the filmmaker trespasses onto the territory of the critic through a dual intervention in aesthetic typologies, which he effects through the exercise of an evaluative function, by providing an expert judgement which is normally the remit of the critic.

Faced with the double transgression that the remake represents, the critic only has a limited number of attitudes to choose from. Before proceeding further, it will be useful to clarify what I mean by the notion of "choice" here. I set out from the hypothesis that the discourse of French cinematographic criticism has not been free to invent its own postures, but rather has always been obliged to model them on, whether in conformity with or opposition to, existing postures drawn from other more established and legitimised fields, such as literature or the visual arts, which had already proved their worth as aesthetic attitudes. This is one way in which the critic can reaffirm cinema's place in the realm of art in spite of all the evidence to the contrary, such as the industrial mode of production of films, the "dumbing-down" of the commentary on cinema found in the media, the absorption of cinema by television, and the impossibility of including within the sphere of cinematic art those popular productions that have found favour with the majority of the public.

It is nonetheless the case that while this critical approach remained just about serviceable throughout the twentieth century, it began to break down once the central question in the aesthetic debate shifted into zones where cinema did not for the most part hold privileged status. This is what took place in the 1990s, when the debate came to focus on the dispute surrounding contemporary art, which formed the subject of a very large number of articles and books, and in which cinema did not seem to feature at all. Cinema was not, admittedly, the only artistic domain to be conspicuous by its absence from this dispute, which, as Jacques Rancière has remarked, was more or less limited to the visual arts (Rancière 2004, 36). In the case of cinema, however, this absence was probably due to quite specific reasons. It shows that the world of art is still struggling to accept cinema as one of its component parts. Consequently, it is up to the critic to constantly proclaim and maintain the artistic nature of cinema, even when this is contradicted by the quality of the films that are released in France and current activity in the cinema industry.

Disappointment/deception as a form of reception

Among the aesthetic strategies that the critics use is the imitation of the scorn of the spectator who does not understand the film. This is often deployed by critics in the context of popular cinema, just as it is by the public in their response to contemporary art. This critical attitude was a fundamental feature of the birth of aesthetics in the eighteenth century, which was, as Yves Michaud has pointed out, linked in particular to the deployment of art in the space of public reception constituted by the Salon (Michaud 2003, 106). Art was now exposed to gazes which were no longer only those of the privileged few (public or private patrons) to whom it was previously addressed, and museums and commissions brought works into direct contact with the public, thus giving the latter the opportunity to express, sometimes noisily, its reactions. The public's reception of contemporary art triggers a similar situation. It is not simply that they express their disapproval. It is rather a feeling of disappointment, of having been let down or indeed deceived. This feeling comes from a mismatch between the expectations of the public, which are formed by its implicit conception of art, and the works of art with which it is presented, which are sanctioned by artistic institutions. This feeling can take the form of simple mistrust and incomprehension, such as "I don't trust any painting that I think I could have done myself" (Chateau 1996)[12], or a much more violent form of rejection, as one finds in the reactions collected by Nathalie Heinich in her study (1998, 75-92) . These responses include the complaints from the inhabitants of La Roche-sur-Yon following the installation of a fountain by Bernard Pagès on the town's central square. These complaints are typical of the recriminations habitually levelled at contemporary art: ugliness, provocativeness, the prosaic character of forms and materials, disfigurement of the environment, and the like. Yet these reactions do in fact pinpoint rather well–and at times they share this criterion with a certain branch of criticism–the uninspired, literally insignificant, in the sense of non-signifying, character of those works that turn any attempt at expert analysis into a useless, even parasitic exercise.

Why, then, look to this sort of complaint in order to shed light on the reaction of elitist criticism to *Boudu*? The film, one might object, is highly conventional as regards its form, its performances, and its distribution. It does not appear to have any of the provocative aspects that can be found in contemporary art, from a Duchamp urinal to Kiki Smith's *Bottles* (an installation in which a series of large flasks are supposed to contain all the forms of secretion produced by the human body, from tears to sperm). The provocation, if it is there at all, can only be perceived by the informed viewers that are the critics. For them, though, it constitutes the most shocking scandal imaginable. For the "new version" of *Boudu,* as Jugnot insists on calling it, is not a form of "readymade" in the way that Gus Van Sant's *Psycho* (1998) is. Far from adhering respectfully to the original, it returns an element of ordinariness to a film that is reputed to be innovative and subversive. What this means for Jugnot is the need to stretch Renoir's satirical fable towards comedy and farce. To this end, he must revive the film's content, as its narrative and spectacle value has eroded with time, and adapt it to new contexts. It is striking that all of the adaptation strategies taken in the 2004 film are similar: they rejuvenate an older model in order to facilitate access to the film for the general public, and for this reason, they go beyond their perceptions, sensations and emotions. The new *Boudu* attempts to reinforce and underline everything that could have faded in the classic film. The documentary approach to filming Parisian exteriors, at which Renoir excelled, but which then became more widespread, has given place to a brassy aesthetic which evokes the boulevard theatre. The descriptive attention of Renoir's camera, respectful of the natural rhythm of word and gesture, gives way to rapid and jerky rhythm, this again very closely linked to vaudeville. Black and white has become very bright polychrome and the colour (the now famous "puke yellow" as described by Ostria) is not only present in the sets, but symbolically represented by the characters who are implicated in forms of parodic artistic activity.

Finally, and above all, the excessive psychological approach to the characters, which is far removed from the Renoirian palette, requires a very forced performance on the part of the actors. Permanent panic, close to hysteria, in the case of Jugnot/Christian who is always overwhelmed by events; complete changes of attitude in mid-flow for Catherine Frot/Yseult who shifts from depression (reclined body, dropping mouth, whining voice) to stunning euphoria, after the revelation brought about by her physical meeting with Boudu. However, it is in relation to Boudu that the most spectacular transformation takes place. In Renoir's film, Simon's performance, light and acrobatic, was of a great physical freedom. The sensuality and anarchy of the characters conveyed an Epicurean effervescence. Depardieu on the contrary moves very little and heavily, he only responds to his physiological needs, occupying the centre of the frame with a massive presence which, rather than embodying a liberating anarchy for the Lespinglet family, actually functions as a cumbersome burden.

If Jugnot claims the symbolic right to take liberties with Renoir's film (and I do not intend to enter the legal domain here), it is because, just as in the sphere of contemporary art, the classic work becomes the mould, the "raw material". Faced with the playful, detached attitude required by the film, or simply required by the passage of time, the discourse of the critics is in a typical mismatched position with regard to the evolution of the object to which it refers. The remake of a great classic is not only expected to be the object of an aesthetic judgement, but makes such a judgement entirely irrelevant. Even if one insists on considering it as a work of art, Jugnot's *Boudu* is part of "that subset of the field of works of art" which Jean-Marie Schaeffer describes as "not always fitting into an aesthetic perspective" (2000, 44).[13] It fits first and foremost into the category of a popular film that is intended to communicate directly with the public. In this respect it is not surprising that the mediation of the critics in their capacity as guide and seer becomes as superfluous here as it does in the field of digital art, which also, according to Edmond Couchot, renders useless and inoperative "the mission of mediation attributed by modernity to art criticism" (la mission de médiation attribuée par la modernité au critique d'art) (2000).

As a remake, *Boudu* is not intended to become the subject of statements of taste. In fact, the rewriting measures which I have outlined aim above all to provoke a new aesthetic experience, in the widest possible sense, by the whole range of stimulations and new emotions that the spectacle sets out to produce within the spectator. However, as Laurent Jullier asserts, most reviewers "refuse to be emotional toys, they want to decide for themselves which moments within the film generate physical reactions" (2002, 143).[14] Less, even, than mainstream comedy, *Boudu* does not comply with this wish, in that it has been rewritten with the objective of being prescriptive of spectator reactions.

Faced with this difficulty and yet still having to evaluate the film, reviewers find a compromise solution by deliberately confusing the registers of reception. Not only do they perceive the remake as an affront to the original, but their protest is directed precisely at the elements which are meant to rejuvenate the older film–that is, to make the new version into a more intense experience for a broader audience which no longer has access to classics that were originally made for them, but which are now perceived as museum pieces. In this way, the rewriting function is similar to the "translation into Hollywood language" that represents the transfer of a French original into an American remake (see Moine 2007).

This attitude, shared by numerous reviewers and which consists of "baptising" an object as art by the very fact that it is considered as not belonging to the field of art, would be underhand were it not part of a well-established process within criticism. As Schaeffer has remarked, "[o]ne can only, in the name of an evaluative definition of art, exclude objects which by virtue of some descriptive criterion will always already have the right to be called art" (1996, 190).[15] Here, to a far greater extent than is the case with the "distaste for other people's tastes" analysed by Bourdieu in *La Distinction* (1979), we are dealing with a specific form of art identification which consists in maintaining, at all costs, the symbolic unity of cinema, in which the best and the worst is necessarily included, in order to protect its artistic status. Critics have been officially entrusted with the task of elevating cinema to the status of art, and are keen to preserve what is left of this prerogative, now shared as it is with museums, schools, cultural institutions and the like. They therefore stay loyal to their mission, beyond the vicissitudes of the commercial world, by framing their reception in terms of disappointment, which at the very least has the result of inscribing the object within a horizon of expectation. Any aesthetic defence requires a counterpoint, and thus declaring that *Boudu* is disgusting has the effect not so much of excluding the film from the field of art, as of pulling it back into the domain of that which can be evaluated in terms of taste.

There can be no doubt, then, that in one sense the act of criticism itself has reached a dead-end, and this is bound to be repeated time and again as long as critics regard themselves as the guardians of the temple. In an ideal world, the pronouncement of a judgement of taste would be confined to its rightful place, which would be marginalised, because a review of this sort would only inform us about the personal preferences of the person writing it. Far more space, then, would be given over to an analysis of the film's properties, which would become much more rigorous, and less influenced by aesthetic prejudices. A trend along these lines has developed in the last few years in French film-studies research (see Jullier 2005). However, in truth, there is precious little chance that things will change, at any rate not in a culture where film criticism and journalistic reviewing remain a literary genre which aims to provide an aesthetic interpretation of works of art, and where films remain in their traditional place within the sphere of art, if not on account of their intrinsic properties, then at least because of the position they occupy in the cultural landscape. For French cinema is currently less of a national cinematography than it is a system, an active environment producing films which, while they are extremely heterogeneous, nonetheless each depend upon the fate of all the others. The system of subsidies, in particular, creates a *de facto* interdependence between all the facets of this activity.[16] Within this configuration, those working within popular cinema are conscious both of their responsibilities and of the fact that, particularly in relation to television, they possess a degree of cinematic legitimacy which critics know it would be vain to try to oppose. They therefore adopt a posture close to that of traditional censorship, denying *Boudu*, through the argument of the "pointlessness" of the remake, its very right to exist. Or perhaps this position is more like that of the self-censorship practised in the Hollywood studios of the golden age, although with the aim not of putting a brake on production, but of stimulating it. The close relationship between criticism and censorship is not a new phenomenon, as they have joined voices in a number of battles in the history of cinematographic taste, for example over the question of praising the subversive genius of Hollywood cinema at the time of the Production Code. However, when French popular cinema, revelling in its right to call itself part of a national cinema, takes every aesthetic liberty imaginable, the most passionate brand of criticism almost naturally reproduces the gesture of the censor, who nominally sets out to clean up and transform works in order to make them conform to dominant aesthetic norms. This reaction, it will have been understood, attests in exemplary fashion to the aesthetic misunderstanding which, in France, is the basis of relations between elitist criticism and popular cinema.

Translated from the French by Jonathan Hensher,
Isabelle Vanderschelden and Darren Waldron

---

[1] "Depuis quelque temps, je suis effaré de l'attitude de la critique vis-à-vis du cinéma français. Je ne me sens pas plus visé qu'un autre (plutôt moins d'ailleurs), mais je lis simplement ce qui s'écrit ici ou là sur nos films. Certains papiers, qui ressemblent à autant d'assassinats prémédités, me font froid dans le dos, comme si leurs auteurs s'étaient donné le mot pour tuer le cinéma français commercial, populaire, grand public." The letter was published along with a manifesto signed by the members of the ARP.

[2] For example, this was the comment passed by the *Nouvel Observateur* on the films of Bruno Dumont, Thomas Vincent and Xavier Beauvois, as cited in the "Nous, cinéastes" manifesto (Anon. 1999): "The Calais region used to produce

beetroot, now it's producing turkeys" (Le Nord produisait des betteraves, il produit maintenant des navets).

[3] For example, see the review in *Le Monde* (Mandelbaum 2005). For a more detailed discussion of *Les Choristes* as a remake, see Vincendeau's article in this volume.

[4] Adapted from the cult *San Antonio* series by Frédéric Dard.

[5] "Nous sommes en France en mars 2005 et on aimerait avoir le recul et le décalage horaire (voire le sachet pour vomir) d'un étranger cinéphile qui débarquerait ici depuis deux semaines et verrait ce qui nous est infligé au quotidien. "

[6] "Oh! saint Jugnot, comédien et martyr, cinéaste et martyr, les intellos ne t'aiment pas (les intellos sont des salauds, les intellos ont des têtes de veau), et d'ailleurs ils n'aiment personne. Mais, à voir comment tu regardes les gens, tu n'aimes personne non plus: les bourges, les riches, des salauds, encroûtés dans leurs désirs minables; les méridionaux, des pitres; les ouvriers, des Espagnols. Alors il te reste Boudu (il est pratique Boudu, il ne fait que passer)."

[7] "...remake repoussant... vulgaire à pleurer... spécial ringue... caricature de décor provençal à dominante jaune gerbant."

[8] "Depardieu étale sa graisse et sa vulgarité jusqu'à la nausée. On se serait bien passé de ce remake."

[9] "Tout cela est un peu court pour du cinéma mais largement suffisant pour le passage en *prime time* sur une chaîne hertzienne pour lequel le film est calibré."

[10] For instance, *Monsieur Batignole* brought in a television audience of twelve million viewers (compared to a million and a half at cinemas), demonstrating the degree to which the success of *Les Choristes* had stimulated the interest and curiosity of television viewers. See comments on the television audience for *Boudu* in the introduction to the present volume.

[11] "Entreprise d'idéalisation presque pétainiste des petits métiers du cinéma."

[12] "Je me méfie de tout tableau que j'estime avoir pu faire moi-même." This is the reaction of a participant to Jackson Pollock's *Cathedral* during a round table on modern art, reported by Chateau (1996). For further development of this idea see Nacache (2001, 309).

[13] "...cette sous-classe du domaine des œuvres d'art [qui] ne s'inscrivent pas toujours dans une perspective esthétique".

[14] "...refusent d'être les jouets de l'émotion; ils veulent décider eux-mêmes de l'endroit du film qui motivera les réactions du corps."

[15] "On ne peut exclure au nom d'une définition évaluative de l'art que des objets qui en vertu d'un critère descriptif quelconque ont toujours déjà droit au titre d'œuvre d'art."

[16] For further investigation of this topic, see Montebello (2004).

CHAPTER FOURTEEN

"VERY FUNNY IF YOU CAN KEEP UP WITH THE SUBTITLES": THE BRITISH RECEPTION OF *LE FABULEUX DESTIN D'AMELIE POULAIN* (*AMELIE*)

INGRID STIGSDOTTER

In 2001, a series of popular film hits helped French cinema take back a considerable share of the market from their Hollywood competitors at the French box office. Among these films, the biggest sensation was Jean-Pierre Jeunet's *Amélie*,[1] which unlike the other national blockbusters had art-house credentials as well as popular appeal.[2] The French reception of *Amélie* involved reports of deeply moved French audiences, high-profile politicians trying to associate themselves with the film, and a critical debate that questioned the appropriateness of the film's nostalgic representation of Paris, as well as its relationship to French cinema on the one hand and Hollywood on the other. Although I will make occasional references to this well-documented debate (Vincendeau 2001a, Andrew 2004) in this chapter, my main focus will be *Amélie's* reception in Britain, where it attracted over a million cinemagoers in the autumn of 2001. *Amélie's* exceptional success in what is reputedly the most difficult market for non-English-language productions in Europe was partly the consequence of an ambitious marketing campaign, but the film also clearly struck an enduring chord with British audiences. It has enjoyed a successful career as a home cinema product, and it was voted "London's favourite French film" by readers of the website *France in London* both in 2004 and 2006, beating the heritage favourites from the 1980s, *Jean de Florette* and *Manon des sources* (Claude Berri, 1986), as well as the successful Franco-Italian co-production *Cinema Paradiso* (Giuseppe Tornatore, 1989)[3] and Luc Besson's action movie *Léon* (1994). This lingering appeal, long after the hype surrounding the theatrical release had subsided, indicates that the high box office figures are not exclusively the effect of publicity and marketing, but that *Amélie* provided viewers with something they found worth remembering. This is where empirical audience research might provide us with some information that cannot be obtained simply by analysing box office figures, marketing and reviews. As we shall see, an overview of the critical response indicates that the film's journey across national, cultural and linguistic boundaries involved a shift in status, and my empirical research confirms that elements of French popular culture recognised in the French reception of *Amélie* were displaced when the film was embraced by the British public.

Methodological considerations

Following Janet Staiger's important work on film reception, I understand film interpretation as a process constantly in change, where the meaning(s) of a particular film depends on the audience viewing the film, as well as the moment and context of reception (Staiger 1992, 2000, 2005). In addition, I share Thomas Austin's view that empirical audience research can be a useful supplementary tool when researching contemporary film reception, as long as we acknowledge that such audience data does not give direct access to the thoughts of respondents, but represents "a mediation of the moment of film reception, an experience which can only ever be retrieved through the operations of language" (Austin 2002, 26). Indeed, in the case of the data that this chapter draws upon, thirty-nine questionnaires collected in 2005 from two separate audience groups, one at the University of Southampton and the other at the Chichester Cinema at New Park, we are dealing with at least two levels of mediation. Firstly, there is each individual respondent's attempt to express in words their immediate reaction to a film, with limitations imposed by the space available on the questionnaire sheet, the time (screenings took place in the evening and some participants were keen to leave as soon as possible) and of course the questions asked in the first place. Secondly, my interpretation of these accounts was encumbered by troubles ranging from the very mundane (illegible handwriting) to the metaphysical difficulties involved in any form of text interpretation. But as Austin points out, these problems do not in themselves constitute an excuse to avoid researching "real audiences" altogether.

My analysis of the empirical audience material referred to above will be combined with a discussion of the critical discourse surrounding the release of *Amélie* in Britain. The point here is not to argue that participants in my research project were directly influenced by reviews or marketing.

Although most respondents were surely affected by extra-textual factors at some point, several years passed between the original theatrical release of the film and the research screening, and in any case, it is not the immediate impact of publicity that interests me here, but rather the more general discourse surrounding French and European cinema in the UK.[4] In particular, I am interested in exploring how audience reactions to *Amélie* fit in with the expectations that the same viewers have of French cinema. But before I turn to these issues, some further background information about the empirical material used in this article is necessary.

The two *Amélie* screenings were programmed within the context of a season of French and Swedish cinema, free to the general public in exchange for their completed questionnaires.[5] For the series as a whole, the goal was to recruit an audience resembling that of an art-house cinema, but it is very difficult to state with any certainty what a typical audience for French, foreign-language or art cinema in Britain today would look like, since research in this area is extremely limited. The Southampton screening of *Amélie* was dominated by students and university staff to a greater extent than later films in the series, probably because it was the first film in the season, and information about the programme had not yet been disseminated widely enough outside of the university community. Because the university accommodates many international students, and the screenings took place at the campus where modern languages are taught, the percentage of non-British and multilingual viewers was also considerably higher in this audience group than would have been the case in, for example, the local art cinema.

The general perception, supported by anecdotal evidence, is that art-house cinemas are frequented primarily by the middle classes, and a UK Film Council-commissioned report indicates that 70% of specialist cinema viewers belongs to the socio-economic category ABC1 (KPMG 2002, 114). Among participants in my study whose occupation was not connected to the education sector, most were employed in administrative, artistic or socially-orientated jobs, associated with the liberal middle classes. Nevertheless, it should be remembered that *Amélie*'s box office record shows that it clearly managed to attract viewers who do not usually watch French film, and the research audience discussed in this article did also include a number of respondents who viewed non-English language film only once or twice per year. In fact, many of the people who came to later screenings in the series appear to have avoided the first one because they had already seen *Amélie*, and/or in some cases because they favoured less accessible/popular films.[6] More than half of the respondents had actually seen the film before, often several times. In this sense, at least part of the audience could be considered *Amélie* fans, bravely facing the very British autumn weather that haunted the season as a whole in order to attend a screening of a film that they already owned on DVD. It is worth noting that the average age of *Amélie* research participants, twenty-seven in Chichester and thirty in Southampton, was considerably lower than in the case of other screenings in the series, which tended to attract viewers of an average age closer to forty.[7] At 60%, female respondents were also slightly overrepresented, although as we shall see, some viewers were of the opinion that *Amélie* specifically addressed a female audience.

In this chapter, the empirical data obtained through these research screenings will be used to highlight the expectations of this audience in relation to the concept of a "French film", to discuss how these viewers define *Amélie* in terms of genre, and how their perception fits in with the idea of a French film and French national culture. But before I turn to this analysis, I will provide a brief account of *Amélie*'s commercial success in the UK, and also say a few words about the complex French reactions to "national" and "international" aspects of the film.

French cultural heritage for the international market

The scale of *Amélie*'s achievement at the British box office becomes apparent when considering the results of the most successful French titles at the British box office in subsequent years.[8]

It is fair to assume that the box office record of *Un Long dimanche de fiançailles* is at least partly related to audience expectations of an *Amélie* sequel, involving as it did the director Jean-Pierre Jeunet and the star Audrey Tautou, as well as other members of the *Amélie* cast. The film was also nick-named "Amélie at war" by commentators, who drew parallels between the characters played by Tautou in the two films (Gentleman, 2004).

Between 2000 and 2005, only two non-English-language films were more successful than *Amélie* in the UK: Ang Lee's *Crouching Tiger, Hidden Dragon* (2000), a multinational co-production with considerable American imput, and Mel Gibson's *The Passion of the Christ* (2004), an American production filmed in Latin, Aramaic and Hebrew. It is interesting in this context to note that although *Amélie* was shot mainly on location in Paris with a largely French cast and crew, it was co-produced by the Cologne-based German company MMC Independent GmbH, making the film eligible for subsidies from the North-Rhine-Westphalia region, and facilitating distribution in Germany.

Film Title (Production Year)	UK Admissions (Release Period)
Le Fabuleux destin d'Amélie Poulain (2001)	1,000,107 (2001)
8 Femmes (2001)	106,413 (2002-2003)
Les Triplettes de Belleville (2003)	135,433 (2003)
Comme une image (2004)	123,673 (2004-2005)
Un Long dimanche de fiançailles (2004)	335,734 (2005)

When *Amélie* was released in France, reviewers were divided between those who thought the film pandered to an American or Americanised market (*L'Humanité*, 2001), and those who emphasised its references to a specifically French cultural heritage. Critics often connected their discussion of *Amélie* to French artistic traditions by reciting key names (Marcel Aymé, Brassaï, Marcel Carné, Philippe Delerm, Robert Doisneau, Georges Méliès, Georges Perec, Raymond Peynet, Jacques Prévert, Raymond Queneau, Jacques Tati, Alexandre Trauner, François Truffaut...) as a kind of quality assurance (Belleret 2001, Heymann 2001, Morrot 2001, T.S. 2001). Homages to historical representations of Paris were, however, also cited by those who saw the film as regressive and nostalgic, as evidence that the film was obsessed with an idealised French past (Kaganski 2001, Ostria 2001), as well as by those who simply thought that Jeunet's postmodern sampling of references was masking a lack of originality (Boujut 2001).

Later on, at the time of Miramax's Oscar campaign, when *Amélie* was screening in American cinemas that reportedly had not shown a French film since *La Cage aux folles* (Edouard Molinaro, 1978), an article in *Le Monde* described the film as international from its conception, and the film's producer Claudie Ossard confirmed that *Amélie* was already intended for an international market at the writing stage: "We sold *Amélie* on the basis of the screenplay to almost all of the big territories, including the US" (Ossard in Mulard and Sotinel 2002).[9]

The British distributor of *Amélie*, Momentum Pictures, explicitly aimed to make it "the biggest French film ever in the UK" (Johnston 2001). The release was backed by an unusually large marketing budget, which among other things paid for trailers being shown with the American blockbuster *Planet of the Apes* (Tim Burton, 2001). *Amélie* went out on about 80 prints, taking over £500,000 on its opening weekend, expanding to 98 prints in the second week, and eventually showing simultaneously at 115 cinemas, including not only art cinemas, but also multiplexes (Morrison 2001, 44).[10] Even a superficial review of how the film was publicised in the British press reveals tie-ins with French food, drink and fashion brands, and quite apart from advertising, the distributors were very successful in gaining space in newspapers and magazines, including popular newspapers that often neglect to cover foreign-language releases (see Bond 2001, Groskop 2001, Le Marie 2001, Roberts 2001, Ross and Ronay 2001).

Even before *Amélie* was released in Britain, reports on the way in which French left-wing commentators had ascribed ideological messages to the film appeared in British newspapers. These articles often took a mocking approach to French intellectual culture; for example, the *Independent* asked:

> Could the most popular French film of the year, or many a year, be a two-hour, party political broadcast for the far-right National Front and Jean-Marie Le Pen? If you watch *Le Fabuleux destin d'Amélie Poulain*, this may not occur to you, unless you are a French intellectual.

For this commentator, Serge Kaganski's attack on *Amélie* demonstrated

> [T]he same mechanical thought pattern–and French left-wing hatred of the popular–that recently attacked Harry Potter as a bourgeois and sexist glorifier of class and gender distinctions, and the middle-class passion for football as a corrupter of the mind. (Lichfield 2001)

In an article portraying Kaganski's cause slightly more sympathetically, if sceptically, Stuart Jeffries drew parallels to the debate surrounding *Notting Hill* (Roger Michell, 1999) in the UK two years earlier (Jeffries 2001), and this comparison was often made in later reviews (Romney 2001b, Mowe 2001a). In general, however, British critics were less concerned with *Amélie's* ideological message, and more interested in its so-called "feel-good" character. This is perhaps partly linked to the fact that the general UK release took place shortly after 9/11, leading critics to contrast the film's optimism with the global shock over the terrorist attacks on New York (Dougan 2001, Preston 2001, Anon. 2001c). Furthermore, it is hardly surprising that *Amélie's* digitally manipulated, glossy and cheerful post-card image of Paris was less controversial in the eyes of British viewers, likely to have visited France as tourists, rather than actually having lived in the country and experienced the economic and social difficulties that had haunted the nation in recent years.

Four years after the original release, not a single participant in my audience research project acknowledged awareness of the media furore surrounding *Amélie's* French release, despite the fact that the audience included several French respondents, and a number of participants who had seen the film in France when it was first released. [11] Certain respondents would have been too young to take an interest in this at the time of the original release (the Chichester group included four seventeen-year-old A-level students), and film buffs who agreed with the idea that *Amélie* was politically reactionary or represented a sickeningly sugary and clichéd image of France would of course be highly unlikely to attend a repertory screening. As I have already mentioned, many participants could be characterised as devoted *Amélie* fans, and it would therefore be surprising if they brought up this issue, except possibly in order to defend the film. When we turn to consider British expectations of French national film culture, and to *Amélie's* generic character, it is however possible to identify some interesting similarities between critical discourse and empirical audience data. There was a very strong sense in British press reactions to *Amélie* that a "feel-good" film, a category associated with popular cinema, clashed with the very idea of a "French film". In the British context, the latter concept seemed to function almost as a generic label, but a label that could only accommodate a small section of France's film production, and not all of the films that are actually distributed in the UK. Among the information gathered at my research screenings, it is possible to distinguish a similar (if less stark) contrast between expectations of "French film" and descriptions of *Amélie*.

A feel-good French film? Challenging generic expectations in Britain

Films can be categorised in terms of genre by the industry, by critics and by audiences. Because the focus in this article is on reception, I will primarily concentrate on the two latter areas. In the case of audiences, genre is often understood in terms of expectations and intertextuality, and I therefore asked participants in my audience research project not only what type of film they would characterise *Amélie* as, but also what kind of audience they thought that it was aiming for, and whether or not it reminded them of any other films. With regards to the first question, the idea of *Amélie* targeting a specific audience was interpreted in different ways. A student in his late twenties, who nurtured a romantic notion of artistic production, rejected this concept outright, claiming that "the film comes from the desire of its creators to express themselves". A more common response was to recognise *Amélie's* popular aspects by stating that it aimed for a broad audience or to think in terms of sex or age, with certain viewers (mainly, but not exclusively, women) claiming that the film had a specific appeal for female spectators.

The age question divided viewers, as some thought *Amélie* was suitable for everyone, while others specified an adult audience. Certain respondents brought up issues such as education, politics, or class. A fifty-six-year-old female social worker thought the film was aimed at "thinkers", a twenty-five-year-old male local government officer imagined that its ideal spectator was an "'arty', intellectual, left-leaning type of viewer", while a seventeen-year-old male student stated that "I think you need to be, to a degree, intellectual". In terms of class, a forty-five-year-old man argued that the film addressed a "middle-class" audience, while a twenty-one-year-old female sociology student was of the opinion that it would appeal to "all classes". One of the youngest participants pointed out that education might be an issue as "it being in French would put some people off". We will return to the question of language at a later stage, but it is worth noting that in most cases, those who specified a target audience group tended to do so in a manner that meant that they were included in that particular age/sex/class category. This might seem self-evident, considering that we are dealing with an audience who held *Amélie* in high esteem, but it is important to keep in mind since inclusion in a group through specific criteria also means the exclusion of others, and this seems to be significant to at least some of those who consider themselves as members of an "art cinema audience". We should also bear in mind that the experience of taking part in an academic study might influence viewers to emphasise *Amélie's* highbrow or artistic connotations, rather than popular aspects of the film.

The notion of art cinema leads to the next question, about *Amélie's* generic traits. I did not use the term "genre", but opted instead for the vaguer "type", so that those who were not in the habit of differentiating between films in this manner would not be forced to do so. In fact, many respondents stated that they found it difficult to classify the film. This is of course not an unusual problem, since genres tend to be flexible and hybrid rather than fixed and clear-cut, but *Amélie* seems to combine generic cues that I would argue are difficult for a British audience to reconcile. Some viewers used the expression "feel-good", and it was also fairly common to use the words "art-house", "independent" or "alternative" but often in combination with something else, as in "Arty with a twist of romcom!", or "French art-house meets chick flick". A twenty-eight-year-old postgraduate student did however describe the film as "independent art-house" and specifically emphasised that she did not understand how it had managed to reach such a wide audience. The terms that appeared most frequently were nevertheless variations on romance and comedy, often in combination, and here the responses of research respondents converge with descriptions in the press. I have already mentioned that British critics were particularly interested in the film's "feel-good" aspect, and reviewers often defined *Amélie* as a romantic comedy (that is, a popular genre film) that contained traces of art cinema. The *Sunday Times*, for example, stated that it combined "art-house experimentalism with the simple, upbeat emotions of mainstream entertainment" (Landesman 2001). Many respondents used the words "French" or "foreign" to qualify their classification–as in "French romantic comedy" –and the *Sunday Times* review cited above suggested that *Amélie* would meet with disapproval from elitist critics in Britain because it defied certain expectations of what a French film should be like, or what French culture was about:

> There is a certain type of British highbrow who will forgive the French anything: the gloom of existentialism, the grossness of snails in garlic, Sartre's apologies for Stalinism, the sight of a starlet with hairy armpits– but a happy, upbeat, feelgood French film? Yeuuch! (Landesman 2001)

The *Spectator* confirmed that *Amélie* violated expectations: "*Amélie* is a feelgood film in the sense that it feels good about the things French films usually make you feel bad about" (Steyn 2001, 74).

Examining the media discourse surrounding *Amélie's* release, it becomes clear that French cinema is often associated with feeling bad rather than good, and that *Amélie* was therefore seen as an aberration from the norm. The *Sunday Times* contrasted the film with the "doom-laden– and commercially unsuccessful–French films beloved of Parisian cinema purists" (Campbell 2001) while the *Daily Telegraph* described *Amélie* as being "miles from the sort of fare that once made French cinema famous, with an almost total absence of existentialist angst or Gauloise smoke" (Bishop 2001). The *Evening Standard* predicted that audiences would be surprised by

> [A] feelgood French movie in which there are no adulterous couples, no gangs of disaffected Algerians or Moroccans roaming the streets and no unshaven flics mooching around in leather jackets planting drugs, consorting with prostitutes or shooting suspects. (Norman 2001)

This description of a typical French film suggests that apart from being associated with the representation of social ills, French cinema was also expected to contain a certain amount of sexual explicitness, or at least illicit sexual adventures. In relation to audience participants' expectations of French and European cinema this is particularly interesting. Although generally their attitude towards such films was much more positive than the press reactions above suggested, as may be expected from an audience including a fair number of regular foreign-language film consumers, terms used to describe French film included "raunchy", "intense", "oversexed", and "sometimes too much". The curious thing about *Amélie* in this context, and something that several reviewers mentioned, is the fact that although the film contains references to sex and pornography, the central romance appears curiously asexual and innocent (Steyn 2001, 74 Romney 2001b). This innocence was a positive factor for a teacher in his early fifties, a self-proclaimed "big fan" of 1970s and 80s French cinema, for whom *Amélie* "restore[d] faith" after his experience of finding French films "becoming a bit Hollywood/psychotic" in the 1990.

A readerly cinema vs. visual pleasure

The *Observer* used the expression "verbose or otherwise difficult art movies" (Jeffries 2001), when describing international expectations of French cinema, and I believe that the word "verbose" is of key importance here, because the reason that dialogue-heavy French films are perceived as difficult is connected to the issue of linguistic difference, and in particular the screen transfer method known as subtitling.

When surveying the critical reception of *Amélie* in Britain, I was struck firstly by how often subtitles were mentioned, secondly by the way in which critics tended to presume that their readers had an aversion to subtitles, and finally how the displeasure of reading subtitles was set in opposition to the pleasure of film viewing. The quote that provided the title for this article appeared in an article in the *Mail on Sunday*, where it was used to describe *Amélie*'s introductory sequence (Bond 2001). In the same vein, the *Birmingham Evening Mail* stated: "Jeunet's achievement can be summed up by the fact that his skill makes you intstantly [sic] forget that this movie has any subtitles at all... they simply melt into the picture" (Young 2001). Similarly, an article in *Time Out* claimed: "it's tempting to skip the subtitles to fully appreciate the visual feast" (Sharpe, 2001, 22-24).

These are only a few examples of the way in which subtitles featured prominently across a wide range of publications, although as these quotes show, subtitles were set in opposition to *Amélie*'s perceived accessibility and potential for visual pleasure and fun.

As Atom Egoyan and Ian Balfour's book *Subtitles: On the Foreignness of Film* suggests, subtitles signify "foreignness" (Egoyan and Balfour 2004), and in Britain the expressions "foreign-language film", "subtitled film" and "art cinema" often seem to be used more or less interchangeably. The association between subtitles and art cinema stems from the perceived difficulty of reading subtitles combined with the fact that these films are generally exhibited in smaller venues known as art or art-house cinemas.

"French language", "subtitles", and "possibly dialogue-heavy" also appeared among answers to the question of what research respondents expected when a film was described as "French", but in contrast with the press discourse summarised in this article, the majority of participants did not have a negative attitude to these issues. Their ideas about French cinema can be divided into four main groups. The first category involved expectations of artistic quality, and was generally unambiguously positive, with terms including for example "intelligent", "artistic", "stylish", "well directed", "interesting", and "good quality". The second group focused on feeling, atmosphere and emotion, with expressions like "depth and emotional feeling", "French flavour–maybe hyper-real", "quirky, intense, emotional", "attention to detail, focus on human relationships", "emotional journey", and "romantic or dark or really funny in a quirky way". This includes some of the comments that I have already referred to as indicating a sense of excess: "psychological/emotional... sometimes too much", "special atmosphere (psychologically daunting, a bit oversexed)". Clearly, psychological and emotional content was sometimes perceived as too intense; this appears to relate to the more controversial aspects of French art cinema; sexually explicit, controversial, and sometimes violent films. The third group defined French film in relation to what it (supposedly) is not; that is, not Hollywood, not conventional, not blockbuster, not traditional, not genre, not action. Evidently, these three categories left little room for French popular genre films within the imagination of this audience. Finally, there was a group of non-evaluative comments that focused on setting, language, and music. Interestingly, when asked directly what aspects of *Amélie* could be seen as specifically French, most respondents tended to avoid the rather abstract concepts that dominated their replies as to what they expected of a "French film", providing instead very concrete answers relating to the soundtrack, such as the French language or the accordion music, or pointing to highly visible aspects of the mise-en-scène, like "location", "setting", "interiors", "colours", "scenery", "fashion", "décor" and "food", or even more specifically "café", "moped", and "market/grocer's". The importance of

Amélie's look was also clearly reflected in the film titles that *Amélie* reminded viewers of; apart from other films directed by Jeunet (*Delicatessen* (1991), *La Cité des enfants perdus* (1995)) and/or starring Tautou (*Un Long dimanche de fiançailles, L'Auberge espagnole* (Cédric Klapisch, 2002)), the titles ranged across nationalities and genres, including among others *The Wizard of Oz* (Victor Fleming, 1939), *Y Tu Mamá También* (Alfonso Cuarón, 2001), *Chocolat* (Lasse Hallström, 2000), *Cinema Paradiso* (Giuseppe Tornatore, 1988), *The Eternal Sunshine of the Spotless Mind* (Michel Gondry, 2004) and *Arizona Dream* (Emir Kusturica, 1993). Although many of these films are romantic, and respondents often referred to similarities on the level of sentiment, the common denominator seems to be the colourfulness or "magic" aspect of the visual style, and indeed a twenty-year old male student explicitly stated that *Amélie*'s "colour schemes remind me of such films as *House of Flying Daggers* [(Yimou Zhang, 2004)]".

It was notably more common for respondents who did not have English as their first language, or who spoke French, to think that knowledge of French culture affected their film interpretation, while viewers whose mother tongue was English and who did not speak any other languages tended to describe this as irrelevant to their enjoyment of the film. Again, clearly audiences draw upon their own experience, but it is interesting, considering the prominent place that the film's use of cinephilic quotations was given in French reviews, and in at least some of the highbrow British newspapers (Romney 2001a and 2001b; Jeffries 2001) that the only mention of *Amélie*'s nods to classic French cinema came from one of the French participants (a male student in his mid twenties) who stated that it contained many references to the 1950s and 60s. If anyone in this audience noticed the nods to poetic realism or François Truffaut, they did not find it interesting or noteworthy enough to bring it to my attention. Furthermore, many respondents were of the opinion that *Amélie* could have been set anywhere in the world and had few links with French national culture.

While this may partly be explained by the fact that a viewer who genuinely enjoys a film is likely to consider aspects that may have gone over his or her head irrelevant, it also does seem to contradict the same audience's description of French film as artistic and culturally specific. Overall, there is a sense that *Amélie* is considered as unique and atypical of French cinema. This leads me to conclude that the expectations of French film culture held by British art cinema audiences, while much more favourable than the negative stereotypes found in much British press discourse, are formed in a way that does not allow the inclusion of a popular genre film except at the very basic levels of setting, language and recognisable iconography. A popular French movie that crosses the channel is generally transformed into something that better matches the art cinema mould into which all foreign-language films are supposed to fit. *Amélie's* success in the British market is related to the fact that despite its iconic Paris setting, it was received above all as a feel-good film transcending national categories. This might at least partly explain why the optimistic prophecies for foreign-language film in the UK following the successful marketing campaigns for *Amélie* and *Crouching Tiger, Hidden Dragon* have failed to materialise; somehow, rather than counteracting what Shane Danielsen, former Director of the Edinburgh Film Festival, has called the "irrational fear of the subtitle" (Danielsen 2003), *Amélie* has become the exception that proves the rule.

---

[1] In the interests of brevity, the British title will be used throughout this chapter
[2] After *Amélie*, the most popular French releases of 2001 were *La Vérité si je mens! 2* (Thomas Gilou), *Le Placard* (Francis Weber) and *Le Pacte des Loups* (Christophe Gans), all productions that followed popular genre conventions to a greater extent than *Amélie*.
[3] A curious contender for the title, considering that the film's language and setting, as well as the majority of the cast, are Italian.
[4] When asked what they knew about *Amélie* before seeing the film and where they had found this information, some questionnaire respondents indicated that they had seen it reviewed in the press or on TV, but the most common sources of knowledge about the film prior to the first viewing were recommendations from friends or family or having noticed the poster.
[5] Participants for the Southampton research group were recruited by distributing leaflets at the Harbour Lights Picturehouse cinema, the Phoenix Film Society, and across the University, in particular at the Union Film Society, the Avenue campus (where most Humanities subjects, including Film, are taught) the Nuffield Theatre, and the Turner Sims Concert Hall. Messages were also posted on university e-mailing lists. Participants for the Chichester research group were recruited through the programme for the Chichester Cinema in New Park, in its electronic and printed formats.
[6] Other titles shown in the series included *La Vie rêvée des anges* (Erick Zonca, 1998) and *Trolösa/Faithless* (Liv Ullmann, 2000), films representing, respectively, grittily realist and Bergmanesquely austere tendencies in a European cinema far removed from the romantic fantasy world of *Amélie*.
[7] While Docherty, Morrison and Tracey reported that the largest group of specialist cinemagoers (47%) in the 1980s was to be found in the age bracket 16-25 (1987, 54-55), most of my research screenings attracted a significantly older crowd. This might of course be the result of other factors, like the popularity of the New Park Cinema among retired people in Chichester, and the fact that it was a repertory

season rather than a showcase for new films. Yet KPMG's report suggested that in 2002, specialist film appealed to "a much older age group when compared directly to the general cinema audience figure", with viewers over thirty-five accounting for more than 57% of the market, the comparable figure among the general cinema audience being 33% (KPMG 2002, 114). Even among the comparatively young *Amélie* research audience, respondents who stated that they viewed foreign-language film more than once a month were generally over 25 years old. If the figures in Docherty *et al.* were correct, it certainly looks as though the audience for foreign-language film in the UK is ageing without being replaced by younger viewers.

[8] Admission data and other statistical information obtained from the Lumiere online database and the UK Film Council (2003, 2004, 2005, 2006). Because box office receipts rather than admissions figures are the norm in the UK, the figures provided by Lumiere have been estimated by dividing box office receipts by the average ticket price for the relevant year.

[9] "Nous avons vendu *Le Fabuleux destin* sur scénario à presque tous les grands territoires, y compris les Etats-Unis."

[10] Blockbusters often open on around 500 British screens, and really big films, like the *Harry Potter* series, can be distributed on over 1000 prints, while the average foreign-language title is released on less than 10 prints (UK Film Council 2003, 2006b. See also Mowe 2001c). Although *Amélie's* opening performance did not come close to the multimillion debut weekends of a *Harry Potter* or *Lord of the Rings* film, the film nevertheless brought in more revenue in its first weekend than most French films do throughout their whole UK run.

[11] A twenty-five-year-old German audience member normally resident in France had followed the debate concerning *Un long dimanche de fiançailles* and the problem of deciding whether or not a film was French, but he did not mention anything about the debate surrounding *Amélie*.

BIBLIOGRAPHY

Anon., "*La Vérité si je mens*: un million d'entrées, purée", *Libération*, 14 May 1997 p. 4.
—. "Nous, cinéastes", *Libération*, 25 November 1999.
—. "Le Retour du scénario", *France Soir*, 8 February 2001.
—. "*Le Fabuleux destin d'Amélie Poulain* de Jean-Pierre Jeunet", *L'Humanité,* 25 April 2001.
—. "*Vidocq*", *Aden*, 19 September 2001.
—. "French Feel-Good Hit of the Summer", *South Wales Echo*, 20 October 2001c.
—. "Luc Besson: le cinéma fait des affaires", *L'Expansion*, 27 November 2002.
—. "*Les Choristes*", *Le Monde*, 17 March 2004.
—. "L'externalisation des murs d'exploitation prend un nouvel essor", *Les Echos*, 17 February 2005, p.28.
—. "Un court samedi de retrouvailles", *Libération*, 26 February 2005.
—. "Des Césars à petit budget", *L'Humanité*, 5 March 2005.
—. "*Boudu* : Remake pas nécessaire ", *La Tribune desfossés*, 9 March 2005.
—. "Outsourcing: Le grand chambardement", *Nouvel Economiste*, 13 May 2005, pp.23-5.
—. "Les distributeurs révolutionnent la promotion des films", *Ecran Total*, 23 November 2005.
Aiach, L., "Yvan Attal entre 4 yeux: Entretien", *Infrarouge*, 2002, http://www.infrarouge.fr/interview.php?ID=44 (accessed 27 November 2006).
Allen, M., "Talking about a Revolution: The Blockbuster as Industrial Advertisement", in J. Stringer (ed), *Movie Blockbusters*, (London & New York: Routledge, 2003), pp.101-13.
Altman, R., *La Comédie musicale hollywoodienne*, (Paris: Armand Colin, 1992).
—. *Film/Genre*, (London: BFI Publishing, 1999).
Andrew, D., "*Amélie*, or Le Fabuleux Destin du Cinéma Français", *Film Quarterly*, vol. 57, no. 3, 2004, pp. 34-46.
Andrews, G., "*Balzac* and the Little Seamstress" in John Pym (ed), *Time Out Film Guide*, no. 13, (London: Time Out Guides Ltd., 2005).

Armanet, F. & B. Vallaeys (eds), "Si le style *Libé* est imité par tout le monde, changez-le! Tavernier cartes sur table", Round Table with Bertrand Tavernier, Olivier Séguret and Gérard Lefort, *Libération*, 2 December 1999.

Attali, D., "Des répliques qui font mouche", *Le Journal du Dimanche*, 4 February 2001a.

—. "Le Sentier toujours lumineux", *Le Journal du Dimanche*, 4 February 2001b.

Austin, G., *Contemporary French Cinema: An Introduction*, (Manchester: Manchester University Press, 1996).

Austin, J. F., "Digitizing Frenchness in 2001", *French Cultural Studies*, vol. 15, no. 3, October 2004, pp. 281-99.

Austin, T., *Hollywood, Hype and Audiences: Selling and Watching Popular Film in the 1990s*, (Manchester: Manchester University Press, 2002).

Azoury, P., "*Boudu* : mettez les bouts !", *Libération*, 9 March 2005.

Barthes, R., *Mythologies*, (Paris: Editions du Seuil, 1957).

Bazin, A., *What is Cinema? Volume 2*, translated by H. Gray, (Berkeley: University of California Press, 1971). Originally published as *Qu'est-ce que le cinéma?* (Paris: Editions du Cerf, 1958-1962).

Baudin, B., "*La Vérité si je mens!*: Le bonheur est dans le Sentier", *Le Figaro*, 30 April 1997, p. 31.

—. "José Garcia, marathonien du rire", *Le Figaro*, 7 February 2001, p. 30.

—. "Jugnot sur les traces de Noël-Noël", *Le Figaro*, 25 August 2003.

Bégaudeau, F., "Esquives (retour sur un film dont on parle)", *Cahiers du cinéma*, July-August, 2004, pp. 78-81.

Belleret, R., "Les bonnes idées de Jean-Pierre Jeunet et de son dialoguiste Guillaume Laurent", *Le Monde*, 9 May 2001.

Bénabent, J., "La Télé va-t-elle tuer la diversité du cinéma?", *Télérama*, 2970, 13 December 2006, pp. 52-4.

Berry, S., "Genre", in Toby Miller & Robert Stam (eds), *A Companion to Film Theory*, (Oxford: Blackwell, 1999).

Bertuccelli, J., "*Since Otar Left...* An Interview with Director Julie Bertuccelli", *Zeitgeist Films*, 2004, 19 March 2005 http://zeitgeistfilms.com/sinceotarleft/interview.html (accessed 20 October 2006)

Bishop, P., "Will we Fall under the Spell of French Film without Tears", *Daily Telegraph*, 10 August 2001.

Bloom, M. E., "Contemporary France-Chinese Cinema: Translation, Citation and Imitation in Dai Sijie's *Balzac and the Little Seamstress* and Tsai Ming-Liang's *What Time is it There?*", *Quarterly Review of Film and Video* no. 22, 2005, pp. 311-325.

Blumenfeld, S., "Le Sentier de la gloire: *La Vérité si je mens!* a fêté son million d'entrées", *Le Monde*, 14 May 1997, p. 29.

—. "Isaac Sharry, un second rôle de premier plan: 'Je suis condamné à jouer toute ma vie le même personnage'", *Le Monde*, 19 January 2000, p. 31.

—. "Un Sentier balisé de poncifs", *Le Monde*, 7 February 2001, p. 32.

Bond, M., "Forsake Sin for Divine *Amélie*", *Mail on Sunday*, 7 October 2001.

Bonnard, O. & E. Lepage, "*Minimoys*, maxifric", *Nouvel observateur*, 30 November 2006.

Bonnaud, F., "The *Amélie* Effect", translated by A. Lovejoy, *Film Comment*, vol. 37, no. 6, November/December 2001, pp. 36-38.

Bordwell, D., *Planet Hong Kong: Popular Cinema and the Art of Entertainment*, (Cambridge, Massachusetts & London: Harvard University Press, 2000).

Boujut, M., "Hurler avec les loups ?" *Charlie Hebdo*, 7 February 2001.

—. "Destins contrariés", *Charlie Hebdo*, 2 May 2001.

Bourdieu, P., & A. Darbel, *L'Amour de l'art: les musées d'art européens et leur public*, (Paris: Editions de Minuit, 1966).

Bourdieu, P., *La Distinction – critique sociale du jugement*, (Paris: Minuit, Le Sens Commun, 1979), translated as *Distinction: a Social Critique of the Judgement of Taste*, by R. Nice, (Cambridge, Mass: Harvard University Press, 1984).

Bouzet A. D., "*Minimoys*, maximarché", *Libération*, 13 December 2006.

Bray, M. & A Catalayud, "The French Film Industry's Current Financial Crisis and its Impact on Creation: The Example of Jacques Doillon's *Raja* (2003)", *Studies in European Cinema*, vol. 2, no. 3, 2005, pp. 199-212.

Bruss, E. W., "Eye for I: Making and Unmaking Autobiography in Film", in J. Olney (ed), *Autobiography: Essays Theoretical and Critical*, (Princeton, New Jersey: Princeton University Press, 1980).

Burch, N. & G. Sellier, *La Drôle de guerre des sexes du cinéma français 1930-1956*, (Paris: Nathan, 1996).

Burdeau, E., "L'Affaire du goût", *Cahiers du cinéma*, April 2000, pp. 4-5.

Campbell, M., "Chirac Pins Hopes on the *Amélie* Effect", *Sunday Times*, 10 June 2001.

Chartier, J-P., "Les 'films à la première personne' et l'illusion de réalité au cinéma", *Revue du Cinéma*, vol. 1, no. 4, 1947, pp. 32-41.

Chateau, D., "L'Art de l'esquisse", in *Légèreté, corps et âme, un rêve d'apesanteur, Autrement,* no. 164, May 1996.

Chaw, W., "The Game of Wife", *Film Freak* Central, 2002, http://www.filmfreakcentral.net/notes/mywifeisanactressinterview.htm (accessed 20 October, 2006)

Chioua, B., "Studio Canal: studio européen d'une major américano-européenne", in *Quelle diversité face à Hollywood? CinémAction,* Hors Série, (Paris: Corlet-Télérama, 2002), p. 93-95.

Ciment, M., "Haro sur le cinéma français!", *Positif,* no. 517, March, 2004, p. 1.

—. "Grandeur et misère du cinéma français", *Positif,* no. 547, September 2006, pp. 78-80.

Cimbalo, G. V., "Coupling On Camera and Off: Yvan Attal and Charlotte Gainsbourg Talk about *My Wife Is an Actress*", *Indiewire: People.* http://www.indiewire.com/people/int_Gainsbourg_Atta_020716.html (accessed 20 October, 2006).

Cluzel, J., *Propos impertinents sur le cinéma français,* (Paris: Presses Universitaires de France, 2003).

Cohen, P. & G. Konopnicki, "Cinq millions d'entrées pour *Les Choristes*", *Marianne,* 17 May 2004.

CNC, *La Production cinématographique en 2005. Bilan statistique des films agréés du 1er janvier au 31 décembre 2005,* CNC, May 2006.

CNC *Géographie du cinéma,* CNC, no. 300, September 2006.

Conter, E., "*Le Goût des autres*: le goût de tous", *Le Film français,* 26 January 2001, p. 25.

Cook, D. A., *Lost Illusions, History of the American Cinema,* vol. 9, (Berkeley: California University Press, 2002).

Coppermann, A., "Comédie au Sentier", *Les Échos,* 3 May 1997.

—. "L'Indien, le bon, la belle et la bête" *Les Echos,* 31 January 2001.

Creton, L. & A. Jäckel, "Business 1960-2004. A Certain Idea of the Film Industry", in M. Temple & M. Witt (eds), *The French Cinema Book,* pp. 209-20, (London: BFI, 2004).

Dacbert, S., "Les Césars 2001: du goût... sans chocolat", *Le Film français,* 2 February, 2001, p. 3.

Danan, M., "French Cinema in the Era of Media Capitalism," *Media, Culture and Society,* no. 22, 2000, pp. 355-364.

Danielsen, S., "Terror of the Subtitle: It's Time we Stopped Labelling All Foreign Films as Arthouse", Leader Pages, *The Guardian,* 16 August, 2003.

Darrigrand, M., "*Les Choristes,* film d'avenir", *Libération,* 25 November 2004.

216   Bibliography

de Bruyn. O., "Les Délices d'Amélie" *Le Point*, 20 April 2001.
—. "Viva Valéria!", *Le Point*, April 18, 2003.
de la Bretèque, F., "Du Miracle des Loups au *Pacte des loups*, " in R. Moine (ed), *Le Cinéma français face aux genres*, (Paris: AFRHC, 2005), pp. 175-187.
De Vany, A. & D. Wells, "Movie Stars, Big Budgets, and Wide Releases: Empirical Analysis of the Blockbuster Strategy", in A. De Vany (ed), *Hollywood Economics: How Extreme Uncertainty Shapes the Film Industry*, (London: Routledge, 2003). Available online at http://pareto.ucalgary.ca/~wdwalls/papers/block.pdf.
Dehée, Y. & C-M. Bosséno, (eds), *Dictionnaire du Cinéma Populaire Français,* (Paris : Nouveau Monde Editions, 2004).
Deymard, C., "*La Vérité si je mens, 2* : Le Sentier de la gloire", *Le Nouvel Observateur*, 1 February 2001, p. 59.
DIRE *Distribution indépendante et concentration: État des lieux*, Paris: DIRE, November, 2005).
Docherty, D., D. Morrison & M. Tracey, *The Last Picture Show? Britain's Changing Film Audiences*, (London: BFI 1987).
Dollfus, A., "La Révolution *Vidocq*", *France-Soir*, 18 September 2001.
Dougan, A., "Feelgood Film of Year", *Glasgow Evening Times*, 4 October 2001.
Douguet, G., "Alchimiste à sa manière", *Le Figaroscope*, 19 September 2001.
Douin, J. L., "*Boudu*: un clodo rédempteur chez les bobos", *Le Monde*, 9 March 2005.
Dupont-Monod, C., J.-C. Jaillette, and G. Kaplan, "La France d'*Amélie Poulain* contre la France de *Loft Story*", *Marianne*, 14 May 2001
Dupy, J. and P. Guillomeau, "Interview avec Mathieu Kassovitz", *Starfix*, no. 14, September/October 2000.
Dyer, R., "Entertainment and Utopia", in *Only Entertainment*, (London & New York: Routledge, 1992).
Dyer, R. & G. Vincendeau (eds), *Popular European Cinema,* (London: Routledge, 1992).
Egoyan, A. & I. Balfour., *Subtitles: On the Foreignness of Film*, (Cambridge MA: The MIT Press, 2004).
Esquenazi, J-P., *Sociologie des publics*, (Paris: La Découverte, 2003).
Everett, W., "The Autobiographical Eye in European Film", *Europa: An International Journal of Language, Art and Culture*, vol. 2, no. I, 1996a, pp. 3-10. Republished online: http://www.intellectbooks.com/europa/number1/everett.htm (accessed 20 October 2006).

—. (ed), *European Identity in Cinema*, (Exeter: Intellect Books, 1996b).

—. "Film at the Crossroads: *Les Roseaux* sauvages", in P. Powrie (ed), *French Cinema of the 1990s: Continuity and Difference*, (Oxford: Oxford University Press, 1999).

—. (ed), *The Seeing Century: Film, Vision, Identity*, (Amsterdam & Atlanta: Rodopi, 2000).

—. "Film" in M. Jolly (ed), *Encyclopedia of Life Writing: Autobiographical and Biographical Forms*, (London & Chicago: Fitzroy Dearborn, 2001).

Ezra, E. & T. Rowden, "What is Transnational Cinema?", in E. Ezra & T. Rowden (eds), *Transnational Cinema: The Film Reader*, (London: Routledge, 2006).

Farchy, J., *L'Industrie du cinéma*, (Paris: PUF, 2004).

Ferenczi, A. *et al.*, "Cinéma français: ils ont fait la différence", *Télérama*, 6 January 1999, pp. 18-21.

Ferran, P., "Violence économique et cinéma français", *Le Monde*, 26 February 2007.

Forest, C., *L'Argent du cinéma. Introduction à l'économie du septième art*, (Paris: Belin, 2002).

Forrest, J. & L. R. Koos (eds), *Dead Ringers: the Remake in Theory and Practice*, (New York: State University of New York Press, 2001).

Fois, E., "*Vidocq*, la révolution numérique HD", *Le Figaro*, 13 August 2001.

Frodon, J-M., "L'envol d'un film au mépris joyeux des lois du genre", *Le Monde*, April 16, 2003.

—. "*Les Choristes*", *Cahiers du cinéma*, no. 589, April 2004a, p. 35.

—. "Etats du cinéma français: Le meilleur", *Cahiers du cinéma*, no. 593, September, 2004b, pp.10-13.

—. "Production: Changement d'ère", *Cahiers du cinéma*, no. 608, January 2006, pp. 12-23.

—. "Produit-on trop de films en France?", *Cahiers du cinéma*, no. 619, January 2007, pp. 37-39.

Gentleman, A., "*Amélie* Goes to War", *The Guardian*, 5 November 2004.

Gévaudan, F., "Changement et continuité dans la misère des laissés pour compte", *Cinéma 76*, 1976, pp. 52-62.

Gianorio, R., "Un Produit marketing", *France-Soir*, 18 February 2004.

Girolami, D. & N. Hadrien, *Le Livre noir du cinéma français*, (Paris: City, 2006).

Goudineau, D., *Rapport sur la distribution des films en salles*, (Paris: CNC / Ministère de la culture et de la communication, 2000).

Grassin, S., & M. Gilles, "Le Sentier de la gloire", *L'Express*, 1 May 1997, pp. 94-97.

——. "La Vérité sur *La Vérité…*", *L'Express*, 1 February 2001, pp. 52-53.

Greene, N., *Landscapes of Loss: The National Past in Post-War French Cinema*, (Princeton, New Jersey: Princeton University Press, 1999).

Gripsrud, J., *The Aesthetics of Popular Art*, (Kristiansand: Høyskole Forlaget, 1999).

Gronval, A., "Interview with Christophe Barratier", *Movie City News*. 2005, http://www.moviecitynews.com/Interviews/barratier.html (accessed 20 October, 2006).

Groskop, V., "Enjoy!: I'm the girl in that movie!", *Sunday Express*, 30 September 2001.

Guiguet, C. & E. Papillon (eds), *Jean Dréville: Propos du cinéaste, filmographie, documents*, (Paris: Dujarric, 1987).

Guiraudon, V., *Immigration Policy in France: U.S.-France Analysis*, 1 January 2002, http://www.brook.edu/fp/cusf/analysis/immigration.htm, (accessed 3 January, 2007).

Guyot, J., *L'Écran publicitaire: Idéologie et savoir-faire des professionnels de la publicité dans l'audiovisuel (1968-1992)*, (Paris: L'Harmattan, 1992).

Haineault, D-L. & J-Y Roy, *Unconscious for Sale: Advertising, Psychoanalysis and the Public*, translated by K. Lockhart with B. Kerslake, (Minneapolis, MN: University of Minnesota Press, 1993). Originally published as *L'Inconscient qu'on affiche*, (Paris: Editions Aubier Montaigne, 1984).

Hall, S., "European Cinema on the Verge of a Nervous Breakdown", in D. Petrie (ed), *Screening Europe: Image and Identity in Contemporary European Cinema*, (London: BFI Publications, 1992), pp. 45-53.

Hammer, C., "Richard Anconina, 'un homme normal, juif'", *Les Nouveaux cahiers*, no. 84, 1986, p. 82.

Harris, S., "Cinema in a Nation of Filmgoers", in W. Kidd & S. Reynolds (eds), *Contemporary French Cultural Studies*, (London: Arnold, 2000), pp. 208-19.

Haski, P., "Dai Sijie, rééduqué sans rancune: L'auteur, qui vit en France, parle d'expérience", *Libération*, 18 July 2001.

Hayes, G. & M. O'Shaughnessy, "French Cinema: Globalisation, Representation and Resistance", *French Politics, Culture and Society*, vol. 23, no. 3, 2005, pp. 1-13.

Hayes, G., "Regulating Multiplexes: The French State between Corporatism and Globalization", *French Politics, Culture and Society*, vol. 23, no. 3, Winter 2005, pp.14-33.

—. "Multiplexes et résistance(s): à la recherche d'Utopia", in G. Hayes & M. O'Shaughnessy, M. (eds), *Cinéma et engagement*, (Paris: L'Harmattan, 2005), pp.199-222.

Hayward, S., *French National Cinema*, (London: Routledge, 1993).

—. *Luc Besson*, (Manchester: Manchester University Press, 1998).

Hayward, S. & G. Vincendeau (eds), *French Film: Texts and Contexts*, (London: Routledge, 2000, second edition).

Heinich, N., *L'Art contemporain exposé aux rejets: Études de cas*, (Nîmes: Jacqueline Chambon, 1998).

Hellman, J., *The Knight-Monks of Vichy France: Uriage, 1940-1945*, (Toronto: McGill-Queen's University Press, 1993).

Hendrykowska, M., "Was the Cinema Fairground Entertainment? The Birth and Role of Popular Cinema in the Polish Territories up to 1908", in R. Dyer & G. Vincendeau (eds), *Popular European Cinema*, (London and New York: Routledge), pp. 112-125.

Herzberg, N. & F. Johannès, "La Galaxie Jamel", *Le Monde*, 27 September 2006.

Heymann, D., "L'Amie *Amélie* repeint la vie aux couleurs du bonheur", *Marianne*, 30 April 2001.

Higbee, W., *Mathieu Kassovitz*, (Manchester: Manchester University Press, 2006)

Hoggard, L., "Vive la différence", *The Guardian*, 30 January 2005. http://film.guardian.co.uk/features/featurepages/0,,1401512,00.html (accessed 27 November 2006).

Jäckel, A. & L. Creton, "Business: A Certain Idea of the Film Industry" in M. Temple and M. Witt (eds), *The French Cinema Book*, (London: BFI, 2004), pp. 209-20.

Jaoui, A. & J-P. Bacri, *Le Goût des autres: Screenplay*, (London: Pathé Distribution Ltd. 2001).

Japrisot, S., *A Very Long Engagement*, translated by L. Coverdale, (New York: Picador, 1994). Originally published as *Un long dimanche de fiançailles*, (Paris: Denoël, 1991).

Jeffries, S., "The French Insurrection", *Observer*, 24 June 2001.

Johnston, S., "A French Fairy Tale", *The Times Magazine*, 29 September 2001.

Journot, M-T., *Le Courant de "l'esthétique publicitaire" dans le cinéma français des années 80: La modernité en crise: Beineix, Besson, Carax*, (Paris: L'Harmattan, 2004).

Joyard, O., "Sexe: la prochaine frontière du cinéma", *Cahiers du cinéma*, no. 574, December 2002.

Jullier, L., *Qu'est-ce qu'un bon film?*, (Paris: La Dispute, 2002).

Kaganski, S., "*Amélie* pas jolie", *Libération*, 31 May 2001.

KPMG., *Film Council Specialised Exhibition and Distribution Strategy*, 2002.

Katelan, J-Y., "Le Goût d'Agnès", *Première*, March 2000, pp. 84-87.

Kassovitz, M., "Les Aventures de Mathieu Kassovitz", *Steadycam* www.mathieukassovitz.com/itw/steadycam.htm, (accessed 19 July 2005).

Keller, M., *The Untutored Eye: Childhood in the Films of Cocteau, Cornell and Brakhage*, (London & Toronto: Associated University Presses 1986).

Konopnicki, G., "*La Vérité si je mens 2*: le Sentier gaulois contre Big Brother", *Marianne*, 19 February 2001,

Lagny, M., "Popular Taste: the Teplum", in R. Dyer & G. Vincendeau (eds), *Popular European Cinema*, (London & New York: Routledge 1992), p. 169.

Lahire, B., *La Culture des individus–Dissonances culturelles et distinction de soi*, (Paris: La Découverte, 2004).

Lalanne, J-M., "Des bobards en bobines", *Libération*, 7 February 2001, p. 36.

Landesman, C., "Joie de Vivre", *Sunday Times*, 7 October 2001.

de Lange, N., *An Introduction to Judaism*, (Cambridge: Cambridge University Press, 2000).

Larcher, J., "Le Cabinet des curiosités", *Cahiers du cinéma*, no. 557, May 2001, p. 112.

Lázaro-Reboll, A. & A. Willis, *Spanish Popular Cinema*, (Manchester: Manchester University Press 2004).

Leconte, P., "Je suis effaré de l'attitude de la critique..." *Libération*, 25 November 1999.

Lejeune, P., "Cinéma et autobiographie: problèmes de vocabulaire", *Revue Belge du Cinéma*, no. 19, 1987, pp. 7-12.

Le Marie, T., "Life: Shopping List", *Express*, 5 October 2001.

Lequeret E. & I. Régnier, "Dossier: État du cinéma français dans le monde", *Cahiers du cinéma*, no. 568, May 2002, pp. 68-99.

Leveratto, J-M., *La Mesure de l'art–Sociologie de la qualité artistique*, (Paris: La Dispute, 2000).

—. *Introduction à l'anthropologie du spectacle*, (Paris: La Dispute, 2006).

Libiot, E., "*Le Pacte des loups* ", *L'Express*, 25 January 2001.

Lichfield, J., "French Elite Horrified as Feelgood Film Seduces Nation", *The Independent*, 2 June 2001.

Lionnet, F., "Afterword: Francophonie, Postcolonial Studies, and Transnational Feminisms", in H. Adlai Murdoch and A. Donadey (eds), *Postcolonial Theory and Francophone Literary Studies*, (Gainsville, Florida: University Press of Florida, 2005), pp. 258-269.

Lorrain, F-G., "*Minimoys* et maxi-business", *Le Point*, 14 December 2006.

Loustalot, G., "Argent efforts: combien ça coûte *Indigènes*?", *Première*, September 2006, p. 7.

Maltby, R., *Hollywood Cinema*, (Oxford: Blackwell Publishing, 2003).

Martin, M., "Jamel: L'icône des jeunes", *Nouvel Observateur*, 15 November 1998.

Mazdon, L., (ed), *France on Film: Essays in Popular French Cinema*, (London: Wallflower, 2001).

Mélinard, M., "'Cette jeunesse n'a pas de place dans le paysage audiovisuel'-Abdellatif Kechiche, *L'Esquive*", *L'Humanité*, 5 January 2004.

—. "Boudu, une version sans odeur", *L'Humanité*, 9 March 2005.

Mérigeau, P., "Le Cinéma français se meurt: La télé est appelée à régner", *Nouvel observateur*, 11 May 2006, pp. 64-65.

—. *Cinéma: autopsie d'un meurtre*, (Paris: Flammarion, 2007).

Mermet, G., *Francoscopie 2005*, (Paris: Larousse, 2004).

Montebello, F., *Le cinéma en France*, (Paris, Armand Colin, 2005).

Michael, C., "French National Cinema and the Martial Arts Blockbuster," *French Politics, Culture and Society*, vol. 23, no. 3, 2005, pp. 55-75.

Michaud, Y., *La Crise de l'art contemporain*, (Paris: PUF, Intervention philosophique, 1997).

—. *L'Art à l'état gazeux–Essai sur le triomphe de l'esthétique*, (Paris: Stock, 2003).

Mieder, B. & Wolfgang., "Traditional and Innovation: Proverbs in Advertising", *Journal of Popular Culture*, no.11, 1997, pp. 308-19.

Moine, R., *Les Genres du cinéma*, (Paris: Armand Colin Cinema, 2005).

—. *Les remakes de films français à Hollywood*, (Paris: CNRS, 2007).

Molia, F-X., "Présences du western dans le jeune cinéma français : autour de la connotation générique" in R. Moine (ed), *Le Cinéma français face aux genres*, (Paris: AFRHC, 2005), pp. 275-284.

Morain, J-B., "La grande trapéziste", *Les Inrockuptibles*, 16 April 2003.

Morrison, A., "Subtitle Bout", *Empire*, no. 150, 2001 p. 44.

Morrot, B., "*Amélie* ou les sensations de la petite enfance", *Marianne*, 14 May 2001.

Mowe, R., "Cherchez la Femme", *Scotsman*, 4 August, 2001a.

—. "Pleasure Principles", *Scotsman*, 11 August, 2001b.

—. "Vive le Cinéma", *Scotsman*, 25 October 2001c.

Mulard, C. & T. Sotinel, "*Amélie Poulain*, un tour du monde en 17 millions d'entrées", *Le Monde*, 1 January 2002.

Mury, C., "*La Vérité si je mens! 2*", *Télérama*, 10 February 2001, p. 45.

Nacache J., "Comment penser les remakes américains?", in A. Masson (ed), *Positif*, no. 460, June 1999, pp. 76-80.

—. *Hollywood, l'ellipse et l'infilmé*, (Paris: L'Harmattan, Champs Visuels, 2001).

—. "Nouvelle Vague et jeune cinéma-Des opérateurs génériques à la genrification du cinéma français", in R. Moine (ed), *Le Cinéma français face aux genres*, (Paris: AFRHC, 2005), pp. 57-66.

Neale, S., "Questions of Genre", *Screen*, vol. 31, no. 1, 1990, pp. 45-66.

Noguez, D., "Notes sur le film subjectif et l'autobiographie", *Revue Belge du Cinéma* no. 19, 1987, pp. 15-17.

Norman, N., "The End of *le Monde* As We Know It", *Evening Standard*, 26 July 2001.

Observatoire Européen de l'audiovisuel, "Focus 2001: Tendances du marché mondial du film",
    http://www.obs.coe.int/online_publication/reports/focus2001.pdf
    (accessed 20 December 2005).

Observatoire de la diffusion et de l'exploitation cinématographiques, *Rapport annuel 2004*, (Paris: Observatoire, 2005).

Observatoire de la diffusion et de l'exploitation cinématographiques, *Rapport annuel 2005*, (Paris: Observatoire, 2006).

O.D.B., "*Vidocq*", *Le Point*, 14 September 2001.

O'Regan, T., "Too popular by far: on Hollywood's International Popularity", *The Australian Journal of Media & Culture*, vol. 5, no. 2, 1992, pp. 302-347.

O'Shaughnessy, M., "The Shifting Identities of French Popular Cinema", *Film-Philosophy*, vol. 6, no. 27, September 2002 http://www.film-philosophy.com/vol6-2002/n27oshaughnessy, (accessed 17 January, 2007).

Ostria, V., "*Vidocq*", *L'Humanité*, 19 September 2001.

—. "Occupons-nous *d'Amélie*", *L'Humanité-Hebdo*, 22 September 2001a.

—. "*Boudu*", *Les Inrockuptibles*, 9 March 2005.

Palmer, T., "Style and Sensation in the Contemporary French Cinema of the Body", *Journal of Film and Video*, vol. 58, no. 3, 2006a, pp. 22-32.

—. "Under Your Skin: Marina de Van and the Contemporary French *cinéma du corps*", *Studies in French Cinema*, vol. 6, no. 3, 2006b, pp. 171-181.

Perkins, V.F., "The Atlantic Divide", in R. Dyer & G. Vincendeau (eds), *Popular European Cinema*, (London & New York: Routledge, 1992), pp. 194-205.

Père, O., "Gans avec les Loups", *Les Inrockuptibles*, 30 January 2001.

Péron, D., "Ça rame sur *Les Rivières pourpres*", *Libération*, 27 September 2000.

—. "Le cinéma défendu", *Libération*, 3 March 2007.

Péron D. and J-M Lalanne, "Gévaudan gâté", *Libération*, 31 January 2001.

Petrie, D., "Introduction", in D. Petrie (ed), *Screening Europe: Image and Identity in Contemporary European Cinema*, (London: BFI Publications, 1992) pp. 1-8.

Priot, F., *Financement et devis des films français*, (Paris: Dixit, 2005).

Powrie, P., *French Cinema in the 1980s: Nostalgia and the Crisis of Masculinity*, (Oxford: Clarendon Press, 1997).

—. (ed), *French Cinema in the 1990s: Continuity and Difference*, (Oxford: Oxford University Press, 1999).

—. "Heritage, History and 'New Realism': French Cinema in the 1990s", in P. Powrie (ed), *French Cinema of the 1990s: Continuity and Difference*, (Oxford: Oxford University Press, 1999), pp.1-21.

Prédal, R., *Le Jeune cinéma français*, (Paris: Nathan, 2002).

Preston, P., "Soft Choux Shuffle", *The Observer*, 7 October 2001.

Quid, "Statistiques générales", http://www.quid.fr/2007/Information/Statistiques_Generales/3?emph= cahier,cahiers,cinémas,cinema,cinéma&query=cahiers+du+cin%E9ma (accessed 25 January, 2007).

Rabourdin, D., "Le Fric est roi, ou les conditions d'accès du spectateur au film français", *Cinéma 76*, 1976, pp. 37-42.

Radstone, S., "Cinema/Memory/History", *Screen*, vol. 36, no. 1, 1995, pp. 35-47.

Rancière, J., *Malaise dans l'esthétique*, (Paris: Galilée, 2004).

Rémond, A., "Je ne vous dirai pas ce que je pense *des Choristes*", *Marianne*, 17 May 2004.

Rémy, V., "*Le Goût des autres*", *Télérama*, 1 March 2000, pp. 30-32.

Rey-Debove, J., "Le Sens de la tautologie", *Le Français moderne: Revue de linguistique française,* no. 46, 1978, pp. 318-32.

Richou, P., "*La Vérité si je mens*", *Cahiers du cinéma*, July 1997, p. 76.

Rigby, B., *Popular Culture in Modern France: A Study of Cultural Discourse*, (London & New York: Routledge, 1991).

Roberts, N., "It Gauls me but *Amélie* is so Good", *The Sun*, 6 October 2001.

Romney, J., "France's New Wave–Big Bucks and Bangs" *The Independent on Sunday*, 10 June, 2001a.

—. "A Sickening Ray of Sunshine," *The Independent on Sunday*, 7 October, 2001b.

Rollet, B., *Coline Serreau*, (Manchester: Manchester University Press, 1998).

Rosello, M., "Third Cinema or Third Degree: The 'Rachid System' in Serge Meynard's *L'Oeil au beurre noir*", in D. Sherzer (ed), *Cinema, Colonialism, Postcolonialism: Perspectives from the French and Francophone Worlds*, (Austin, Texas: University of Texas Press, 1996), pp. 147-172.

—. *Declining the Stereotype: Ethnicity and Representation in French Cultures*, (Hanover & London: University Press of New England, 1998).

—. *Postcolonial Hospitality: The Immigrant as Guest*, (Stanford, California: Stanford University Press, 2002).

Ross, P. & S. Ronay, "French Dressing is Sweet and Sour", *News of the World*, 30 September 2001.

Rouyer, P. & C. Vassé, "Entretien: Valéria Bruni-Tedeschi, la foi et la richesse", *Positif*, no. 507, May 2003.

Roy, J., "Un grand méchant loup face à Hollywood", *L'Humanité*, 31 January 2001.

Royer, P., "Terreur sur le Gévaudan", *La Croix*, 31 January 2001.

Rutherford, J., "The Third Space: Interview with Homi Bhabha", in J. Rutherford (ed), *Identity: Community, Culture, Difference*, (London: Lawrence & Wishart, 1990), pp. 207-221.

Sadoul, G., "*La Cage aux rossignols*", *Les Lettres françaises*, 22 September 1945.

Scatton-Tessier, M., "*Le Petisme:* Flirting with the Sordid in *Le Fabuleux Destin d'Amélie Poulain*", *Studies in French Cinema*, vol. 4, no. 3, November 2004, pp. 197-207.

Schaeffer, J-M., *Les Célibataires de l'art–Pour une esthétique sans mythes*, (Paris: Gallimard, 1996).

—. *Adieu à l'esthétique,* (Paris: P.U.F., 2000).

Sen-Lun, Y., "Romantic Boyhood Memories of Chinese Filmmaker", *Taipei Times*, 20 May 2002.

Sharpe, S., "Tautou Recall", *Time Out*, 5-12 September 2001.

Sherzer, D., (ed), *Cinema, Colonialism, Postcolonialism: Perspectives from the French and Francophone Worlds*, (Austin, TX: University of Texas Press, 1996).

—. "Comedy and Interracial Relationships: *Romuald et Juliette* (Serreau, 1987) and *Métisse* (Kassovitz, 1993)", in P. Powrie (ed), *French Cinema in the 1990s: Continuity and Difference*, (Oxford & New York: Oxford University Press, 1999), pp. 148-159.

Sorin, C., "Quand l'Europe fait du cinéma européen au second degré", in *Quelle diversité face à Hollywood? CinémAction*, Hors Série, (Paris: Corlet-Télérama, 2002), pp. 104-109.

Sorlin, P., "Ce qu'était un film populaire dans l'Europe des années cinquante", in Bertin-Maghit, J-P. (ed), *Les Cinémas européens des années cinquante*, (Paris, AFRHC, 2000), pp. 19-46.

Sotinel, T., "*Le Fabuleux destin d'Amélie Poulain*: Quand Georges Perec rencontre Marcel Carné", *Le Monde*, 25 April 2001.

—. "Cinéma: Financement sur le fil", *Le Monde*, 13 April 2007.

Staiger, J., *Interpreting Films: Studies in the Historical Reception of American Cinema*, (Princeton: Princeton University Press, 1992).

—. *Perverse Spectators: The Practices of Film Reception*, (New York: New York University Press, 2000).

—. *Media Reception Studies*, (New York: New York University Press, 2005).

Steyn, M., "Relentlessly Quirky", *Spectator*, 13 October 2001.

Stratton, J., "Not Really White – Again: Performing Jewish Difference in Hollywood Films since the 1980s", *Screen*, vol. 42, 2001, pp. 142-66.

Strauss, F., "Opération portes ouvertes. *Cahiers du cinéma*", no. 481, June 1994, pp. 8-9.

Suozzo, J., "*Les Choristes* : Q&A with Director Christophe Barratier", in *Storyboard: the Newsletter for the Washington DC Film Society 2005*, http://www.dcfilmsociety.org/storyboard0502.htm#chorus   (accessed 20 October, 2006).

Suzer, A., "Christophe Barratier, le musicien-cinéaste", *Marianne*, 7 June 2004.

Tarr, C., "Ethnicity and Identity in the *Cinéma de Banlieue*" in P. Powrie (ed), *French Cinema in the 1990s: Continuity and Difference*, (Oxford University Press: Oxford & New York, 1999), pp. 172-184.

—. *Reframing Difference: Beur and Banlieue Filmmaking in France.* (Manchester: Manchester University Press, 2005).

—. Special issue "Transnational Cinema", *Modern and Contemporary France* vol. 15, no. 1, 2007, pp. 3-7.

Tessé, J.-P., "Cité dans le texte", *Cahiers du cinéma*, no. 586, January 2004, pp. 52-3.

Théate, B., "Anconina dans le Sentier, l'humour juif en dix leçons", *Le Journal du Dimanche*, 27 April 1997.

Tranchant, M-N. & C. Gans : "L'Instinct des feuilletonistes", *Le Figaro*, 31 January 2001.

Truffaut, F., "Une certaine tendance du cinéma français", *Cahiers du cinéma*, no. 31, January 1954, pp. 15-29, translated as "A Certain Tendency of French Cinema", B. Nichols (ed), *Movies and Methods*, (Berkeley: University of California Press, 1985), pp. 224-237.

T. S., "Quand Georges Perec rencontre Marcel Carné", *Le Monde*, 25 April 2001.

UK Film Council, *Film in the UK 2002 Statistical Yearbook*, 2003.

UK Film Council, *UK Film Council Statistical Yearbook Annual Review 2003-2004*, 2004.

UK Film Council, *UK Film Council Statistical Yearbook Annual Review 2004-2005*, 2005.

UK Film Council, *RSU Statistical Yearbook 2005-2006*, 2006a.

UK Film Council, "UK Film Council Increases Film Viewing Choices for UK Audiences", UK Film Council web site News section 18 October, 2006b.

Vanderschelden, I., "Jamel Debbouze: A New Popular Star in French Cinema", *Studies in French Cinema,* vol. 5, no. 1, 2005, pp. 61-72.

—. "New Strategies for a Transnational/French Popular Cinema" in C. Tarr (ed), *Modern and Contemporary France*, vol. 15, no. 1, February 2007, pp. 37-50.

Vincendeau, G., "France 1945-1965 and Hollywood: the *Policier* as International Text", *Screen*, vol. 33, no.1, 1992, pp. 50-80.

—. "Café Society", *Sight and Sound* vol. 11, no. 8, 2001a, pp. 22-25.

—. "The Art of Spectacle: The Aesthetics of Classical French Cinema", in M. Temple, & M. Witt (eds), *The French Cinema Book*, (London: BFI, 2004), pp. 137-152.

Vulser, N., "*Un long dimanche de fiançailles* reste privé du financement du CNC", *Le Monde*, 2 June 2005

Vulser, N., "La forte bipolarisation du marché", *Le Monde*, 13 April 2007.

Waintrop, E., "Sentier lumineux: la comédie est facile mais généreuse", *Libération*, 14 May 1997, p. 4.

Waldron, D., "Incorporating Qualitative Audience Research into French Film Studies: the Case of *Gazon maudit* (Balasko, 1995)", *Studies in French Cinema*, vol. 4, no. 2, 2004, pp. 121-133.

Williams, R., *Keywords: A Vocabulary of Culture and Society*, (Glasgow: Fontana, 1976).

Wilson, E., *French Cinema since 1950: Personal Histories*, (London: Duckworth 1999).

Young, G., "*Amélie's* a True Ray of Sunshine", *Birmingham Evening Mail*, 5 October, 2001.

FILMOGRAPHY

17 rue bleue (Chad Chenouga, 2001)
37,2 le matin / Betty Blue (Jean-Jacques Beineix, 1986)
5x2 (François Ozon, 2004)
8 Femmes / 8 Women (François Ozon, 2001)
8½ (Federico Fellini, 1963)
Adémaï au moyen âge (Jean de Marguenat, 1934)
Adémaï aviateur (Jean Tarride, 1933)
Adémaï bandit d'honneur (Gilles Grangier, 1943)
Agents secrets (Frédéric Schoendoerffer, 2004)
Arizona Dream (Emir Kusturica 1993)
Assault on Precinct 13 (Jean-François Richet, 2005)
Astérix et Obélix contre César (Claude Zidi, 1999)
Astérix et Obélix: mission Cléopâtre (Alain Chabat, 2002)
Au coeur du mensonge (Claude Chabrol, 1999)
Au revoir les enfants (Louis Malle, 1987)
Baise-moi (Virginie Despentes and Coralie Trinh Thi, 2000)
Balzac et la petite tailleuse chinoise (Dai Sijie, 2002)
Banlieue 13/B.13 (Pierre Morel, 2004)
Beauty Shop (Billie Woodruff, 2005)
Belphégor, le fantôme du Louvre (Jean-Paul Salomé, 2001)
Billy Elliott (Stephen Daldry, 2000)
Bloody Mallory (Julien Magnat, 2002)
Blueberry: L'expérience secrète (Jan Kounen, 2004)
Boudu (Gérard Jugnot, 2005)
Boudu sauvé des eaux / Boudu Saved from Drowning (Jean Renoir, 1932)
Brice de Nice (James Huth, 2005)
Bride of Chucky (Ronny Yu, 1998, USA)
Bye Bye (Karim Dridi, 1995)
Caché / Hidden (Michael Haneke, 2005)
Catwoman (Pitof, 2004)
Cette femme-là (Guillaume Nicloux, 2003)
Chaos (Coline Serreau, 2001)
Chicken Little (Mark Dindal, 2005)
Chocolat (Lasse Hallström, 2000)
Cinema Paradiso (Giuseppe Tornatore, 1989)

Citizen Kane (Orson Welles, 1941)
Comme une image/Look at Me (Agnès Jaoui, 2004)
Corps à corps (François Hanss, 2003)
Crouching Tiger, Hidden Dragon / Wo hu cang long (Ang Lee, 2000)
Cuisine et dépendances (Olivier Muyl, 1993)
De l'amour (Jean-François Richet, 2001)
Dead Poets' Society (Peter Weir, 1989)
Déjà mort (Olivier Dahan, 1997)
Delicatessen (Marc Caro and Jean-Pierre Jeunet, 1991)
Demain et encore demain (Dominique Cabrera, 1997)
Demonlover (Olivier Assayas, 2001)
Depuis qu'Otar est parti / Since Otar Left (Julie Bertuccelli, 2003)
Deuce Bigalow: European Gigolo (Mike Bigelow, 2005)
Diabolo Menthe (Diane Kurys, 1977)
Dieu est grand, je suis toute petite / God is Great and I'm not (Pascale
    Bailly, 2001)
Diva (Jean-Jacques Beineix, 1981)
Dobermann (Jan Kounen, 2000)
Dog Star Man (Stan Brakhage, 1961-1964)
Douce France (Malik Chibane 1995)
Down and Out in Beverly Hills (Paul Mazursky,1986)
Elle est des nôtres / She's One of Us (Siegrid Alnoy, 2003)
Etat des Lieux Jean-François Richet, 1995
The Eternal Sunshine of the Spotless Mind (Michel Gondry, 2004)
Être et avoir (Nicolas Philibert, 2002)
Eye Myth (Stan Brakhage, 1967)
Fahrenheit 9/11 (Michael Moore, 2004)
Fanny and Alexandre (Ingmar Bergman, 1982)
Fantasia (James Algar, Samual Armstrong, 1940)
Fauteuils d'orchestre / Orchestra Seats (Danielle Thomson, 2006)
Gabrielle (Patrice Chéreau, 2005)
Gazon maudit / French Twist (Josiane Balasko, 1995)
Gothika (Mathieu Kassovitz, 2003)
Harry Potter and the Goblet of Fire (Mike Newell, 2005)
Harry Potter and the Prisoner of Azkaban (Alfonso Cuarón, 2004)
Harry, un ami qui vous veut du bien / Harry , He is Here to Help
    (Dominik Moll, 2000)
Haute tension / High Tension (Alexandre Aja, 2003)
Hexagone (Malik Chibane, 1994)
Hostage (Florent Emilio Siri, 2005)
Hôtel de France (Patrice Chéreau, 1987)

The House of Flying Daggers / Shi mian mai fu (Yimou Zhang, 2004)
I mostri (Dino Risi, 1963)
Il est plus facile pour un chameau.../It Easier for a Camel... (Valeria Bruni-Tedeschi, 2003)
Il était une fois dans l'Oued (La légende de Johnny Bachir) (Djamel Bensalah, 2005)
Ils / Them (David Moreau and Xavier Palud, 2006)
Inch'Allah Dimanche (Yamina Benguigui, 2001)
Indigènes / Days of Glory (Rachid Bouchareb, 2006)
Innocence (Lucile Hadzihalilovic, 2004)
Intimité (Patrice Chéreau, 2001)
Irreversible (Gaspar Noé, 2002)
J'aime la vie, je fais du vélo, je vais au cinéma (Francis Fourcou, 2005)
Jaws (Steven Spielberg, 1975)
Jean de Florette (Claude Berri. 1986)
Jeanne d'Arc / The Messenger (Luc Besson, 1999)
Jet Set (Fabien Onteniente, 2000)
Jeunesse dorée (Zaïda Ghorab-Volta, 2002)
Jeux interdits /Forbidden Games (René Clément, 1952)
King Kong (Peter Jackson, 2005)
Kirikou et les bêtes sauvages (Bénédicte Galup & Michel Ocelot, 2005)
Le Baiser mortel du Dragon / Kiss of the Dragon (Chris Nahon, 2001)
Krim, Ahmed Bouchaala, 1995
L'Amoureuse (Jacques Doillon, 1987)
L'Auberge espagnole / Pot Luck (Cédric Klapisch, 2002)
L'Enquête corse (Alain Berbérian, 2004)
L'Esquive / Games of Love and Chance (Abdellatif Kechiche, 2004)
L'Homme est une femme comme les autres (Jean-Jacques Zilbermann, 1998)
L'Intrus / The Intruder (Claire Denis, 2005)
La Baule-les-Pins /C'est la Vie (Diane Kurys, 1990)
La Boum (Claude Pinoteau, 1980)
La Cage aux folles (Edouard Molinaro, 1978)
La Cage aux rossignols / A Cage of Nightingales (Jean Dréville, 1945)
La Cité des Enfants Perdus /The City of Lost Children (Marc Caro and Jean-Pierre Jeunet, 1995)
La Crise Coline Serreau, 1992
La Doublure / The Valet (Francis Veber, 2006)
La Faute à Voltaire (Abdellatif Kechiche, 2004)
La Gifle (Claude Pinoteau, 1974)
La Gloire de mon père (Yves Robert, 1990)

La Grande bouffe (Marco Ferreri 1973)
La Grande vadrouille (Gérard Oury, 1966)
La Guerre des boutons (Yves Robert, 1962)
La Haine / Hate (Mathieu Kassovitz, 1995)
La Marche de l'Empereur / The March of the Penguins (Luc Jacquet, 2005)
La Môme / La Vie en Rose (Olivier Dahan, 2007)
La Nuit Américaine / Day for Night (François Truffaut, 1973)
La Petite Jérusalem (Karin Albou, 2005)
La Pianiste / The Piano Teacher (Michael Haneke, 2001)
La Squale (Fabrice Génestal, 2000)
La Vérité si je mens! /Would I Lie to You (Thomas Gilou, 1997)
La Vérité si je mens! 2 / Would I Lie to You 2 (Thomas Gilou, 2001)
Le Baiser mortel du dragon / Kiss of the Dragon (Chris Nahon, 2001)
Le Château de ma mère (Yves Robert, 1990)
Le Ciel, les oiseaux... et ta mère (Djamel Bensalah, 1999)
Le Cinquième élément / Fifth Element (Luc Besson, 1997)
Le Corniaud (Gérard Oury, 1965)
Le Derrière (Valérie Lemercier, 1999).
Le Dîner de cons / The Dinner Game (Francis Veber, 1998)
Le Fabuleux destin d'Amélie Poulain / Amelie (Jean-Pierre Jeunet, 2001)
Le Goût des autres / The Taste of Others (Agnès Jaoui, 2000)
Le Grand bleu /The Big Blue (Luc Besson, 1988)
Le Maître d'école (Claude Berri, 1981)
Le Manège enchanté / The Magic Roundabout (Dave Borthwick, Jean Duval, Frank Passingham, 2005)
Le Pacte des loups /Brotherhood of the Wolf (Christophe Gans, 2001)
Le Père tranquille (René Clément, 1946)
Le Placard / The Closet (Francis Véber, 2001)
Le Plaisir et ses petits tracas (Nicolas Boukhrief, 1998)
Le Plus beau métier du monde (Gérard Lauzier, 1996)
Le Raïd (Djamel Bensalah, 2002)
Le Tango des Rashevski (Sam Garbarski, 2003)
Le Thé à la menthe (Abdelkrim Bahloul, 1985)
Le Thé au harem d'Archimède (Mehdi Charef, 1985)
Léon (Luc Besson. 1994. France).
Les 400 coups / The 400 Blows (François Truffaut, 1959)
Les Aventures de Rabbi Jacob. (Gérard Oury, 1973)
Les Bronzés (Patrice Leconte, 1978)
Les Bronzés 3: Amis pour la vie (Patrice Leconte, 2006)
Les Bronzés font du ski (Patrice Leconte, 1979)

Les Choristes / The Chorus (Christophe Barratier, 2004)
Les Clefs de bagnole / The Car Keys (Laurent Baffie, 2003)
Les Enfants du marais / Children of the marshland (Jean Becker, 1999)
Les Enfants du paradis Children of Paradise (Marcel Carné, 1945)
Les Gens normaux n'ont rien d'exceptionnel (Laurence Ferreira-Barbosa, 1993)
Les Morsures de l'aube (Antoine de Caunes, 2001)
Les Rivières pourpres / Crimson Rivers (Mathieu Kassovitz, 2000)
Les Roseaux Sauvages / The Wild Reeds (André Techiné, 1994).
Les Triplettes de Belleville / Belleville rendez-Vous (Sylvain Chomet, 2003).
Les Visiteurs (Jean Marie Poiré, 1993)
Les Visiteurs 2: Les Couloirs du temps (Jean-Marie Poiré, 1998)
Les Yeux sans visage / Eyes without a Face (Georges Franju, 1960)
Lévy et Goliath (Gérard Oury, 1987)
Ma 6-T va crack-er (Jean-François Richet, 1997)
Ma Femme est une actrice / My Wife is an Actress (Yvan Attal, 2001)
Madison (William Bindley, 2001)
Maléfique (Eric Valette, 2002)
Manon des sources (Claude Berri, 1985)
Métisse, (Mathieu Kassovitz, 1993)
Mimi (Claire Simon, 2003)
Mimic (Guillermo del Toro, 1997)
Mina Tannenbaum (Martine Dugowson, 1994)
Mirror (Andrei Tarkovsky, 1974)
Mona Lisa Smile (Mike Newell, 2003)
Monsieur Batignole (Gérard Jugnot, 2002)
Mothlight (Stan Brakhage, 1963)
Mr. Holland's Opus (Stephen Herek, 1995)
Mulholland Drive (David Lynch, 2001)
Music of the Heart (Wes Craven, 1999)
Neg'Marron (Jean-Claude Flamand-Barny, 2005)
Nénette et Boni (Claire Denis, 1996)
Nid de guêpes / The Nest (Florent Emilio Siri, 2002)
Nightwatch (Ole Bornedal, 1997)
Notting Hill (Roger Michell, 1999)
Olé (Florence Quentin, 2005)
Omelette (Rémi Lange, 1994)
Oublie-moi (Noémie Lvovsky, 1994)
Partir revenir (Claude Lelouch, 1985)
Pas de Repos pour les braves (Alain Guiraudie, 2003)

Petits frères (Jacques Doillon, 1999)

Planet of the Apes (Tim Burton, 2001)

Promenons-nous dans les bois / *Deep in the Woods* (Lionel Delplanque, 2000)

Psycho (Gus Van Sant, 1998)

Quand la Mer monte... / When the Sea Rises (Gilles Porte & Yolande Moreau, 2004)

Quand on sera grand (Renaud Cohen, 2001)

Qui a tué Bambi?/ *Who Killed Bambi* ? (Gilles Marchand, 2003)

Raï (Thomas Gilou, 1995)

Rencontre avec le Dragon (Hélène Angel, 2001)

Rois et Reine / King and Queen (Arnaud Desplechin, 2004)

Romance (Catherine Breillat, 1999)

Romuald et Juliette (Coline Serreau, 1989)

Rue Cases-Nègres (Euzhan Palcy, 1983)

Samia (Philippe Faucon, 2001)

San Antonio (Frédéric Auburtin, 2004)

Sex Is Comedy (Catherine Breillat, 2002)

Seven (David Fincher 1995)

Sheitan (Kim Chapiron, 2006)

Shrek 2 (Andrew Adamson, Kelly Asbury and Conrad Vernon, 2004)

Silence of the Lambs (Jonathan Demme 1991)

Silent Hill (Christophe Gans, 2006)

Smoking/No Smoking (Alain Resnais, 1993)

Sombre (Philippe Grandrieux, 1998)

Souviens-toi de moi (Zaïda Ghorab-Volta, 1996)

Spider-Man 2 (Sam Raimi, 2004)

Stand and Deliver (Ramon Mendéndez, 1988)

Star Wars: The Empire Strikes Back (George Lucas, 1980)

Star Wars, episode I : The Phantom Menace (George Lucas, 1998)

Star Wars, episode II : Attack of the Clones (George Lucas, 2002)

Subway (Luc Besson, 1985)

Tarnation (Jonathan Caouette, 2003)

Taxi (Gérard Pirès, 1998)

Taxi 2 (Gérard Krawczyk, 2000)

Taxi 3 (Gérard Krawczyk, 2003)

Taxi 4 (Gérard Krawczyk, 2007)

Tchao Pantin. Dir. Claude Berri. Pathé Distribution. 1983

The Chronicles of Narnia: The Lion, the Witch and the Wardrobe (Andrew Adamson, 2005)

The Corn is Green (Irving Rapper, 1945)

The Emperor's Club (Michael Hoffman, 2002)
The Great Dictator (Charles Chaplin, 1940)
The Hills Have Eyes (Alexandre Aja, 2006)
The Lord of the Rings: The Fellowship of the Rings (Peter Jackson, 2001)
The Man Who Shot Liberty Valance (John Ford, 1962)
The Matrix (Andy et Larry Wachovski, 1999)
The Passion of the Christ (Mel Gibson. 2004)
The Wild Bunch (Sam Peckinpah, 1969)
Thelma and Louise (Ridley Scott, 1990)
To Sir with Love (James Clavell, 1967)
Tous les garçons et les filles de leur âge (various directors, 1994)
Trois hommes et un couffin / Three Men and a Cradle (Coline Serreau, 1985)
Trouble Every Day (Claire Denis, 2001)
Twenty-nine Palms (Bruno Dumont, 2003)
Un air de famille /Family Ressemblances (Cédric Klapisch, 1996)
Un fil à la patte (Michel Deville, 2005).
Un indien dans la ville (Hervé Palud, 1994)
Un long dimanche de fiançailles/ A Very Long Engagement (Jean-Pierre Jeunet, 2004)
Vendredi soir / Friday Night (Claire Denis, 2001)
Vidocq (Pitof, 2001)
Voisins, voisines (Malik Chibane, 2005)
Wesh wesh, qu'est-ce qui se passe? (Rabah Ameur-Zaïmèche, 2002)
Wizard of Oz, The (Victor Fleming. 1939. USA)
XXL (Ariel Zeïtoun, 1997)
Y Tu Mamá También (Alfonso Cuarón, 2001)
Yamakasi (Ariel Zeitoun, 2001)
Zéro de conduite (Jean Vigo, 1933)

CONTRIBUTORS

Graeme Hayes is Lecturer in French and European studies at Aston University. His work on French cinema concentrates on the political economy of film, particularly concerning the relationships between industry, public policy and citizens' mobilisation. He is the editor of *Cinéma et engagement* (L'Harmattan, 2005) and of a special issue of *French Politics, Culture and Society* (2005) on French cinema and globalisation, both in conjunction with Martin O'Shaughnessy. His other articles include a short study of Alain Delon and various pieces on *Les Amants du Pont Neuf*, *Delicatessen* and *Du Rififi chez les Hommes*.

Will Higbee is Deputy Director of Film Studies in the Department of Modern Languages at the University of Exeter. His research interests include representations of ethnicity, postcolonial and diasporic cultures in contemporary French cinema. He has published a monograph on Mathieu Kassovitz as part of Manchester University Press's series on French Directors. He is currently working on a study of Algerian émigré directors.

Sarah Leahy is a Lecturer in French at the University of Newcastle upon Tyne. She has authored several articles on female stars in French cinema and a monograph on *Casque d'or* (IB Tauris, 2007). Research interests include cinema audiences, cultural and national identities, spectatorship, theories of gender and sexuality. She is currently undertaking a project investigating film culture and cinema-going in Newcastle upon Tyne.

Joseph McGonagle is a Lecturer in French Studies at The University of Manchester. His research interests include representations of ethnicity in French and Francophone film and photography. He has published articles on French television and photography in *French Cultural Studies* (2002) and *Modern & Contemporary France* (2005) and an interview with the artist Zineb Sedira in *Signs* (2006). His PhD thesis considers representations of ethnicity in French film and photography since the 1980s.

Binita Mehta is Chair of the French Department at Manhattanville College in Purchase, New York, USA, where she teaches courses in French language, literature, culture and film. Her book *Widows, Pariahs, and 'Bayadères': India as Spectacle* was by published by Bucknell University Press in 2002. Her article, "Emigrants Twice Displaced: Race, Color, and Identity in Mira Nair's *Mississippi Masala*" was a chapter in *Between the Lines: South Asians and Postcoloniality*, published by Temple University Press in 1996.

Raphaëlle Moine is "Professeure en études Cinématographiques" at the Université de Paris X-Nanterre. Her books include: *France/Hollywood. Echanges cinématographiques et identités nationales* (2002, with Martin Barnier), *Les Genres du cinéma* (2005), *Le Cinéma français face aux genres* (2005), and *Les remakes de films français à Hollywood* (2007).

François-Xavier Molia is completing his doctorate in Film Studies at the University of Paris X-Nanterre. His research interests include genres in contemporary French popular cinema. He has published "Présence du western dans le jeune cinéma français : autour de la connotation générique", in Raphaëlle Moine (ed) *Les Genres du cinéma français* (Paris: AFRHC, 2005) and "Plus de peur que de mal : politique du film-catastrophe" in Laurent Véray (ed) *Les Peurs de Hollywood* (Lausanne: éditions Antipodes, 2006).

Tim Palmer is Assistant Professor of Film Studies at the University of North Carolina in Wilmington, USA. He specialises in French, classical Hollywood, and Asian cinema; his research has been published in *Cinema Journal, Studies in French Cinema, Journal of Film and Video, Film International,* and *Senses of Cinema*. His chapter on Jean-Pierre Melville's *Le Samouraï* recently appeared in *The Cinema of France* (London: Wallflower, 2006). He is currently writing a book, *Brutal Intimacy: Contemporary French Cinema*, for Wesleyan University Press.

Jacqueline Nacache lectures at the University of Paris VII. She has published extensively on Hollywood cinema. Her most important publications include *L'Acteur de cinéma* (2003) and *Le Film Hollywoodien classique* (2005).

Deirdre Russell is a doctoral student in French Studies at The University of Manchester. Her thesis entitled 'Narrative Identities in Contemporary French Autobiographical Literature and Film' explores the social dimensions of autobiographical identity. Forthcoming publications include 'Narrating Colonial Memories and Selves in Claire Denis' *Chocolat*' in *Time and Memory in Narrative*, ed. Karl Simms and Shilpa Venkatachalam.

Michelle Scatton-Tessier is an Assistant Professor of French at the University of North Carolina Wilmington, USA. She has a Ph.D. from The University of Iowa. She has published on women writers in France, early French television, and contemporary French cinema.

Ingrid Stigsdotter is a doctoral student in Film Studies at the University of Southampton, where she also teaches on the degree programme. Her doctoral research examines the reception of contemporary European cinema in Britain, with particular focus on recent French and Swedish films, and the impact of cultural and linguistic difference on film interpretation. Other research interests include artists' film and video, and independent film exhibition and distribution.

Carrie Tarr is Research Fellow in the Faculty of Arts and Sciences at Kingston University. She has many publications in the areas of ethnicity and gender in French cinema. She has recently published an edited edition with Brigitte Rollet entitled *Cinema and the Second Sex: Women's Filmmaking in France in the 1980s and 1990s* (2001) and *Reframing Difference: Beur and Banlieue Cinema in France* (2005).

Isabelle Vanderschelden is Senior Lecturer in French Studies at Manchester Metropolitan University. She has published a monograph on *Le Fabuleux destin d'Amélie Poulain* (IB Tauris, 2007) and several articles on contemporary popular cinema in France, including a study of Jamel Debbouze in *Studies in French Cinema* (2005), a chapter on *Les Visiteurs* in the *Cinema of France* (2006) and a discussion of the transnational in *Modern and Contemporary France* (2007).

Ginette Vincendeau is Professor of Film Studies and Director of the Film Studies Programme at King's College, London. She has written widely on popular French and European cinema. Among her books are *Pépé le Moko* (BFI, 1998); *Stars and Stardom in French Cinema* (Continuum, 2000 and 2006); *Jean-Pierre Melville: An American in Paris* (BFI, 2003); and *La Haine* (I.B. Tauris, 2005). She is also the editor of *The Encyclopedia of European Cinema* (BFI/Cassell, 1995); co-editor, with Susan Hayward, of *French Film: Texts and Contexts* (Routledge, 1990 and 2000) and, with Alastair Phillips, of *Journeys of Desire, European Actors in Hollywood* (BFI, 2006).

Darren Waldron is Lecturer in French Screen Studies at the University of Manchester. His scholarly interests include representations of gender and sexuality in contemporary French cinema and audience research. He has published an article on *Gazon maudit* in (Mazdon (ed), 2001) and another on spectator responses to the same film in *Studies in French Cinema* (2004). He has also published a study of sexuality in *Pédale douce, L'Homme est une femme comme les autres, Le Derrière* and *Le Placard* in *Modern and Contemporary France*.

INDEX